Shan

SHAKSPERE GEMS

BY THE AUTHOR OF

'*THE BOOK OF FAMILIAR QUOTATIONS*'

BOSTON

LEE & SHEPARD, PUBLISHERS

NEW YORK

LEE, SHEPARD, & DILLINGHAM

1872

Printed by R. Clark, *Edinburgh.*

TO

SAMUEL SIMPSON, ESQ. OF STRETFORD,

NEAR MANCHESTER,

THIS VOLUME OF EXTRACTS

FROM THE WORKS OF SHAKSPERE

IS DEDICATED

BY HIS SINCERE FRIEND

THE COMPILER.

PREFACE.

WHILST numerous selections from Shakspere have been published, it is to be feared that, for the most part, they contain many passages which it is scarcely expedient to place before youthful readers. One object of this compilation is to present a book specially adapted to the youth of both sexes for use in scholastic and family circles, which, whilst embodying the most prominent beauties, excludes everything which may be deemed objectionable by the most fastidious persons. Another aim of the Compiler has been to make the book one which it is believed cannot fail to impart to its readers some knowledge of

Shakspere's works generally; thus, extracts from every play have been included, varying in length according to its interest and popularity, and at the commencement of each play a short account of the plot or fable is given.

The communications which the Compiler has received from the principals of high-class educational establishments in various parts of the kingdom, on the desirability of imparting Shaksperean knowledge to their pupils, prove conclusively that some acquaintance with the undying works of Shakspere is by many instructors deemed a desideratum, if not a necessity.

CONTENTS.

—ooo—

TEMPEST.

Prospero, the rightful Duke of Milan, is cheated out of his dukedom by the intrigues of his brother Antonio, and is sent to sea with his infant daughter Miranda; in the frail boat in which they are embarked they reach an island, where, educated by her father, Miranda grows to womanhood. Prospero, who is a magician, with the help of Ariel, a familiar spirit, causes the king of Naples, with his son Ferdinand, and Antonio, the usurping brother, to be shipwrecked on the island. Ferdinand encounters Miranda, falls in love with her, and is accepted as her future husband. The play concludes with the resolution of Prospero to abandon magic and revisit his dukedom. The chief characters in the play are Prospero, the rightful Duke; Antonio, his usurping brother; Alonso, King of Naples; Ferdinand, his son; Ariel, an airy spirit; Caliban, a savage and deformed slave; Gonzalo, an honest old counsellor of Naples, and Miranda, daughter of Prospero.

Act I.

Ariel's Description of Managing the Storm.

I boarded the king's ship; now on the beak,
Now in the waist, the deck, in every cabin,
I flamed amazement; sometimes I'd divide,
And burn in many places; on the top-mast,
The yards, and bowsprit, would I flame distinctly,
Then meet, and join; Jove's lightnings, the precursors

O' the dreadful thunder-claps, more momentary
And sight outrunning were not: the fire, and cracks
Of sulphurous roaring, the most mighty Neptune
Seem'd to besiege, and make his bold waves tremble,
Yea, his dread trident shake.——
——Not a soul
But felt a fever of the mad, and play'd
Some tricks of desperation: all but mariners
Plung'd in the foaming brine, and quit the vessel,
Then all afire with me: the king's son, Ferdinand,
With hair up-staring (then like reeds, not hair),
Was the first man that leap'd.

Caliban's Curses.

CALIBAN. As wicked dew as e'er my mother brush'd
With raven feather from unwholesome fen,
Drop on you both! a south-west blow on ye,
And blister you all o'er!
PROSPERO. For this, be sure, to-night thou shalt have cramps,
Side-stitches that shall pen thy breath up; urchins*
Shall, for that vast of night that they may work,
All exercise on thee: thou shalt be pinch'd
As thick as honeycombs, each pinch more stinging
Than bees that made them.
CALIBAN. I must eat my dinner.
This island's mine, by Sycorax my mother,
Which thou takest from me. When thou camest first
Thou strokedst me, and madest much of me; wouldst give me
Water with berries in't: and teach me how
To name the bigger light, and how the less,
That burn by day and night: and then I lov'd thee,

* Imps, fairies.

And shew'd thee all the qualities o' the isle,
The fresh springs, brine pits, barren place, and fertile;
Cursed be I that did so!—All the charms
Of Sycorax, toads, beetles, bats, light on you!
For I am all the subjects that you have,
Which first was mine own king: and here you sty me
In this hard rock, whiles you do keep from me
The rest of the island.

Music.

Where should this music be? i' the air, or the earth?
It sounds no more: and sure it waits upon
Some god of the island. Sitting on a bank,
Weeping again the king my father's wreck,
This music crept by me upon the waters:
Allaying both their fury and my passion,
With its sweet air.

Ariel's Song.

Full fathom five thy father lies;
 Of his bones are coral made;
Those are pearls, that were his eyes:
 Nothing of him that doth fade,
But doth suffer a sea change
Into something rich and strange.
Sea-nymphs hourly ring his knell:
Hark! now I hear them,—ding-dong, bell.

A Lover's Speech.

My spirits, as in a dream, are all bound up.
My father's loss, the weakness which I feel,
The wreck of all my friends, or this man's threats.

To whom I am subdued, are but light to me,
Might I but through my prison once a day
Behold this maid: all corners else o' the earth
Let liberty make use of: space enough
Have I in such a prison.

Act II.

Description of Ferdinand's Swimming ashore.

I saw him beat the surges under him,
And ride upon their backs; he trod the water,
Whose enmity he flung aside, and breasted
The surge most swoln that met him: his bold head
'Bove the contentious waves he kept, and oar'd
Himself with his good arms in lusty stroke
To the shore, that o'er his wave-worn basis bow'd,
As stooping to relieve him: I not doubt
He came alive to land.

Sleep.

Do not omit the heavy offer of it:
It seldom visits sorrow; when it doth,
It is a comforter.

Caliban's Curses.

All the infections that the sun sucks up
From bogs, fens, flats, on Prosper fall, and make him
By inch-meal a disease! His spirits hear me,
And yet I needs must curse. But they'll nor pinch,
Fright me with urchin shows, pitch me i' the mire,
Nor lead me like a fire-brand in the dark
Out of my way, unless he bid them; but
For every trifle are they set upon me:
Sometimes like apes, that moe* and chatter at me,

* To make faces

And after, bite me; then like hedge-hogs, which
Lie tumbling in my bare-foot way, and mount
Their pricks at my footfall; sometimes am I
All wound with adders, who, with cloven tongues,
Do hiss me into madness.

Satire on English Curiosity.

What have we here? a man or a fish? Dead or alive? A fish; he smells like a fish; a very ancient and fish-like smell; a kind of, not of the newest, Poor-John. A strange fish! Were I in England now (as once I was), and had but this fish painted, not a holiday fool there but would give a piece of silver; there would this monster make a man; any strange beast there makes a man: when they will not give a doit to relieve a lame beggar, they will lay out ten to see a dead Indian.

Caliban's Promises.

I'll shew thee the best springs; I'll pluck thee berries;
I'll fish for thee, and get thee wood enough.
A plague upon the tyrant that I serve!
I'll bear him no more sticks, but follow thee,
Thou wondrous man.
I pr'ythee, let me bring thee where crabs grow:
And I with my long nails will dig thee pig-nuts:
Show thee a jay's nest, and instruct thee how
To snare the nimble marmozet; I'll bring thee
To clustering filberds, and sometimes I'll get thee
Young sea-mells* from the rock.

* The sea-mell is pronounced by some commentators to be a species of sea gull. In the original text the word is "scamels."

Act III.

Ferdinand and Miranda. Prospero at a distance.

Miranda. Alas, now! pray you,
Work not so hard: I would the lightning had
Burnt up those logs, that you are enjoin'd to pile!
Pray, set it down, and rest you: when this burns,
'Twill weep for having wearied you. My father
Is hard at study; pray now, rest yourself;
He's safe for these three hours.

Ferdinand. O most dear mistress,
The sun will set, before I shall discharge
What I must strive to do.

Miranda. If you will sit down
I'll bear your logs the while: pray give me that;
I'll carry it to the pile.

Ferdinand. No, precious creature;
I had rather crack my sinews, break my back,
Than you should such dishonour undergo,
While I sit lazy by.

Miranda. It would become me
As well as it does you: and I should do it
With much more ease; for my good will is to it,
And yours against.

Prospero. Poor worm! thou art infected;
This visitation shews it.

Miranda. You look wearily.

Ferdinand. No, noble mistress; 'tis fresh morning with me
When you are by at night. I do beseech you
(Chiefly that I might set it in my prayers),
What is your name?

Miranda. Miranda:—O my father,
I have broke your hest* to say so!

* Disobeyed her father's injunctions.

FERDINAND. Admired Miranda!
Indeed the top of admiration; worth
What's dearest to the world! Full many a lady
I have eyed with best regard; and many a time
The harmony of their tongues hath into bondage
Brought my too diligent ear: for several virtues
Have I liked several women; never any
With so full soul, but some defect in her
Did quarrel with the noblest grace she owed,*
And put it to the foil: But you, O you,
So perfect, and so peerless, are created
Of every creature's best.

MIRANDA. I do not know
One of my sex: no woman's face remember,
Save, from my glass, mine own; nor have I seen
More that I may call men, than you, good friend,
And my dear father: how features are abroad,
I am skill-less of; but, by my modesty,
(The jewel in my dower) I would not wish
Any companion in the world but you;
Nor can imagination form a shape,
Besides yourself, to like of: but I prattle
Something too wildly, and my father's precepts
Therein forget.

FERDINAND. I am, in my condition,
A prince, Miranda; I do think, a king;
(I would, not so!) and would no more endure
This wooden slavery, than I would suffer
The flesh-fly blow my mouth.—Hear my soul speak;
—The very instant that I saw you, did
My heart fly to your service; there resides,
To make me slave to it; and, for your sake,
Am I this patient log-man.

* Owned.

MIRANDA. Do you love me?

FERDINAND. O heaven, O earth, bear witness to this sound,
And crown what I profess with kind event,
If I speak true; if hollowly, invert
What best is boded me, to mischief! I,
Beyond all limit of what else i' the world,
Do love, prize, honour you.

MIRANDA. I am a fool,
To weep at what I am glad of.

A Guilty Conscience.

O, it is monstrous! monstrous!
Methought the billows spoke and told me of it;
The winds did sing it to me; and the thunder,
That deep and dreadful organ pipe, pronounced
The name of Prosper.

ACT IV.

Vanity of Human Nature.

These our actors,
As I foretold you, were all spirits, and
Are melted into air, into thin air:
And, like the baseless fabric of this vision,
The cloud-capp'd towers, the gorgeous palaces,
The solemn temples, the great globe itself;
Yea, all which it inherit shall dissolve;
And, like this insubstantial pageant faded,
Leave not a rack* behind. We are such stuff
As dreams are made on, and our little life
Is rounded with a sleep.

* *Rack* refers to the clouds when in motion; some critics suppose that *track* was the original word used.

Drunkards Enchanted by Ariel.

I told you, sir, they were red-hot with drinking;
So full of valour, that they smote the air
For breathing in their faces; beat the ground
For kissing of their feet: yet always bending
Towards their project. Then I beat my tabor,
At which, like unback'd colts, they prick'd their ears,
Advanced their eyelids, lifted up their noses,
As they smelt music; so I charm'd their ears,
That, calf-like, they my lowing followed through
Tooth'd briers, sharp furzes, pricking goss, and thorns,
Which entered their frail shins: at last I left them
I' the filthy mantled pool beyond your cell,
There dancing up to their chins.

Act V.

Prospero's Abjuration of Magic.

Ye elves of hills, brooks, standing lakes, and groves,
And ye, that on the sands with printless foot
Do chase the ebbing Neptune, and do fly him
When he comes back; you demi-puppets, that
By moonshine do the green-sour ringlets make,
Whereof the ewe not bites; and you, whose pastime
Is to make midnight-mushrooms; that rejoice
To hear the solemn curfew; by whose aid
(Weak masters though ye be) I have bedimm'd
The nood-tide sun, call'd forth the mutinous winds,
And 'twixt the green sea and the azured vault
Set roaring war; to the dread rattling thunder
Have I given fire, and rifted Jove's stout oak
With his own bolt: the strong-based promontory
Have I made shake; and by the spurs pluck'd up

The pine and cedar: graves at my command
Have waked their sleepers; ope'd and let them forth
By my so potent art; but this rough magic
I here abjure: and, when I have requir'd
Some heavenly music (which even now I do)
To work mine end upon their senses, that
This airy charm is for, I'll break my staff,
Bury it certain fathoms in the earth,
And deeper than did ever plummet sound,
I'll drown my book.

Senses returning.

The charm dissolves apace,
And as the morning steals upon the night,
Melting the darkness, so their rising senses
Begin to chase the ignorant fumes that mantle
Their clearer reason.—O my good Gonzalo,
My true preserver, and a loyal sir
To him thou follow'st: I will pay thy graces
Home, both in word and deed.—Most cruelly
Didst thou, Alonso, use me and my daughter;
Thy brother was a furtherer in the act:—
Thou'rt pinch'd for't now, Sebastian.—Flesh and blood,
You brother mine, that entertain'd ambition,
Expell'd remorse* and nature; who, with Sebastian
(Whose inward pinches are most strong),
Would here have kill'd our king: I do forgive thee,
Unnatural though thou art! Their understanding
Begins to swell; and the approaching tide
Will shortly fill the reasonable shores,
That now lie foul and muddy. Not one of them
That yet looks on me, or would know me.

* Used here in the sense of compassion.

Ariel's Song.

Where the bee sucks, there suck I;
In a cowslip's bell I lie;
There I couch when owls do cry.
On the bat's back I do fly,
After summer, merrily:
Merrily, merrily, shall I live now,
Under the blossom that hangs on the bough.

—ooo—

TWELFTH NIGHT.

Orsino, Duke of Illyria, is a suitor for the hand of Olivia, a rich countess. Sebastian and Viola, who are twin brother and sister, have been shipwrecked, but are saved; Viola, however, misses her brother in the wreck, and, believing him to be drowned, dresses herself in male attire, and, assuming the name of Cesario, enters the service of Orsino, of whom she becomes enamoured. Olivia rejects the proffered hand of Orsino, and falls passionately in love with Viola, believing her, from her costume, to be a man. Eventually Sebastian reaches Illyria, and his exact likeness to his twin sister occasions numerous amusing mistakes. In the end Orsino is accepted by Viola as her husband, and Sebastian by Olivia. The play is enlivened by a number of comic incidents, in which Malvolio (Olivia's steward), Sir Toby Belch (her uncle), and Sir Andrew Aguecheek, are the chief actors.

Act I.

Music.

If music be the food of love, play on,
Give me excess of it; that, surfeiting,

The appetite may sicken and so die,——
That strain again; it had a dying fall:
O, it came o'er my ear like the sweet south,
That breathes upon a bank of violets,
Stealing, and giving odour.

Escape from Shipwreck.

I saw your brother,
Most provident in peril, bind himself
(Courage and hope both teaching him the practice)
To a strong mast that lived upon the sea;
Where, like Arion on the dolphin's back,
I saw him hold acquaintance with the waves,
So long as I could see.

Description of a Beautiful Boy.

Dear lad, believe it;
For they shall yet belie thy happy years
That say, thou art a man: Diana's lip
Is not more smooth and rubious; thy small pipe
Is, as the maiden's organ, shrill and sound,
And all is semblative a woman's part.

Act II.

Disguise.

Disguise, I see, thou art a wickedness,
Wherein the pregnant enemy does much.
How easy is it for the proper false*
In women's waxen hearts to set their forms!
Alas, our frailty is the cause, not we;
For, such as we are made of, such we be.

* *Proper* is here used to signify *handsome*.

True Love.

Come hither, boy; if ever thou shalt love,
In the sweet pangs of it remember me:
For, such as I am, all true lovers are;
Unstaid and skittish in all motion else,
Save in the constant image of the creature
That is beloved.

The Wife should be Younger than the Husband.

Let still the woman take
An elder than herself; so wears she to him,
So sways she level in her husband's heart.
For, boy, however we do praise ourselves,
Our fancies are more giddy and unfirm,
More longing, wavering, sooner lost and worn,
Than women's are.

Character of an Old Song.

Mark it, Cesario; it is old and plain:
The spinsters and the knitters in the sun,
And the free maids, that weave their thread with bones,*
Do use to chant it: it is silly sooth,†
And dallies with the innocence of love,
Like the old age.

Song.

Come away, come away, death,
And in sad cypress let me be laid;
Fly away, fly away, breath;
I am slain by a fair cruel maid.
My shroud of white, stuck all with yew,
O, prepare it;

* Lace-makers. † Simple truth.

My part of death no one so true
Did share it.

Not a flower, not a flower sweet,
On my black coffin let there be strown;
Not a friend, not a friend greet
My poor corpse, where my bones shall be thrown.
A thousand thousands sighs to save,
Lay me, O, where
Sad true lover ne'er find my grave
To weep there.

Viola, attired as a Page, speaks of her concealed Love for the Duke.

VIOLA. Ay, but I know,—
DUKE. What dost thou know?
VIOLA. Too well what love women to men may owe:
In faith, they are as true of heart as we.
My father had a daughter lov'd a man,
As it might be, perhaps, were I a woman,
I should your lordship.
DUKE. And what's her history?
VIOLA. A blank, my lord: She never told her love,
But let concealment, like a worm i' the bud,
Feed on her damask cheek: she pin'd in thought,
And, with a green and yellow melancholy,
She sat like Patience on a monument,
Smiling at grief. Was not this love, indeed?
We men may say more, swear more: but, indeed,
Our shows are more than will; for still we prove
Much in our vows, but little in our love.

Act III.

A Jester.

This fellow's wise enough to play the fool;
And, to do that well, craves a kind of wit;
He must observe their mood on whom he jests,
The quality of persons and the time;
And, like the haggard,* check at every feather
That comes before his eye. This is a practice,
As full of labour as a wise man's art:
For folly, that he wisely shews, is fit;
But wise men, folly-fallen, quite taint their wit.

Unsought Love.

Cesario, by the roses of the spring,
By maidhood, honour, truth, and every thing,
I love thee so, that maugre† all thy pride,
Nor wit, nor reason can my passion hide.
Do not extort thy reasons from this clause,
For, that I woo, thou therefore hast no cause;
But, rather, reason thus with reason fetter:
Love sought is good, but given unsought is better.

—*ooo*—

TWO GENTLEMEN OF VERONA.

Valentine and Proteus, the two gentlemen of Verona, are in love severally with Silvia, daughter of the Duke of Milan, and Julia, a lady of Verona. Valentine leaves Verona for the court of Milan, where he is joined by Proteus, Julia following her lover in male attire. Proteus proves inconstant and becomes enamoured of Silvia, whose intended elopement and marriage with Valentine

* A hawk not properly trained. † Notwithstanding.

he betrays to her father the Duke, who designs to wed her tc Thurio an empty braggart. On discovering this the Duke banishes Valentine from his dominions, who, journeying towards Mantua, encounters in a forest certain outlaws, who make him their captain. After Valentine's exile, Proteus, dissembling his love for Silvia, promises the Duke to urge her to accept Thurio; she rejects both suitors and follows Valentine, on whom her father at length bestows her. The treachery of Proteus being discovered, he becomes repentant, and is pardoned by Julia, who accepts him as her husband. The more serious parts of the play are relieved by the comic scenes in which Speed and Launce, servants to Valentine and Proteus, appear.

Act I.

Love Commended and Censured.

Proteus. Yet writers say, As in the sweetest bud
The eating canker dwells, so eating love
Inhabits in the finest wits of all.
Valentine. And writers say, As the most forward bud
Is eaten by the canker ere it blow,
Even so by love the young and tender wit
Is turn'd to folly; blasting in the bud,
Losing his verdure even in the prime,
And all the fair effects of future hopes.

Love Froward and Dissembling.

Maids, in modesty say "*No*" to that
Which they would have the profferer construe *Aye.*
Fie, fie! how wayward is this foolish love;
That, like a testy babe will scratch the nurse,
And presently, all humbled, kiss the rod!

Advantage of Travelling.

He cannot be a perfect man,
Not being try'd and tutor'd in the world;

Experience is by industry achieved,
And perfected by the swift course of time.

Love compared to an April day.

O, how this spring of love resembleth
The uncertain glory of an April day;
Which now shews all the beauty of the sun,
And by and bye a cloud takes all away!

Act II.

An accomplished young Gentleman.

His years but young, but his experience old;
His head unmellow'd, but his judgment ripe;
And, in a word (for far behind his worth
Come all the praises that I now bestow),
He is complete in feature, and in mind,
With all good grace to grace a gentleman.

Contempt of Love punished.

I have done penance for contemning love;
Whose high imperious thoughts have punish'd me
With bitter fasts, with penitential groans,
With nightly tears, and daily heart-sore sighs;
For, in revenge of my contempt of love,
Love hath chased sleep from my enthralled eyes,
And made them watchers of mine own heart's sorrow.
O, gentle Proteus, Love's a mighty lord,
And hath so humbled me, as, I confess,
There is no woe to his correction,
Nor, to his service, no such joy on earth!
Now, no discourse, except it be of love;
Now can I break my fast, dine, sup, and sleep,
Upon the very naked name of love.

Love increased by Attempts to suppress it.

JULIA. Didst thou but know the inly touch of love;
Thou wouldst as soon go kindle fire with snow,
As seek to quench the fire of love with words.
LUCETTA. I do not seek to quench your love's hot fire;
But qualify the fire's extreme rage,
Lest it should burn above the bounds of reason.
JULIA. The more thou damm'st it up, the more it burns;
The current, that with gentle murmur glides,
Thou know'st, being stopp'd, impatiently doth rage;
But, when his fair course is not hindered,
He makes sweet music with the enamell'd stones,
Giving a gentle kiss to every sedge
He overtaketh in his pilgrimage;
And so by many winding nooks he strays,
With willing sport, to the wild ocean.
Then let me go, and hinder not my course;
I'll be as patient as a gentle stream,
And make a pastime of each weary step,
Till the last step have brought me to my love;
And there I'll rest, as, after much turmoil,
A blessed soul doth in Elysium.

A faithful Lover.

His words are bonds, his oaths are oracles;
His love sincere, his thoughts immaculate;
His tears pure messengers sent from his heart,
His heart as far from fraud as heaven from earth.

Act III.

Presents prevail with Woman.

Win her with gifts, if she respect not words ;
Dumb jewels often, in their silent kind,
More than quick words do move a woman's mind.

Beauty petitioning in vain.

Ay, ay ; and she hath offer'd to the doom,
(Which unreversed, stands in effectual force),
A sea of melting pearl, which some call tears :
Those at her father's churlish feet she tender'd ;
With them, upon her knees, her humble self ;
Wringing her hands, whose whiteness so became them,
As if but now they waxed pale for woe ;
But neither bended knees, pure hands held up,
Sad sighs, deep groans, nor silver-shedding tears,
Could penetrate her uncompassionate sire.

Hope.

Hope is a lover's staff ; walk hence with that,
And manage it against despairing thoughts.

Three Things in Man disliked by Women.

The best way is to slander Valentine
With falsehood, cowardice, and poor descent ;
Three things that women highly hold in hate.

The Power of Poetry with Women.

Say, that upon the altar of her beauty
You sacrifice your tears, your sighs, your heart
Write till your ink be dry ; and with your tears
Moist it again, and frame some feeling line,
That may discover such integrity :—

For Orpheus' lute was strung with poet's sinews;
Whose golden touch could soften steel and stones,
Make tigers tame, and huge leviathans
Forsake unsounded deeps to dance on sands.

Act V.

A Lover in Solitude.

How use doth breed a habit in a man!
This shadowy desert, unfrequented woods,
I better brook than flourishing peopled towns.
Here can I sit alone, unseen of any,
And, to the nightingale's complaining notes,
Tune my distresses, and record my woes.
O thou that dost inhabit in my breast,
Leave not the mansion so long tenantless;
Lest, growing ruinous, the building fall,
And leave no memory of what it was!
Repair me with thy presence, Sylvia;
Thou gentle nymph, cherish thy forlorn swain!

Love unreturned.

What dangerous action, stood it next to death,
Would I not undergo for one calm look?
O, 'tis the curse in love, and still approved,
When women cannot love where they're beloved.

Infidelity in a Friend.

Who should be trusted now, when one's right hand
Is perjur'd to the bosom? Proteus,
I am sorry I must never trust thee more,
But count the world a stranger for thy sake.
The private wound is deepest.

Repentance.

Who by repentance is not satisfied,
Is not of heaven nor earth.

Inconstancy in Man.

O heaven! were man
But constant, he were perfect: that one error
Fills him with faults.

—ooo—

WINTER'S TALE.

Polixenes, King of Bohemia, is on a visit to his friend Leontes, King of Sicilia, and is about to take his leave, when he is induced, chiefly by the courteous solicitations of Hermione wife of Leontes, to prolong his visit. Suddenly Leontes, who has hitherto been a kind husband, changes his love for Hermione to the bitterest hate, orders her to prison, and commands Antigonus, a Sicilian lord, to take away her infant daughter, and leave the child exposed in a remote and desert place in Bohemia. An old shepherd finds the little princess and brings her up as his own child under the name of Perdita. When she has arrived at womanhood, she is encountered by Florizel, the son of Polixenes, and they become enamoured of each other, she being then supposed to be the daughter of the old shepherd. The play concludes with the discovery of the royal descent of Perdita, and Hermione (who for a number of years has been supposed to be dead, but who has been only in concealment) is restored to Leontes, who deeply repents of his cruel persecution of her.

Act I.

Fondness of a Father for his Child.

If at home, sir,
He's all my exercise, my mirth, my matter:

Now my sworn friend, and then mine enemy:
My parasite, my soldier, statesman, all:
He makes a July's day short as December:
And, with his varying childness, cures in me
Thoughts that would thick my blood.

Regicides hateful.

To do this deed,
Promotion follows; if I could find example
Of thousands, that had struck anointed kings,
And flourished after, I'd not do't: but since
Nor brass, nor stone, nor parchment, bears not one,
Let villany itself forswear't.

Act II.

Eloquence of silent Innocence.

The silence often of pure innocence
Persuades, when speaking fails.

Exposing an Infant.

Come on, poor babe:
Some powerful spirit instruct the kites and ravens,
To be thy nurses! Wolves and bears, they say,
Casting their savageness aside, have done
Like offices of pity.

Act III.

Innocence.

Innocence shall make
False accusation blush, and tyranny
Tremble at patience.

Despair of Pardon.

But, O thou tyrant!
Do not repent these things; for they are heavier
Than all thy woes can stir: therefore betake thee,
To nothing but despair. A thousand knees
Ten thousand years together, naked, fasting,
Upon a barren mountain, and still winter
In storm perpetual, could not move the gods
To look that way thou wert.

Infant exposed.

Poor wretch,
That, for thy mother's fault, art thus exposed
To loss, and what may follow!—Weep I cannot,
But my heart bleeds: and most accursed am I,
To be by oath enjoin'd to this.—Farewell!
The day frowns more and more; thou art like to have
A lullaby too rough.

A Rustic's Description of a Shipwreck.

I would you did but see how it chafes, how it rages, how it takes up the shore! but that's not to the point. O, the most piteous cry of the poor souls! sometimes to see 'em, and not to see 'em; now the ship boring the moon with her main-mast; and anon swallowed with yest and froth, as you'd thrust a cork into a hogshead. And then for the land service,—To see how the bear tore out his shoulder-bone; how he cried to me for help, and said his name was Antigonus, a nobleman.—But to make an end of the ship: to see how the sea flap-dragoned* it:—but, first, how the poor souls roared, and the sea mocked them;—and how the

* Engulphed.

poor gentleman roared, and the bear mocked him, both roaring louder than the sea or weather.

Act IV.

True Love.

He says, he loves my daughter;
I think so too; for never gazed the moon
Upon the water, as he'll stand, and read
As 'twere, my daughter's eyes: and, to be plain,
I think there is not half a kiss to choose
Who loves another best.

A Father the best Guest at his Son's Nuptials.

Polixenes. Methinks, a father
Is, at the nuptial of his son, a guest
That best becomes the table. Pray you, once more
Is not your father grown incapable
Of reasonable affairs? is he not stupid
With age, and altering rheums? can he speak? hear?
Know man from man? dispute his own estate?
Lies he not bed-rid? and again does nothing,
But what he did being childish?
Florizel. No, good sir:
He has his health, and ampler strength, indeed,
Than most have of his age.
Polixenes. By my white beard,
You offer him, if this be so, a wrong
Something unfilial. Reason, my son,
Should choose himself a wife; but as good reason,
The father (all whose joy is nothing else
But fair posterity), should hold some counsel
In such a business.

Rural Simplicity.

I was not much afeard: for once or twice
I was about to speak; and tell him plainly,
The self-same sun, that shines upon his court,
Hides not his visage from our cottage, but
Looks on alike.

Love cemented by Prosperity, but loosened by Adversity.

Prosperity's the very bond of love;
Whose fresh complexion and whose heart together
Affliction alters.

Act V.

A Statue.

Leontes. What was he that did make it?—See, my lord,
Would you not deem it breath'd?—and that those veins
Did verily bear blood?
Polixenes. Masterly done:
The very life seems warm upon her lip.
Leontes. The fixure of her eye hath motion in't
As* we are mock'd with art.
* * * * *
Still, methinks,
There is an air comes from her. What fine chisel
Could ever yet cut breath? Let no man mock me,
For I will kiss her.

—ooo—

HAMLET.

Claudius, the reigning king of Denmark, has killed his brother, the former king, and placed himself on the throne, marrying

* As if.

at the same time the widow of the murdered monarch, whose ghost appears to his son Hamlet, urging him to avenge his death. In order the better to effect this object, Hamlet feigns madness, and causes a play to be acted before the king and queen which represents a scene similar to the murder of his father. The agitation of the king and queen at witnessing this representation, convinces Hamlet of their guilt, and he eventually avenges his father's death by killing the guilty Claudius; the queen drinks poison which is intended by the king for Hamlet, who, in a fencing bout with Laertes, son of Polonius, a foolish old lord, is wounded by a rapier anointed with poison and dies. Ophelia, the daughter of Polonius, goes mad, and drowns herself in a distraught state, whilst Polonius himself is stabbed by Hamlet. The play, perhaps more than any other of Shakspere's, abounds in tragic incidents. "If," says Dr. Johnson, speaking of this play, "the dramas of Shakspere were to be characterized each by the particular excellence which distinguishes it from the rest, we must allow to the tragedy of Hamlet the praise of variety; the incidents are so numerous that the argument of the play would make a long tale."

Act I.

Ghosts vanish at the Crowing of a Cock.

Bernardo. It was about to speak when the cock crew.

Horatio. And then it started, like a guilty thing
Upon a fearful summons. I have heard,
The cock, that is the trumpet of the morn,
Doth with his lofty and shrill-sounding throat
Awake the god of day; and, at his warning,
Whether in sea or fire, in earth or air,
The extravagant and erring spirit hies
To his confine.

The Reverence paid to Christmas Time.

It faded on the crowing of the cock.
Some say, that ever 'gainst that season comes

Wherein our Saviour's birth is celebrated,
This bird of dawning singeth all night long :
And then, they say, no spirit dares stir abroad ;
The nights are wholesome ; then no planets strike,
No fairy takes, nor witch hath power to charm,
So hallow'd and so gracious is the time.

Morning.

But, look, the morn, in russet mantle clad,
Walks o'er the dew of yon high eastern hill.

Real Grief.

'Tis not alone my inky cloak, good mother,
Nor customary suits of solemn black,
Nor windy suspiration of forced breath,
No, nor the fruitful river in the eye,
Nor the dejected 'haviour of the visage,
Together with all forms, modes, shows of grief,
That can denote me truly ; these, indeed, seem,
For they are actions that a man might play:
But I have that within, which passeth show ;
These, but the trappings and the suits of woe.

Immoderate Grief reproved.

'Tis sweet and commendable in your nature, Hamlet,
To give these mourning duties to your father :
But, you must know, your father lost a father ;
That father lost his, and the survivor bound
In filial obligation, for some term
To do obsequious sorrow : But to persevere
In obstinate condolement, is a course
Of impious stubbornness ; 'tis unmanly grief ;
It shows a will most incorrect to heaven ;
A heart unfortified, or mind impatient ;

An understanding simple and unschool'd:
For what we know must be, and is as common
As any the most vulgar thing to sense,
Why should we, in our peevish opposition,
Take it to heart? Fie! 'tis a fault to heaven,
A fault against the dead, a fault to nature,
To reason most absurd; whose common theme
Is death of fathers, and who still hath cried
From the first corse, till he that died to-day,
"This must be so."

Hamlet's Soliloquy on his Mother's Marriage.

O that this too too solid flesh would melt,
Thaw, and resolve* itself into a dew!
Or that the Everlasting had not fixed
His canon† 'gainst self-slaughter! O God! O God!
How weary, stale, flat, and unprofitable
Seem to me all the uses of this world!
Fie on't! O fie! 'tis an unweeded garden,
That grows to seed; things rank and gross in nature
Possess it merely. That it should come to this!
But two months dead!—nay, not so much, not two:
So excellent a king; that was, to this
Hyperion‡ to a satyr: so loving to my mother,
That he might not beteem§ the winds of heaven
Visit her face too roughly. Heaven and earth!
Must I remember? why, she would hang on him,
As if increase of appetite had grown
By what it fed on: and yet, within a month,—
Let me not think on't;—Frailty, thy name is woman!—
A little month; or ere those shoes were old,
With which she follow'd my poor father's body,

* Dissolve. † Law. ‡ A name for Apollo.
§ Allow.

Like Niobe, all tears;—why she, even she,—
O heaven! a beast, that wants discourse of reason,
Would have mourn'd longer,—married with my uncle,
My father's brother; but no more like my father,
Than I to Hercules: Within a month;
Ere yet the salt of most unrighteous tears
Had left the flushing in her galled eyes,
She married.

The Extent of Human Perfection.

He was a man, take him for all in all,
I shall not look upon his like again.

Cautions to young Women.

For Hamlet, and the trifling of his favour,
Hold it a fashion and a toy in blood;
A violet in the youth of primy nature,
Forward, not permanent, sweet, not lasting.
The perfume and suppliance of a minute:
No more.

Satire on ungracious Pastors.

I shall the effect of this good lesson keep,
As watchman to my heart: But, good my brother,
Do not, as some ungracious pastors do,
Show me the steep and thorny way to heaven;
Whilst, like a puff'd and reckless libertine,
Himself the primrose path of dalliance treads,
And recks not his own reed.*

Advice to a Son going to Travel.

Give thy thoughts no tongue,
Nor any unproportion'd thought his act.

* Regards not his own lessons.

Be thou familiar, but by no means vulgar.
The friends thou hast, and their adoption tried,
Grapple them to thy soul with hooks of steel;
But do not dull thy palm* with entertainment
Of each new-hatch'd, unfledged comrade. Beware
Of entrance to a quarrel: but, being in,
Bear it that the opposer may beware of thee.
Give every man thine ear, but few thy voice:
Take each man's censure,† but reserve thy judgment.
Costly thy habit as thy purse can buy,
But not express'd in fancy; rich, not gaudy:
For the apparel oft proclaims the man;
And they in France, of the best rank and station,
Are most select and generous, chief‡ in that.
Neither a borrower nor a lender be:
For loan oft loses both itself and friend;
And borrowing dulls the edge of husbandry.
This above all,—To thine own self be true;
And it must follow, as the night the day,
Thou canst not then be false to any man.

Hamlet's Address to his Father's Ghost.

Angels and ministers of grace defend us!—
Be thou a spirit of health, or goblin damn'd,
Bring with thee airs from heaven, or blasts from hell,
Be thy intents wicked or charitable,
Thou com'st in such a questionable shape,
That I will speak to thee; I'll call thee, Hamlet,
King, father, royal Dane: O, answer me:
Let me not burst in ignorance! but tell
Why thy canoniz'd bones, hearsed in death,
Have burst their cerements! why the sepulchre,
Wherein we saw thee quietly in-urn'd,

* Palm of the hand. † Opinion. ‡ Chiefly.

Hath oped his ponderous and marble jaws,
To cast thee up again! What may this mean,
That thou, dead corse, again, in complete steel,
Revisit'st thus the glimpses of the moon,
Making night hideous; and we fools of nature,
So horribly to shake our disposition,
With thoughts beyond the reaches of our souls?

The Dangers attendant on following the Ghost.

What, if it tempt you toward the flood, my lord,
Or to the dreadful summit of the cliff,
That beetles* o'er his base into the sea?
And there assume some other horrible form,
Which might deprive your sovereignty of reason,
And draw you into madness? think of it:
The very place puts toys† of desperation,
Without more motive, into every brain,
That looks so many fathoms to the sea,
And hears it roar beneath.

Ghost and Hamlet.

HAMLET. Whither wilt thou lead me? speak; I'll go no further.
GHOST. Mark me.
HAMLET. I will.
GHOST. My hour is almost come,
When I to sulphurous and tormenting flames
Must render up myself.
HAMLET. Alas, poor ghost!
GHOST. Pity me not, but lend thy serious hearing
To what I shall unfold.
HAMLET. Speak, I am bound to hear.

* Impends. † Whims.

GHOST. So art thou to revenge, when thou shalt hear.
HAMLET. What?
GHOST. I am thy father's spirit;
Doom'd for a certain term to walk the night;
And, for the day, confin'd to fast in fires,
Till the foul crimes, done in my days of nature,
Are burn'd and purg'd away. But that I am forbid
To tell the secrets of my prison house,
I could a tale unfold, whose lightest word
Would harrow up thy soul; freeze thy young blood;
Make thy two eyes, like stars, start from their spheres;
Thy knotted and combined locks to part,
And each particular hair to stand on end,
Like quills upon the fretful porcupine:
But this eternal blazon must not be
To ears of flesh and blood:—List, list, O list!
If thou didst ever thy dear father love,—
HAMLET. O heaven!
GHOST. Revenge his foul and most unnatural murder.
HAMLET. Murder?
GHOST. Murder most foul, as in the best it is;
But this most foul, strange, and unnatural.
HAMLET. Haste me to know it; that I with wings as swift
As meditation, or the thoughts of love,
May sweep to my revenge.
GHOST. I find thee apt;
And duller shouldst thou be than the fat weed
That rots itself in ease on Lethe's Wharf,
Wouldst thou not stir in this. Now, Hamlet, hear:
'Tis given out, that, sleeping in mine orchard,
A serpent stung me; so the whole ear of Denmark
Is, by a forged process of my death,
Rankly abus'd: but know, thou noble youth,

The serpent that did sting thy father's life
Now wears his crown.
HAMLET. O, my prophetic soul! my uncle!

The Ghost's Description of the Murder.

But soft! methinks I scent the morning air;
Brief let me be:—Sleeping within mine orchard,
My custom always of the afternoon,
Upon my secure hour thy uncle stole,
With juice of cursed hebenon* in a vial,
And in the porches of mine ears did pour
The leperous distilment; whose effect
Holds such an enmity with blood of man,
That, swift as quicksilver, it courses through
The natural gates and alleys of the body;
And, with a sudden vigour, it doth posset
And curd, like eager droppings into milk,
The thin and wholesome blood: so did it mine;
And a most instant tetter† bark'd about,
Most lazar‡ like, with vile and loathsome crust,
All my smooth body.
Thus was I, sleeping, by a brother's hand,
Of life, of crown, of queen, at once dispatch'd;§
Cut off even in the blossoms of my sin,
Unhousell'd,‖ disappointed, unanel'd;¶
No reckoning made, but sent to my account
With all my imperfections on my head.

Approach of Dawn.

The glow-worm shews the matin to be near,
And 'gins to pale his uneffectual fire.

* Henbane. † Scurf. ‡ Leprous.
§ Deprived. ‖ Without having received the sacrament.
¶ Without extreme unction.

Act II.

Old Age.

Beshrew my jealousy!
It seems, it is as proper to our age
To cast beyond ourselves in our opinions,
As it is common for the younger sort
To lack discretion.

Reflections on Man.

I have of late (but wherefore I know not) lost all my mirth, foregone all custom of exercises: and, indeed, it goes so heavily with my disposition, that this goodly frame, the earth, seems to me a sterile promontory: this most excellent canopy, the air, look you, this brave o'er-hanging firmament, this majestical roof fretted with golden fire, why, it appears no other thing to me, than a foul and pestilent congregation of vapours. What a piece of work is man! How noble in reason! how infinite in faculties! in form, and moving, how express and admirable! in action, how like an angel! in apprehension, how like a god! the beauty of the world! the paragon of animals! And yet, to me, what is this quintessence of dust? Man delights not me,—nor woman neither; though, by your smiling, you seem to say so.

Hamlet's Reflections on the Player.

O, what a rogue and peasant slave am I!
Is it not monstrous, that this player here,
But in a fiction, in a dream of passion,
Could force his soul thus to his own conceit,
That, from her working, all his visage wann'd;
Tears in his eyes, distraction in 's aspect,

A broken voice, and his whole function suiting
With forms to his conceit? And all for nothing!
For Hecuba!
What's Hecuba to him, or he to Hecuba,
That he should weep for her? What would he do,
Had he the motive and the cue for passion
That I have? He would drown the stage with tears,
And cleave the general ear with horrid speech;
Make mad the guilty, and appal the free,
Confound the ignorant; and amaze, indeed,
The very faculties of eyes and ears.
Yet I,
A dull and muddy-mettled rascal, peak,
Like John a-dreams, unpregnant of my cause,
And can say nothing; no, not for a king,
Upon whose property, and most dear life,
A damn'd defeat* was made. Am I a coward?
Who calls me villain? breaks my pate across?
Plucks off my beard, and blows it in my face?
Tweaks me by the nose? gives me the lie i' the throat,
As deep as to the lungs? Who does me this?
Ha!
Why, I should take it; for it cannot be,
But I am pigeon-liver'd, and lack gall
To make oppression bitter; or, ere this,
I should have fatted all the region kites
With this slave's offal.

Effect of a Play on the Mind.

I have heard
That guilty creatures, sitting at a play,
Have by the very cunning of the scene

* Alluding to his father's murder and the usurpation of the crown by his uncle.

Been struck so to the soul, that presently
They have proclaim'd their malefactions !*
For murder, though it have no tongue, will speak
With most miraculous organ. I 'll have these players
Play something like the murder of my father,
Before mine uncle : I 'll observe his looks ;
I 'll tent him to the quick ;† if he do blench
I know my course. The spirit that I have seen
May be a devil : and the devil hath power
To assume a pleasing shape ; yea, and, perhaps,
Out of my weakness and my melancholy
(As he is very potent with such spirits)
Abuses me to damn me. I 'll have grounds
More relative than this. The play 's the thing
Wherein I' ll catch the conscience of the king.

Act III.

Hamlet's Soliloquy on Life and Death.

To be, or not to be, that is the question :—
Whether 'tis nobler in the mind to suffer
The slings and arrows of outrageous fortune ;
Or to take arms against a sea of troubles,
And, by opposing, end them ?—To die,—to sleep,—
No more ;—and, by a sleep, to say we end
The heart-ache, and the thousand natural shocks
That flesh is heir to,—'tis a consummation
Devoutly to be wish'd. To die ;—to sleep ;—
To sleep ! perchance to dream ;—ay, there 's the rub ;
For in that sleep of death what dreams may come,
When we have shuffled off this mortal coil,‡
Must give us pause ; there 's the respect§

* Their crimes. † Particularly note if he betrays his guilt
‡ Confusion. § Reason.

That makes calamity of so long life:
For who would bear the whips and scorns of time,
The oppressor's wrong, the proud man's contumely,*
The pangs of despis'd love, the law's delay,
The insolence of office, and the spurns
That patient merit of the unworthy takes,
When he himself might his quietus† make
With a bare bodkin?‡ who would fardels§ bear,
To grunt and sweat under a weary life;
But that the dread of something after death,—
The undiscovered country, from whose bourn‖
No traveller returns,—puzzles the will;
And makes us rather bear those ills we have,
Than fly to others that we know not of?
Thus conscience does make cowards of us all;
And thus the native hue of resolution
Is sicklied o'er with the pale cast of thought;
And enterprises of great pith and moment,
With this regard, their currents turn awry,
And lose the name of action.

Calumny.

Be thou as chaste as ice, as pure as snow, thou shalt not escape calumny.

A Disordered Mind.

O, what a noble mind is here o'erthrown!
The courtier's, soldier's, scholar's, eye, tongue, sword,
The expectancy and rose of the fair state,
The glass of fashion, and the mould¶ of form,

* Contempt. † Acquittance.
‡ A dagger was in our author's time sometimes called a bodkin.
§ Burthens. ‖ Confines.
¶ The model by which others might frame themselves.

The observed of all observers! quite, quite down!
And I, of ladies most deject and wretched,
That suck'd the honey of his music vows,
Now see that noble and most sovereign reason,
Like sweet bells jangled, out of tune and harsh;
That unmatch'd form and feature of blown youth,
Blasted with ecstasy.*

Hamlet's Instructions to the Players.

HAMLET. Speak the speech, I pray you, as I pronounced it to you, trippingly on the tongue; but if you mouth it, as many of our players do, I had as lief the town-crier spoke my lines. Nor do not saw the air too much with your hand, thus; but use all gently: for in the very torrent, tempest, and (as I may say) whirlwind of your passion, you must acquire and beget a temperance that may give it smoothness. O, it offends me to the soul, to hear a robustious periwig-pated fellow tear a passion to tatters, to very rags, to split the ears of the groundlings; † who, for the most part, are capable of nothing but inexplicable dumb show and noise: I would have such a fellow whipped for out-doing Termagant; it out-herods Herod. Pray you avoid it.

PLAYER. I warrant your honour.

HAMLET. Be not too tame neither, but let your own discretion be your tutor; suit the action to the word, the word to the action; with this special observance, that you o'erstep not the modesty of nature: for any thing so overdone is from the purpose of playing, whose end, both at the first, and now, was, and is, to hold, as 'twere, the mirror up to nature; to show virtue her own feature, scorn her own image, and the very age and body

* Insanity.

† That portion of the audience occupying the pit of the theatre.

of the time, his form and pressure. Now this, over-done, or come tardy off, though it make the unskilful laugh, cannot but make the judicious grieve; the censure of which one must, in your allowance, overweigh a whole theatre of others. O, there be players, that I have seen play,—and heard others praise, and that highly—not to speak it profanely, that neither having the accent of Christians, nor the gait of Christian, Pagan, nor man, have so strutted, and bellowed, that I have thought some of nature's journeymen had made men, and not made them well, they imitated humanity so abominably.

Player. I hope we have reformed that indifferently with us.

Hamlet. O, reform it altogether. And let those that play your clowns speak no more than is set down for them: for there be of them that will themselves laugh, to set on some quantity of barren spectators to laugh too; though, in the mean time, some necessary question of the play be then to be considered: that's villanous: and shows a most pitiful ambition in the fool that uses it.

Hamlet's Esteem for his friend Horatio.

Nay, do not think I flatter:
For what advancement may I hope from thee,
That no revenue hast but thy good spirits
To feed and clothe thee? Why should the poor be flatter'd?
No, let the candied tongue lick absurd pomp;
And crook the pregnant* hinges of the knee,
Where thrift may follow fawning. Dost thou hear?
Since my dear soul was mistress of her choice.

* Prompt, facile.

And could of men distinguish her election,
She hath seal'd thee for herself; for thou hast been
As one in suffering all, that suffers nothing;
A man that fortune's buffets and rewards
Hast ta'en with equal thanks: and bless'd are those
Whose blood and judgment are so well co-mingled,
That they are not a pipe for fortune's finger
To sound what stop she please: Give me that man
That is not passion's slave, and I will wear him
In my heart's core, ay, in my heart of hearts,
As I do thee.

Midnight.

'Tis now the very witching time of night;
When churchyards yawn, and hell itself breathes out
Contagion to this world: Now could I drink hot blood,
And do such bitter business as the day
Would quake to look on. Soft; now to my mother—
O, heart, lose not thy nature; let not ever
The soul of Nero enter this firm bosom:
Let me be cruel, not unnatural:
I will speak daggers to her, but use none.

The King's Despairing Soliloquy.

O, my offence is rank, it smells to heaven;
It hath the primal eldest curse upon't,
A brother's murder!—Pray can I not,
Though inclination be as sharp as will;
My stronger guilt defeats my strong intent;
And, like a man to double business bound,
I stand in pause where I shall first begin,
And both neglect. What if this cursed hand
Were thicker than itself with brother's blood?
Is there not rain enough in the sweet heavens

To wash it white as snow? Whereto serves mercy,
But to confront the visage of offence?
And what's in prayer, but this two-fold force,—
To be forestalled ere we come to fall,
Or pardoned, being down? Then I'll look up;
My fault is past. But, O, what form of prayer
Can serve my turn? Forgive me my foul murder!—
That cannot be; since I am still possess'd
Of those effects for which I did the murder,
My crown, mine own ambition, and my queen.
May one be pardon'd, and retain the offence?
In the corrupted currents of this world,
Offence's gilded hand may shove by justice;
And oft 'tis seen, the wicked prize itself
Buys out the law. But 'tis not so above:
There is no shuffling, there the action lies
In his true nature; and we ourselves compell'd,
Even to the teeth and forehead of our faults,
To give in evidence. What then? what rests?
Try what repentance can: What can it not?
Yet what can it, when one cannot repent?
O wretched state! O bosom, black as death!
O limed soul, that, struggling to be free,
Art more engag'd! Help, angels, make assay!
Bow, stubborn knees! and, heart, with strings of steel,
Be soft as sinews of the new-born babe;
All may be well!

Hamlet and his Mother.

QUEEN. What have I done, that thou darest wag thy tongue
In noise so rude against me?
HAMLET. Such an act
That blurs the grace and blush of modesty;

Calls virtue hypocrite; takes off the rose
From the fair forehead of an innocent love,
And sets a blister there; makes marriage vows
As false as dicers' oaths: O, such a deed
As from the body of contraction* plucks
The very soul; and sweet religion makes
A rhapsody of words: heaven's face doth glow;
Yea, this solidity and compound mass,
With tristful† visage, as against the doom,
Is thought-sick at the act.

QUEEN. Ah me, what act,
That roars so loud, and thunders in the index?

HAMLET. Look here, upon this picture, and on this;
The counterfeit presentment of two brothers.
See, what a grace was seated on this brow:
Hyperion's‡ curls; the front of Jove himself;
An eye like Mars, to threaten and command;
A station like the herald Mercury,
New-lighted on a heaven-kissing hill;
A combination, and a form, indeed,
Where every god did seem to set his seal,
To give the world assurance of a man:
This was your husband.—Look you now, what follows;
Here is your husband; like a mildew'd ear,
Blasting his wholesome brother. Have you eyes?
Could you on this fair mountain leave to feed,
And batten on this moor? Ha! have you eyes?
You cannot call it love: for, at your age,
The hey-day in the blood is tame, 'tis humble,
And waits upon the judgment: and what judgment
Would step from this to this? Sense, sure you have,
Else could you not have motion: but, sure that sense
Is apoplex'd: for madness would not err;

* Contract of wedlock. † Mournful. ‡ Apollo's.

Nor sense to ecstasy* was ne'er so thrall'd,
But it reserved some quantity of choice,
To serve in such a difference. What devil was't
That thus hath cozen'd you at hoodman-blind?†
Eyes without feeling, feeling without sight,
Ears without hands or eyes, smelling sans‡ all,
Or but a sickly part of one true sense
Could not so mope.§
O shame! where is thy blush? Rebellious hell,
If thou canst mutine in a matron's bones,
To flaming youth let virtue be as wax,
And melt in her own fire: proclaim no shame,
When the compulsive ardour gives the charge;
Since frost itself as actively doth burn,
And reason panders will.

QUEEN. O Hamlet, speak no more:
Thou turn'st mine eyes into my very soul;
And there I see such black and grained spots,
As will not leave their tinct.||

Enter Ghost.

HAMLET. Save me, and hover o'er me with your wings,
You heavenly guards! — What would your gracious figure?

QUEEN. Alas, he's mad.

HAMLET. Do you not come your tardy son to chide,
That, lapsed in time and passion, lets go by
The important acting of your dread command?
O, say!

GHOST. Do not forget: this visitation
Is but to whet thy almost blunted purpose.

* Frenzy. † Blindman's-buff. ‡ Without. § Could not be so absurd. || Tinge, hue.

But, look! amazement on thy mother sits:
O, step between her and her fighting soul;
Conceit* in weakest bodies strongest works;
Speak to her, Hamlet.
HAMLET. How is it with you, lady?
QUEEN. Alas, how is't with you?
That you do bend your eye on vacancy,
And with the incorporal air do hold discourse?
Forth at your eyes your spirits wildly peep;
And, as the sleeping soldiers in the alarm,
Your bedded hair, like life in excrements,
Starts up, and stands on end. O gentle son,
Upon the heat and flame of thy distemper
Sprinkle cool patience. Whereon do you look?
HAMLET. On him! On him! Look you, how pale he glares!
His form and cause conjoin'd, preaching to stones,
Would make them capable.† Do not look upon me;
Lest with this piteous action, you convert
My stern effects;‡ then what I have to do
Will want true colour; tears, perchance, for blood.
QUEEN. To whom do you speak this?
HAMLET. Do you see nothing there?
QUEEN. Nothing at all; yet all that is I see.
HAMLET. Nor did you nothing hear?
QUEEN. No, nothing, but ourselves.
HAMLET. Why look you there! look, how it steals away!
My father, in his habit as he lived!
Look, where he goes, even now, out at the portal!
[*Exit Ghost*
QUEEN. This is the very coinage of your brain:

* Fancy. † Would make them comprehend. ‡ Actions.

This bodiless creation ecstasy
Is very cunning in.
HAMLET. Ecstasy!
My pulse, as yours, doth temperately keep time,
And makes as healthful music: it is not madness
That I have utter'd: bring me to the test,
And I the matter will re-word; which madness
Would gambol from. Mother, for love of grace,
Lay not that flattering unction to your soul,
That not your trespass, but my madness speaks:
It will but skin and film the ulcerous place;
Whiles rank corruption, mining all within,
Infects unseen. Confess yourself to heaven;
Repent what's past; avoid what is to come.

ACT IV.

Hamlet's Irresolution.

How all occasions do inform against me,
And spur my dull revenge! what is a man
If his chief good, and market* of his time,
Be but to sleep and feed? a beast, no more.
Sure, he that made us with such large discourse,†
Looking before and after, gave us not
That capability and god-like reason
To fust‡ in us unused. Now, whether it be
Bestial oblivion, or some craven scruple
Of thinking too precisely on the event,—
A thought which quarter'd hath but one part wisdom
And, ever, three parts coward,—I do not know
Why yet I live to say, "This thing's to do;"
Sith I have cause, and will, and strength, and means
To do't. Examples gross as earth exhort me.

* Profit. † Capacity. ‡ Moulder.

Sorrows rarely single.

When sorrows come, they come not single spies,
But in battalions!

The Divinity of Kings.

There's such divinity doth hedge a king,
That treason can but peep to what it would,
Acts little of his will.

Act V.

Hamlet's Reflections on Yorick's Skull.

Grave-digger. A pestilence on him for a mad rogue! he poured a flagon of Rhenish on my head once. This same skull, Sir, was Yorick's skull, the king's jester.

Hamlet. This?

Grave-digger. E'en that.

Hamlet. Alas poor Yorick!—I knew him, Horatio; a fellow of infinite jest; of most excellent fancy; he hath borne me on his back a thousand times; and now, how abhorred in my imagination it is! my gorge rises at it. Here hung those lips that I have kissed I know not how oft. Where be your gibes now? your gambols? your songs? your flashes of merriment, that were wont to set the table on a roar? Not one now to mock your own grinning: quite chap-fallen? Now get you to my lady's chamber, and tell her, let her paint an inch thick, to this favour* she must come; make her laugh at that.

Ophelia's Interment.

Lay her i' the earth;
And from her fair and unpolluted flesh,

* Condition.

May violets spring !—I tell thee, churlish priest,
A minist'ring angel shall my sister be,
When thou liest howling.

Melancholy.

This is mere madness ;
And thus a while the fit will work on him :
Anon, as patient as the female dove,
When that her golden couplets are disclosed,
His silence will sit drooping.

Providence directs our Actions.

There's a divinity that shapes our ends,
Rough-hew them how we will.

—*ooo*—

JULIUS CÆSAR.

Brutus and Cassius, noble Romans, envious of the popularity of Cæsar, conspire with Casca, Decius, and others to assassinate him. Cæsar is warned by his wife Calphurnia and a soothsayer against attending the Capitol ; he however disregards their admonitions, and is killed by the conspirators at the foot of Pompey's statue. In the commotion which ensues Brutus harangues the citizens, and wins them over to his side, but Mark Antony (called in the play Marcus Antonius), who is a strong adherent of Cæsar's, afterwards addresses the populace, and excites in them a desire to avenge the death of Cæsar. Octavius, Antony, and Lepidus, march with an army against Brutus and Cassius, who have fled from Rome and await with their forces the attack of Antony and his confederates. A quarrel ensues between Brutus and Cassius in the tent of the former, prior to the battle which is to decide their fates ; their differences, however, are soon healed, and they meet the hostile army at Philippi where they are defeated, and, rather than fall into the hands of their foes, kill themselves. Portia, the wife of Brutus, has, prior to this period, ended her life by poison. An eloquent tribute from Octavius and Antony to the character of Brutus ends the play.

Act I.

Patriotism.

What is it that you would impart to me?
If it be aught toward the general good,
Set honour in one eye, and death i' the other,
And I will look on both indifferently.
For, let the gods so speed me, as I love
The name of honour more than I fear death.

Contempt of Cassius for Cæsar.

Cassius. I was born free as Cæsar; so were you.
We both have fed as well; and we can both
Endure the winter's cold as well as he.
For once, upon a raw and gusty day,
The troubled Tiber chafing with her shores,
Cæsar said to me, "Dar'st thou, Cassius, now,
Leap in with me into this angry flood,
And swim to yonder point?" Upon the word,
Accoutred as I was, I plunged in,
And bade him follow: so, indeed, he did.
The torrent roar'd; and we did buffet it
With lusty sinews; throwing it aside,
And stemming it with hearts of controversy.
But ere we could arrive the point propos'd,
Cæsar cried, "Help me, Cassius, or I sink."
I, as Æneas, our great ancestor,
Did from the flames of Troy upon his shoulder
The old Anchises bear, so from the waves of Tiber
Did I the tired Cæsar: And this man
Is now become a god; and Cassius is

A wretched creature, and must bend his body,
If Cæsar carelessly but nod on him.
He had a fever when he was in Spain,
And, when the fit was on him, I did mark
How he did shake; 'tis true, this god did shake:
His coward lips did from their colour fly;
And that same eye, whose bend doth awe the world,
Did lose its lustre: I did hear him groan:
Ay, and that tongue of his, that bade the Romans
Mark him, and write his speeches in their books,
Alas! it cried, "Give me some drink, Titinius,"
As a sick girl. Ye gods, it doth amaze me,
A man of such a feeble temper should
So get the start of the majestic world,
And bear the palm alone. [*Shouts.*

BRUTUS. Another general shout!
I do believe that these applauses are
For some new honours that are heap'd on Cæsar.

CASSIUS. Why, man, he doth bestride the narrow world
Like a Colossus; and we petty men
Walk under his huge legs, and peep about
To find ourselves dishonourable graves.
Men at some time are masters of their fates:
The fault, dear Brutus, is not in our stars,
But in ourselves, that we are underlings.
Brutus and Cæsar: What should be in that Cæsar?
Why should that name be sounded more than yours?
Write them together, yours is as fair a name;
Sound them, it doth become the mouth as well;
Weigh them, it is as heavy; conjure them,
Brutus will start a spirit as soon as Cæsar.
Now in the names of all the gods at once,
Upon what meat doth this our Cæsar feed,

That he is grown so great? Age, thou art sham'd!
Rome, thou hast lost the breed of noble bloods!
When went there by an age, since the great flood,
But it was fam'd with more than with one man?
When could they say, till now, that talk'd of Rome,
That her wide walks encompass'd but one man?

Cæsar's suspicions of Cassius.

'Would he were fatter:—but I fear him not:
Yet if my name were liable to fear,
I do not know the man I should avoid
So soon as that spare Cassius. He reads much;
He is a great observer, and he looks
Quite through the deeds of men: he loves no plays,
As thou dost, Antony; he hears no music:
Seldom he smiles; and smiles in such a sort,
As if he mock'd himself, and scorn'd his spirit,
That could be mov'd to smile at any thing
Such men as he be never at heart's ease,
Whiles they behold a greater than themselves;
And therefore are they very dangerous.
I rather tell thee what is to be fear'd,
Than what I fear, for always I am Cæsar.

Act II.

Ambition clad in Humility.

But 'tis a common proof,
That lowliness is young ambition's ladder
Whereto the climber upward turns his face:
But when he once attains the upmost round,
He then unto the ladder turns his back,
Looks in the clouds, scorning the base degrees
By which he did ascend.

Conspiracy dreadful till executed.

Between the acting of a dreadful thing
And the first motion, all the interim is
Like a phantasma, or a hideous dream:
The genius, and the mortal instruments,
Are then in council: and the state of man,
Like to a little kingdom, suffers then
The nature of an insurrection.

Conspiracy.

O conspiracy!
Shamest thou to shew thy dangerous brow by night
When evils are most free? O then, by day,
Where wilt thou find a cavern dark enough
To mask thy monstrous visage? Seek none, conspiracy;
Hide it in smiles and affability;
For if thou path, thy native semblance on,
Not Erebus itself were dim enough
To hide thee from prevention.

Sleep.

Enjoy the honey-heavy dew of slumber:
Thou hast no figures nor no fantasies,
Which busy care draws in the brains of men;
Therefore thou sleep'st so sound.

Portents attend Royal Deaths.

When beggars die, there are no comets seen:
The heavens themselves blaze forth the death of princes.

The Fear of Death.

Cowards die many times before their deaths:
The valiant never taste of death but once.

Of all the wonders that I yet have heard,
It seems to me most strange that men should fear;
Seeing that death, a necessary end,
Will come when it will come.

Envy.

My heart laments that virtue cannot live
Out of the teeth of emulation.*

Act III.

Brutus's Address to the Citizens.

Brutus. Be patient till the last.
Romans, countrymen, and lovers! hear me for my cause; and be silent, that you may hear: believe me for mine honour; and have respect to mine honour, that you may believe: censure me in your wisdom; and awake your senses, that you may the better judge. If there be any in this assembly, any dear friend of Cæsar's, to him I say, that Brutus's love to Cæsar was no less than his. If then that friend demand why Brutus rose against Cæsar, this is my answer,—Not that I loved Cæsar less, but that I loved Rome more. Had you rather Cæsar were living and die all slaves; than that Cæsar were dead, to live all free men? As Cæsar loved me, I weep for him; as he was fortunate, I rejoice at it; as he was valiant, I honour him: but, as he was ambitious, I slew him. There is tears for his love; joy for his fortune; honour for his valour; and death for his ambition. Who is here so base, that would be a bondman? If any, speak; for him have I offended. Who is here so rude, that would not be a Roman? If any, speak, for him have I offended. Who is here so vile,

* Malice.

that will not love his country? If any, speak, for him have I offended. I pause for a reply.

CITIZENS. None, Brutus, none.

BRUTUS. Then none have I offended. I have done no more to Cæsar, than you should do to Brutus. The question of his death is enrolled in the Capitol; his glory not extenuated, wherein he was worthy; nor his offences enforced, for which he suffered death. Here comes his body, mourn'd by Mark Antony: who, though he had no hand in his death, shall receive the benefit of his dying, a place in the commonwealth; as which of you shall not? With this I depart: that, as I slew my best lover for the good of Rome, I have the same dagger for myself, when it shall please my country to need my death.

Antony's Oration over Cæsar's Body.

Friends, Romans, countrymen, lend me your ears!
I come to bury Cæsar, not to praise him;
The evil that men do, lives after them;
The good is oft interred with their bones;
So let it be with Cæsar. The noble Brutus
Hath told you, Cæsar was ambitious:
If it were so, it was a grievous fault;
And grievously hath Cæsar answer'd it.
Here, under leave of Brutus, and the rest
(For Brutus is an honourable man;
So they are all, all honourable men),
Come I to speak in Cæsar's funeral.
He was my friend, faithful and just to me;
But Brutus says, he was ambitious;
And Brutus is an honourable man.
He hath brought many captives home to Rome,
Whose ransoms did the general coffers fill:

Did this in Cæsar seem ambitious?
When that the poor have cried, Cæsar hath wept;
Ambition should be made of sterner stuff;
Yet Brutus says, he was ambitious;
And Brutus is an honourable man.
You all did see, that on the Lupercal,
I thrice presented him a kingly crown,
Which he did thrice refuse. Was this ambition?
Yet Brutus says, he was ambitious;
And, sure, he is an honourable man.
I speak not to disprove what Brutus spoke,
But here I am to speak what I do know.
You all did love him once, not without cause,
What cause withholds you then to mourn for him?
O judgment, thou art fled to brutish beasts,
And men have lost their reason!—Bear with me;
My heart is in the coffin there with Cæsar,
And I must pause till it comes back to me.

* * * * *

But yesterday the word of Cæsar might
Have stood against the world: now lies he there,
And none so poor to do him reverence.
O masters! if I were disposed to stir
Your hearts and minds to mutiny and rage,
I should do Brutus wrong, and Cassius wrong,
Who, you all know, are honourable men;
I will not do them wrong; I rather choose
To wrong the dead, to wrong myself, and you,
Than I will wrong such honourable men.
But here's a parchment, with the seal of Cæsar;
I found it in his closet, 'tis his will:
Let but the commons hear this testament
(Which, pardon me, I do not mean to read),
And they would go and kiss dead Cæsar's wounds,

And dip their napkins in his sacred blood;
Yea, beg a hair of him for memory,
And, dying, mention it within their wills,
Bequeathing it as a rich legacy,
Unto their issue.

* * * * *

If you have tears, prepare to shed them now.
You all do know this mantle: I remember
The first time ever Cæsar put it on;
'Twas on a summer's evening in his tent;
That day he overcame the Nervii:—
Look! in this place ran Cassius' dagger through:
See what a rent the envious Casca made:
Through this the well-beloved Brutus stabb'd;
And, as he pluck'd his cursed steel away,
Mark how the blood of Cæsar follow'd it,
As rushing out of doors, to be resolved,
If Brutus so unkindly knock'd or no:
For Brutus, as you know, was Cæsar's angel.
Judge, O you gods, how dearly Cæsar loved him!
This was the most unkindest cut of all:
For when the noble Cæsar saw him stab,
Ingratitude, more strong than traitor's arms,
Quite vanquish'd him: then burst his mighty heart;
And, in his mantle muffling up his face,
Even at the base of Pompey's statue,
Which all the while ran blood, great Cæsar fell
O, what a fall was there, my countrymen!
Then I, and you, and all of us, fell down,
Whilst bloody treason flourished over us.
O, now you weep; and, I perceive, you feel
The dint* of pity: these are gracious drops.
Kind souls, what, weep you, when you but behold

* Impression.

Our Cæsar's vesture wounded? Look you here,
Here is himself, marr'd, as you see, by traitors.

* * * * *

Good friends, sweet friends, let me not stir you up
To such a sudden flood of mutiny.
They that have done this deed are honourable:
What private griefs* they have, alas, I know not,
That made them do it; they are wise and honourable,
And will, no doubt, with reasons answer you.
I come not, friends, to steal away your hearts;
I am no orator, as Brutus is:
But, as you know me all, a plain blunt man,
That love my friend, and that they know full well
That gave me public leave to speak of him,
For I have neither wit, nor words, nor worth,
Action, nor utterance, nor the power of speech,
To stir men's blood: I only speak right on;
I tell you that which you yourselves do know;
Show you sweet Cæsar's wounds, poor, poor dumb mouths,
And bid them speak for me: but were I Brutus,
And Brutus Antony, there were an Antony
Would ruffle up your spirits, and put a tongue
In every wound of Cæsar's, that should move
The stones of Rome to rise and mutiny.

Act IV.

Ceremonious Courtesy insincere.

Ever note, Lucillus,
When love begins to sicken and decay,
It useth an enforced ceremony.
There are no tricks in plain and simple faith:

* Wrongs.

But hollow men, like horses hot at hand,
Make gallant show and promise of their mettle:
But when they should endure the bloody spur,
They fall their crests, and, like deceitful jades,
Sink in the trial.

The Quarrel Scene between Brutus and Cassius.

CASSIUS. That you have wronged me, doth appear in this:
You have condemn'd and noted Lucius Pella,
For taking bribes here of the Sardians;
Wherein my letters, praying on his side,
Because I knew the man, were slighted off.
BRUTUS. You wrong'd yourself to write in such a case.
CASSIUS. In such a time as this, it is not meet
That every nice* offence should bear his comment.
BRUTUS. Let me tell you, Cassius, you yourself
Are much condemn'd to have an itching palm;
To sell and mart your offices for gold
To undeservers.
CASSIUS. I an itching palm?
You know that you are Brutus that speak this,
Or, by the gods, this speech were else your last.
BRUTUS. The name of Cassius honours this corruption,
And chastisement doth therefore hide his head.
CASSIUS. Chastisement!
BRUTUS. Remember March, the ides of March remember!
Did not great Julius bleed for justice' sake?
What villain touch'd his body, that did stab,
And not for justice? What, shall one of us,

* Every trivial matter.

That struck the foremost man of all this world,
But for supporting robbers; shall we now
Contaminate our fingers with base bribes?
And sell the mighty space of our large honours,
For so much trash as may be grasped thus?—
I had rather be a dog, and bay the moon,
Than such a Roman.

CASSIUS. Brutus, bay not me,
I'll not endure it: you forget yourself
To hedge me in; I am a soldier, I,
Older in practice, abler than yourself
To make conditions.

BRUTUS. Go to; you're not, Cassius.

CASSIUS. I am.

BRUTUS. I say, you are not.

CASSIUS. Urge me no more, I shall forget myself:
Have mind upon your health, tempt me no further.

BRUTUS. Away, slight man!

CASSIUS. Is't possible?

BRUTUS. Hear me, for I will speak.
Must I give way and room to your rash choler?
Shall I be frighted when a madman stares?

CASSIUS. O, ye gods! ye gods! must I endure all this!

BRUTUS. All this? ay, more: fret till your proud heart break;
Go, show your slaves how choleric you are,
And make your bondmen tremble. Must I budge?
Must I observe you? Must I stand and crouch
Under your testy humour? By the gods
You shall digest the venom of your spleen
Though it do split you: for, from this day forth,
I'll use you for my mirth, yea, for my laughter,
When you are waspish.

CASSIUS. Is it come to this?

BRUTUS. You say you are a better soldier:
Let it appear so; make your vaunting true,
And it shall please me well: for mine own part,
I shall be glad to learn of noble men.

CASSIUS. You wrong me, every way you wrong me, Brutus;
I said an elder soldier, not a better:
Did I say better?

BRUTUS. If you did, I care not.

CASSIUS. When Cæsar liv'd, he durst not thus have mov'd me.

BRUTUS. Peace, peace; you durst not so have tempted him.

CASSIUS. I durst not?

BRUTUS. No.

CASSIUS. What? durst not tempt him?

BRUTUS. For your life you durst not.

CASSIUS. Do not presume too much upon my love,
I may do that I shall be sorry for.

BRUTUS. You have done that you should be sorry for.
There is no terror, Cassius, in your threats:
For I am arm'd so strong in honesty,
That they pass by me, as the idle wind,
Which I respect not. I did send to you
For certain sums of gold, which you denied me;—
For I can raise no money by vile means:
By heaven, I had rather coin my heart,
And drop my blood for drachmas,* than to wring
From the hard hands of peasants their vile trash
By any indirection. I did send
To you for gold to pay my legions,
Which you denied me: was that done like Cassius?

* Money.

Should I have answer'd Caius Cassius so?
When Marcus Brutus grows so covetous,
To lock such rascal counters from his friends,
Be ready, gods, with all your thunderbolts,
Dash him to pieces!

CASSIUS. I denied you not.

BRUTUS. You did.

CASSIUS. I did not: he was but a fool
That brought my answer back.—Brutus hath rived* my heart:
A friend should bear his friend's infirmities,
But Brutus makes mine greater than they are.

BRUTUS. I do not, till you practise them on me.

CASSIUS. You love me not.

BRUTUS. I do not like your faults.

CASSIUS. A friendly eye could never see such faults.

BRUTUS. A flatterer's would not, though they do appear
As huge as high Olympus.

CASSIUS. Come, Antony, and young Octavius come,
Revenge yourselves alone on Cassius,
For Cassius is aweary of the world:
Hated by one he loves; braved by his brother;
Check'd like a bondman; all his faults observed,
Set in a note-book, learn'd, and conn'd by rote,
To cast into my teeth. O, I could weep
My spirit from mine eyes!—There is my dagger,
And here my naked breast; within, a heart
Dearer than Plutus' mine, richer than gold;
If that thou be'st a Roman, take it forth:
I, that denied thee gold, will give my heart:
Strike, as thou didst at Cæsar; for, I know,

* Riven.

When thou didst hate him worst, thou lov'dst him better
Than ever thou lov'dst Cassius.
BRUTUS. Sheath your dagger:
Be angry when you will, it shall have scope;
Do what you will, dishonour shall be humour.
O Cassius, you are yoked with a lamb
That carries anger as the flint bears fire;
Who, much enforced, shows a hasty spark,
And straight is cold again.
CASSIUS. Hath Cassius lived
To be but mirth and laughter to his Brutus,
When grief and blood ill-temper'd vexeth him?
BRUTUS. When I spoke that I was ill-temper'd too.
CASSIUS. Do you confess so much? Give me your hand.
BRUTUS. And my heart too.
CASSIUS. O Brutus!
BRUTUS. What's the matter?
CASSIUS. Have you not love enough to bear with me,
When that rash humour, which my mother gave me,
Makes me forgetful?
BRUTUS. Yes, Cassius; and henceforth,
When you are over-earnest with your Brutus,
He'll think your mother chides, and leave you so.

Chances occur for Success in Life.

There is a tide in the affairs of men,
Which, taken at the flood, leads on to fortune;
Omitted, all the voyage of their life
Is bound in shallows and in miseries.
On such a full sea are we now afloat,
And we must take the current when it serves,
Or lose our ventures.

Act V.

The Parting of Brutus and Cassius before the Battle of Philippi.

Cassius. Then, if we lose this battle,
You are contented to be led in triumph
Through the streets of Rome?
Brutus. No, Cassius, no: think not, thou noble Roman,
That ever Brutus will go bound to Rome:
He bears too great a mind. But this same day
Must end that work the ides of March begun;
And whether we shall meet again I know not.
Therefore our everlasting farewell take:—
For ever, and for ever, farewell Cassius!
If we do meet again, why we shall smile;
If not, why then this parting was well made.
Cassius. For ever, and for ever, farewell, Brutus!
If we do meet again, we'll smile indeed;
If not, 'tis true, this parting was well made.
Brutus. Why, then, lead on.—O, that a man might know
The end of this day's business ere it come?
But it sufficeth that the day will end,
And then the end is known.

Antony's Description of Brutus.

This was the noblest Roman of them all;
All the conspirators, save only he,
Did that they did in envy of great Cæsar;
He, only, in a general honest thought,
And common good to all, made one of them.
His life was gentle; and the elements
So mix'd in him, that Nature might stand up,
And say to all the world "This was a man!"

KING LEAR.

Lear, King of Britain, desirous to "shake all cares and business from his age," resolves to divide his kingdom between his daughters, Goneril, Regan, and Cordelia. He inquires from them the degree of love each feels for him, and deceived by the extravagant professions of Goneril and Regan (wives of the Dukes of Albany and Cornwall), apportions his realm equally between them, to the unjust exclusion of Cordelia, his youngest daughter, whose affection for her father, though less strongly expressed than her sisters', is deep and genuine. The Earl of Kent strongly, but in vain, pleads against the disinherison of Cordelia, and is banished by Lear for his urgent pleading in her behalf. Notwithstanding her portionless condition, the King of France marries Cordelia for her beauty and worth, and takes her with him to France. Goneril and Regan, being mistresses of the kingdom, agree in turns to entertain their father and his retinue, but they treat the old king with cruelty, and he goes mad. Cordelia, now Queen of France, advised of her sisters' unfilial conduct, advances with an army to vindicate her father's cause, but her forces are defeated, and she and Lear are taken prisoners; she is executed, and he expires over her dead body. A dispute has occurred between Goneril and Regan, the latter of whom is poisoned by her sister, who kills herself. In a combat between Edmund and Edgar, half-brothers and sons of the Earl of Glo'ster, the former, whose conduct throughout the play is marked by the deepest villany, is slain, and dies confessing his crimes.

Act I.

Goneril's profession of Love for her Father.

Sir, I
Do love you more than words can wield the matter,
Dearer than eye-sight, space and liberty;
Beyond what can be valued, rich or rare;

No less than life, with grace, health, beauty, honour;
As much as child e'er lov'd, or father found.
A love that makes breath poor, and speech unable;
Beyond all manner of so much I love you.

Regan's profession of Filial Love.

I am made of that self metal as my sister,
And prize me at her worth. In my true heart
I find, she names my very deed of love;
Only she comes too short,—that I profess
Myself an enemy to all other joys,
Which the most precious square of sense possesses;
And find, I am alone felicitate
In your dear highness' love.

The King of France's approval of Cordelia's conduct.

Fairest Cordelia, thou art most rich, being poor;
Most choice, forsaken; and most loved, despised!
Thee and thy virtues here I seize upon:
Be it lawful, I take up what's cast away.
Gods, gods! 'tis strange that from their cold'st neglect
My love should kindle to inflamed respect.—
Thy dowerless daughter, king, thrown to my chance,
Is queen of us, of ours, and our fair France.
Not all the dukes of wat'rish Burgundy
Shall buy this unpriz'd precious maid of me.—
Bid them farewell, Cordelia, though unkind:
Thou losest here, a better where* to find.

Ingratitude in a Child.

Ingratitude! thou marble-hearted fiend,
More hideous, when thou show'st thee in a child,
Than the sea-monster!

* Here and where are in this place used as nouns.

Act II.

Lear's indignation at Goneril's unkindness.

I pr'ythee, daughter, do not make me mad;
I will not trouble thee, my child; farewell:
We'll no more meet, no more see one another:—
But yet thou art my flesh, my blood, my daughter;
Or, rather, a disease that's in my flesh,
Which I must needs call mine: thou art a boil,
A plague-sore, an embossed* carbuncle,
In my corrupted blood. But I'll not chide thee;
Let shame come when it will, I do not call it:
I do not bid the thunder-bearer shoot,
Nor tell tales of thee to high-judging Jove.

Lear on the Ingratitude of his Daughters.

You see me here, you gods, a poor old man,
As full of grief as age; wretched in both!
If it be you that stir these daughters' hearts
Against their father, fool me not so much
To bear it tamely; touch me with noble anger!
O, let not women's weapons, water-drops,
Stain my man's cheeks!—No, you unnatural hags,
I will have such revenges on you both,
That all the world shall—I will do such things,—
What they are, yet I know not: but they shall be
The terrors of the earth. You think I'll weep:
No, I'll not weep:—
I have full cause of weeping, but this heart
Shall break into a hundred thousand flaws,
Or ere I'll weep.

* Swollen.

Act III.

Lear's Exclamations in the Tempest.

Blow, wind, and crack your cheeks! rage! blow!
You cataracts and hurricanoes spout
Till you have drench'd our steeples, drowned the cocks!
You sulphurous and thought-executing fires,
Vaunt couriers to oak-cleaving thunderbolts,
Singe my white head! And thou, all-shaking thunder,
Strike flat the thick rotundity o' the world!
* * * * *
Rumble thy bellyful! Spit, fire! spout, rain!
Nor rain, wind, thunder, fire, are my daughters:
I tax you not, you elements with unkindness,
I never gave you kingdom, call'd you children,
You owe me no subscription;* why then, let fall
Your horrible pleasure; here I stand, your slave,
A poor, infirm, weak, and despis'd old man:—
But yet I call you servile ministers,
That have with two pernicious daughters join'd
Your high-engender'd battles 'gainst a head
So old and white as this. O! O! 'tis foul!

Reflections on Man.

Is man no more than this? Consider him well: thou owest the worm no silk, the beast no hide, the sheep no wool, the cat no perfume!—Ha! here's three of us are sophisticated!—Thou art the thing itself: unaccommodated man is no more but such a poor, bare, forked animal as thou art.—Off, off, you lendings.

* Allegiance.

Act IV.

Cordelia's emotion on hearing of her Sister's cruelty.

Patience and sorrow strove
Who should express her goodliest. You have seen
Sunshine and rain at once: her smiles and tears
Were like a better day: Those happy smiles,
That play'd on her ripe lip, seem'd not to know
What guests were in her eyes; which parted thence,
As pearls from diamonds dropp'd.

Description of Dover Cliff.

How fearful
And dizzy 'tis to cast one's eyes so low!
The crows, and choughs, that wing the midway air,
Show scarce so gross as beetles: half way down
Hangs one that gathers samphire; dreadful trade!
Methinks he seems no bigger than his head:
The fishermen, that walk upon the beach,
Appear like mice; and yon tall anchoring bark,
Diminished to her cock;* her cock, a buoy
Almost too small for sight: the murmuring surge
That on the unnumber'd idle pebbles chafes,
Cannot be heard so high:—I'll look no more;
Lest my brain turn, and the deficient sight
Topple down headlong.

Glos'ter's Farewell to the World.

O you mighty gods!
This world I do renounce; and, in your sights,
Shake patiently my great affliction off:
If I could bear it longer, and not fall

* Cock-boat, a small boat belonging to the "anchoring bark."

To quarrel with your great opposeless wills,
My snuff, and loathed part of nature should
Burn itself out.

Lear on his Flatterers.

They flatter'd me like a dog; and told me I had white hairs in my beard, ere the black ones were there. To say *ay* and *no*, to everything I said!—Ay and no too was no good divinity. When the rain came to wet me once, and the wind to make me chatter; when the thunder would not peace at my bidding; there I found them, there I smelt them out. Go to, they are not men o' their words; they told me I was everything; 'tis a lie; I am not ague-proof.

Scene between Lear and Cordelia.

CORDELIA. How does my royal lord? How fares your majesty?
LEAR. You do me wrong to take me out o' the grave.
Thou art a soul in bliss: but I am bound
Upon a wheel of fire, that mine own tears
Do scald like molten lead.
CORDELIA. Sir, do you know me?
LEAR. You are a spirit, I know; when did you die?
CORDELIA. Still, still, far wide!
PHYSICIAN. He's scarce awake; let him alone awhile.
LEAR. Where have I been?—Where am I?—Fair day-light?—
I am mightily abused.—I should even die with pity,
To see another thus.—I know not what to say.—
I will not swear these are my hands: let's see;
I feel this pin prick. Would I were assured
Of my condition.
CORDELIA. O, look upon me, sir,

And hold your hands in benediction o'er me :—
No, sir, you must not kneel.
LEAR. Pray do not mock me :
I am a very foolish fond old man,
Fourscore and upwards ; and, to deal plainly,
I fear I am not in my perfect mind.
Methinks I should know you, and know this man :
Yet I am doubtful : for I am mainly ignorant
What place this is ; and all the skill I have
Remembers not these garments, nor I know not
Where I did lodge last night. Do not laugh at me ;
For, as I am a man, I think this lady
To be my child Cordelia.
CORDELIA. And so I am, I am.
LEAR. Be your tears wet ? Yes, faith, I pray, weep not :
If you have poison for me, I will drink it.
I know you do not love me ; for your sisters
Have, as I do remember, done me wrong :
You have some cause, they have not.
CORDELIA. No cause, no cause.
LEAR. Am I in France ?
KENT. In your own kingdom, sir.
LEAR. Do not abuse me.
PHYSICIAN. Be comforted, good madam : the great rage,
You see, is cured in him ; and yet it is danger
To make him even o'er the time he has lost ;
Desire him to go in ; trouble him no more,
Till further settling.
CORDELIA. Will't please your highness walk ?
LEAR. You must bear with me :
Pray now forget and forgive : I am old and foolish.

Act V.

Lear to Cordelia when taken Prisoners.

Come, let's away to prison :
We two alone will sing like birds i' the cage :
When thou dost ask me blessing, I'll kneel down,
And ask of thee forgiveness : so we'll live,
And pray, and sing, and tell old tales, and laugh
At gilded butterflies and hear poor rogues
Talk of court news ; and we'll talk with them too,—
Who loses, and who wins ; who's in, who's out ;
And take upon us the mystery of things,
As if we were God's spies : and we'll wear out,
In a wall'd prison, packs and sects of great ones,
That ebb and flow by the moon.

Edgar's defiance of Edmund.

Draw thy sword ;
That if my speech offend a noble heart,
Thy arm may do thee justice : here is mine.
Behold, it is the privilege of mine honours,
My oath, and my profession : I protest,—
Maugre thy strength, youth, place, and eminence,
Despite thy victor sword, and fire-new fortune,
Thy valour, and thy heart,—thou art a traitor :
False to thy gods, thy brother, and thy father ;
Conspirant 'gainst this high illustrious prince ;
And from the extremest upward of thy head,
To the descent and dust beneath thy feet,
A most toad-spotted traitor. Say thou, *No,*
This sword, this arm, and my best spirits, are bent
To prove upon thy heart, whereto I speak,
Thou liest.

Lear on the Death of Cordelia.

Howl, howl, howl, howl!—O you are men of stones;
Had I your tongues and eyes, I'd use them so
That heaven's vault should crack:—O, she is gone for
ever!—
I know when one is dead, and when one lives;
She's dead as earth.—Lend me a looking-glass;
If that her breath will mist or stain the stone,
Why then she lives.

* * * * *

This feather stirs: she lives! if it be so,
It is a chance that does redeem all sorrows
That ever I have felt.

—ooo—

MACBETH.

Macbeth and Banquo, generals in the army of Duncan, king of Scotland, returning from a victorious campaign, encounter, on a blighted heath, three witches, who hail Macbeth as the future king of Scotland. Inspired thus with a craving for royalty, Macbeth, in a letter, informs his wife, an ambitious and unscrupulous woman, of the greatness that is predicted for him, and in order to obtain the sovereignty he resolves to murder the good king Duncan. The virtues of the king cause him to hesitate, but his scruples are overcome by Lady Macbeth, and he assassinates Duncan whilst a guest in Inverness Castle. With the connivance of his wife, Macbeth endeavours to cast suspicion of the murder on the guards who sleep at the entrance to the king's chamber; he is, however, himself suspected of the crime, especially by Banquo, who has heard the prediction of the witches; and Macbeth, remembering this, causes Banquo to be slain. Malcolm and Donalbain, sons of the deceased monarch, fly from Scotland; the former escapes to England, where he is joined by Macduff, a nobleman of Scotland. They obtain assistance from England, and, with an army commanded by Siward, Earl of Northumberland, besiege Macbeth's castle, where the tyrant is slain by Macduff. Lady Macbeth, a prey to remorse, and "troubled with thick-coming fancies," dies, and Malcolm is proclaimed King.

Act I.

Description of the Witches.

What are these,
So wither'd, and so wild in their attire;
That look not like the inhabitants o' the earth,
And yet are on't? Live you? or are you aught
That man may question? You seem to understand me,
By each at once her choppy finger laying
Upon her skinny lips:—You should be women,
And yet your beards forbid me to interpret
That you are so.

Macbeth's Disposition.

Yet do I fear thy nature;
It is too full o' the milk of human kindness,
To catch the nearest way: Thou would'st be great;
Art not without ambition; but without
The illness should attend it. What thou would'st highly,
That would'st thou holily: would'st not play false,
And yet would'st wrongly win.

Macbeth's Irresolution.

If it were done, when 'tis done, then 'twere well
It were done quickly: if the assassination
Could trammel up the consequence, and catch,

With his surcease, success; that but this blow
Might be the be-all and the end-all here;
But here, upon this bank and shoal of time,—
We'd jump the life to come.—But, in these cases,
We still have judgment here; that we but teach
Bloody instructions, which, being taught, return
To plague the inventor: this even-handed justice
Commends the ingredients of our poison'd chalice
To our own lips. He's here in double trust:
First, as I am his kinsman and his subject,
Strong both against the deed; then, as his host,
Who should against his murderer shut the door,
Not bear the knife myself. Besides, this Duncan
Hath borne his faculties so meek, hath been
So clear in his great office, that his virtues
Will plead like angels, trumpet-tongued, against
The deep damnation of his taking off:
And pity, like a naked new-born babe,
Striding the blast, or heaven's cherubim, hors'd
Upon the sightless couriers* of the air,
Shall blow the horrid deed in every eye,
That tears shall drown the wind.—I have no spur
To prick the sides of my intent, but only
Vaulting ambition, which o'erleaps itself,
And falls on the other.

Courage.

I dare do all that may become a man;
Who dares do more is none.

* An allusion to the winds; sightless is used for invisible.

Act II.

The Visionary Dagger Scene.

Is this a dagger which I see before me,
The handle toward my hand? Come, let me clutch thee:
I have thee not, and yet I see thee still.
Art thou not, fatal vision, sensible
To feeling as to sight? or art thou but
A dagger of the mind; a false creation,
Proceeding from the heat-oppressed brain?
I see thee yet, in form as palpable
As this which now I draw.
Thou marshall'st me the way that I was going,
And such an instrument I was to use.
Mine eyes are made the fools o' the other senses,
Or else worth all the rest; I see thee still;
And on thy blade, and dudgeon,* gouts† of blood,
Which was not so before.—There's no such thing:
It is the bloody business, which informs
Thus to mine eyes.

Act III.

Macbeth's Remorse.

We have scotch'd the snake, not kill'd it;
She'll close, and be herself; whilst our poor malice
Remains in danger of her former tooth.
But let the frame of things disjoint, both the worlds suffer,
Ere we will eat our meal in fear, and sleep
In the affliction of these terrible dreams,
That shake us nightly: better be with the dead,

* The handle of the dagger. † Spots of blood.

Whom we, to gain our place, have sent to peace,
Than on the torture of the mind to lie
In restless ecstasy.* Duncan is in his grave;
After life's fitful fever, he sleeps well;
Treason has done his worst; nor steel, nor poison,
Malice domestic, foreign levy, nothing,
Can touch him further.

Macbeth's Terror at the Ghost of Banquo.

What man dare, I dare:
Approach thou like the rugged Russian bear,
The arm'd rhinoceros, or the Hyrcan tiger,
Take any shape but that, and my firm nerves
Shall never tremble; or, be alive again,
And dare me to the desert with thy sword;
If trembling I inhibit thee,† protest me
The baby of a girl. Hence, horrible shadow!
Unreal mockery, hence!

Act IV.

Malcolm's Description of the Character of Macbeth.

I grant him bloody,
Luxurious, avaricious, false, deceitful,
Sudden, malicious, smacking of every sin
That has a name.

The Qualities which become a King.

The king-becoming graces,
As justice, verity, temperance, stableness,
Bounty, perseverance, mercy, lowliness,

* Mental torture.

† Inhibit means to forbid; the original reading is *inhabit then*.

Devotion, patience, courage, fortitude,
I have no relish of them.

A Distracted Kingdom.

Alas, poor country:
Almost afraid to know itself! It cannot
Be call'd our mother, but our grave: where nothing,
But who knows nothing, is once seen to smile;
Where sighs, and groans, and shrieks that rend the air,
Are made, not mark'd: where violent sorrow seems
A modern ecstasy: the dead man's knell
Is there scarce ask'd, for who; and good men's lives
Expire before the flowers in their caps,
Dying, or ere they sicken.

Act V.

Lady Macbeth in the Sleep-walking Scene.

Gentlewoman. Lo you, here she comes! This is her very guise; and, upon my life, fast asleep. Observe her: stand close.

Doctor. How came she by that light?

Gentlewoman. Why, it stood by her: she has light by her continually; 't is her command.

Doctor. You see, her eyes are open.

Gentlewoman. Ay, but their sense is shut.

Doctor. What is it she does now? Look, how she rubs her hands.

Gentlewoman. It is an accustomed action with her, to seem thus washing her hands; I have known her continue in this a quarter of an hour.

Lady Macbeth. Yet here's a spot.

Doctor. Hark! she speaks: I will set down what

comes from her, to satisfy my remembrance the more strongly.

Lady Macbeth. Out, damned spot! out, I say!— One; two; why, then, 'tis time to do't:——Hell is murky!—Fie, my lord; fie! a soldier and afeard? What need we fear who knows it, when none can call our power to account?—Yet who would have thought the old man to have had so much blood in him?

Doctor. Do you mark that?

Lady Macbeth. The thane of Fife had a wife; where is she now?——What, will these hands ne'er be clean?—No more o' that, my lord, no more o' that: you mar all with this starting.

Doctor. Go to, go to; you have known what you should not.

Gentlewoman. She has spoke what she should not, I am sure of that: heaven knows what she has known.

Lady Macbeth. Here's the smell of the blood still; all the perfumes of Arabia will not sweeten this little hand. Oh! oh! oh!

Doctor. What a sigh is there! The heart is sorely charged.

Gentlewoman. I would not have such a heart in my bosom for the dignity of the whole body.

Doctor. Well, well, well,—

Gentlewoman. 'Pray God it be, sir.

Doctor. This disease is beyond my practice: yet I have known those which have walked in their sleep, who have died holily in their beds.

Lady Macbeth. Wash your hands, put on your nightgown; look not so pale:—I tell you yet again, Banquo's buried; he cannot come out of his grave.

Doctor. Even so.

Lady Macbeth. To bed, to bed; there's knocking

at the gate. Come, come, come, come, give me your hand; what's done, cannot be undone: to bed, to bed, to bed.

Despised Old Age.

I have liv'd long enough: my way of life
Is fallen into the sear, the yellow leaf;
And that which should accompany old age,
As honour, love, obedience, troops of friends,
I must not look to have; but in their stead,
Curses, not loud, but deep, mouth-honour, breath,
Which the poor heart would fain deny, but dare not.

Diseases of the Mind Incurable.

Canst thou not minister to a mind diseas'd;
Pluck from the memory a rooted sorrow;
Raze out the written troubles of the brain;
And, with some sweet oblivious antidote,
Cleanse the stuff'd bosom of that perilous stuff
Which weighs upon the heart?

Macbeth's Defiance of the Hostile Army.

Hang out our banners on the outward walls;
The cry is still, *They come:* Our castle's strength
Will laugh a siege to scorn: here let them lie.
Till famine and the ague eat them up:
Were they not forc'd with those that should be ours,
We might have met them dareful, beard to beard,
And beat them backward home.

Reflections on Life.

To-morrow, and to-morrow, and to-morrow,
Creeps in this petty pace from day to day,
To the last syllable of recorded time;

And all our yesterdays have lighted fools
The way to dusty death. Out, out, brief candle!
Life's but a walking shadow; a poor player,
That struts and frets his hour upon the stage,
And then is heard no more; it is a tale
Told by an idiot, full of sound and fury,
Signifying nothing.

—*ooo*—

TIMON OF ATHENS.

Timon, a noble Athenian, lavishes his wealth on a host of flatterers whose worthlessness he discovers when misfortunes overtake him. Convinced of the heartlessness of his professed friends, he revenges himself on them by inviting them to a banquet, at which the dishes contain nothing but hot water, which he flings in the faces of his guests, and himself retires to the woods and becomes a confirmed misanthrope. In the meantime Alcibiades, an Athenian general, has been banished from Athens by the Senate for too vehemently interceding on behalf of a friend under sentence of death. The banished general levies an army and besieges Athens, the gates of which are opened to him, and the play concludes with the death of Timon and the resolve of Alcibiades to punish his own and Timon's enemies. Apemantus, a churlish philosopher, and Flavius, Timon's steward, are, in addition to those named, somewhat prominent characters in the drama. Dr. Johnson speaks of this play as "a domestic tragedy which strongly fastens on the attention of the reader; in the plan there is not much art, but the incidents are natural, and the characters various and exact."

Act I.

Friendship in Adversity.

I am not of that feather, to shake off
My friend when he must need me. I do know him

A gentleman, that well deserves a help,
Which he shall have: I'll pay the debt and free him.

The pleasure of doing good.

O, you gods, think I, what need we have any friends, if we should never have need of them? they were the most needless creatures living, should we ne'er have use for them: and would most resemble sweet instruments hung up in cases, that keep their sounds to themselves. Why, I have often wished myself poorer, that I might come nearer to you. We are born to do benefits: and what better or properer can we call our own, than the riches of our friends? O, what a precious comfort 'tis, to have so many, like brothers, commanding one another's fortunes.

Act II.

Timon's reckless Extravagance.

No care, no stop! so senseless of expense,
That he will neither know how to maintain it,
Nor cease his flow of riot: takes no account
How things go from him; nor resumes no care
Of what is to continue.

Faithless Friends.

They answer, in a joint and corporate voice,
That now they are at fall, want treasure, cannot
Do what they would; are sorry—you are honourable,—
But yet they could have wish'd—they know not—but
Something hath been amiss—a noble nature
May catch a wrench—would all were well—'tis pity—
And so, intending other serious matters,
After distasteful looks, and these hard fractions,*

* Abrupt excuses.

With certain half-caps, and cold moving nods
They froze me into silence.

Act IV.

A Friend Forsaken.

As we do turn our backs
From our companion thrown into his grave,
So his familiars to his buried fortunes
Slink all away; leave their false vows with him,
Like empty purses pick'd; and his poor self,
A dedicated beggar to the air,
With his disease of all-shunn'd poverty,
Walks, like contempt, alone.

The Vanity of Riches.

O, the fierce wretchedness that glory brings us!
Who would not wish to be from wealth exempt,
Since riches point to misery and contempt?
Who'd be so mock'd with glory? or to live
But in a dream of friendship?
To have his pomp, and all what state compounds,
But only painted, like his varnish'd friends?

Apemantus's Appeal to Timon in the Woods.

Thou hast cast away thyself, being like thyself;
A madman so long, now a fool. What, think'st
That the bleak air, thy boisterous chamberlain,
Will put thy shirt on warm! Will these moss'd trees,
That have outliv'd the eagle, page thy heels,
And skip when thou point'st out? Will the cold brook,
Candied with ice, caudle thy morning taste,
To cure thy o'er-night's surfeit? Call the creatures,—
Whose naked natures live in all the spite

Of wreakful heaven;* whose bare unhoused trunks,
To the conflicting elements exposed,
Answer mere nature,—bid them flatter thee.

The Bounties of Nature.

Why should you want? Behold, the earth hath roots;
Within this mile break forth a hundred springs:
The oaks bear mast, the briars scarlet hips;
The bounteous housewife, nature, on each bush
Lays her full mess before you.

Act V.

Promising and Performance.

Promising is the very air o' the time; it opens the eyes of expectation: performance is ever the duller for his act; and, but in the plainer and simpler kind of people the deed of saying is quite out of use. To promise is most courtly and fashionable: performance is a kind of will or testament, which argues a great sickness in his judgment that makes it.

Timon's message to the Athenians.

Come not to me again: but say to Athens,
Timon hath made his everlasting mansion
Upon the beached verge of the salt flood;
Which once a day with his embossed froth
The turbulent surge shall cover; thither come,
And let my grave-stone be your oracle.—
Lips, let sour words go by, and language end.
What is amiss, plague and infection mend!
Graves only be men's works: and death, their gain!
Sun, hide thy beams! Timon hath done his reign.

* Exposed to the elements.

TITUS ANDRONICUS.

Dr. Johnson says, speaking of this play: "All the editors and critics agree with Mr. Theobald in supposing it spurious. I see no reason for differing from them; for the colour of the style is wholly different from that of the other plays, and there is an attempt at regular versification and artificial closes, not always inelegant, yet seldom pleasing. That Shakspere wrote any part,* though Theobald declares it incontestable, I see no reason for believing." The play is, however, now generally recognized as Shakspere's, and is included in all editions of his works, though its inferiority to his unquestioned plays cannot be disputed.

Act I.

Mercy.

Wilt thou draw near the nature of the gods?
Draw near them then in being merciful:
Sweet mercy is nobility's true badge.

Thanks.

Thanks, to men
Of noble minds, is honourable meed.

Act II.

Morning.

As when the golden sun salutes the morn,
And, having gilt the ocean with his beams,
Gallops the Zodiack in his glistering coach,
And overlooks the highest-peering hills.

* Most of the critics who considered the authorship doubtful, admitted that Shakspere had written some portions of the play.

A Hunting Morning.

The hunt is up, the morn is bright and grey.
The fields are fragrant, and the woods are green:
Uncouple here, and let us make a bay,
And wake the emperor, and his lovely bride.

The Charms of Nature.

The birds chant melody on every bush:
The snake lies rolled in the cheerful sun;
The green leaves quiver with the cooling wind,
And make a chequer'd shadow on the ground.

A Gloomy Vale Described.

A barren, detested vale, you see, it is:
The trees, though summer, yet forlorn and lean,
O'ercome with moss, and baleful mistletoe.
Here never shines the sun; here nothing breeds,
Unless the nightly owl, or fatal raven.

Lavinia Singing to her Lute.

O, had the monster seen those lily hands
Tremble, like aspen leaves, upon a lute,
And make the silken strings delight to kiss them,
He would not then have touch'd them for his life;
Or, had he heard the heavenly harmony,
Which that sweet tongue hath made,
He would have dropp'd his knife and fell asleep.

Act III.

A Father's Appeal for Mercy.

Hear me, grave fathers! noble tribunes, stay
For pity of mine age, whose youth was spent

In dangerous wars, whilst you securely slept;
For all my blood in Rome's great quarrel shed;
For all the frosty nights that I have watch'd;
And for these bitter tears, which now you see
Filling the aged wrinkles in my cheeks;
Be pitiful to my condemned sons.

Titus's Vain Appeal to the Tribunes.

If they did hear,
They would not mark me; or, if they did mark,
All bootless to them, they'd not pity me.
Therefore I tell my sorrows to the stones;
Who, though they cannot answer my distress,
Yet in some sort they're better than the tribunes,
For that they will not intercept my tale:
When I do weep, they humbly at my feet
Receive my tears, and seem to weep with me;
And, were they but attired in grave weeds,
Rome could afford no tribune like to these.
A stone is soft as wax, tribunes more hard than stones;
A stone is silent, and offendeth not;
And tribunes with their tongues doom men to death.

Cruelty.

But how, if that fly had a father and mother,
How would he hang his slender gilded wings,
And buzz lamenting doings in the air?
Poor harmless fly!
That with his pretty buzzing melody,
Came here to make us merry; and thou hast kill'd him.

Act V.

Revenge.

I am revenge, sent from the infernal kingdom,
To ease the gnawing vulture of thy mind,
By working wreakful vengeance on thy foes.
Come down, and welcome me to this world's light;
Confer with me of murder and of death.

—*ooo*—

TROILUS AND CRESSIDA.

This play describes the siege of Troy by the Greeks. Troilus, son of Priam king of Troy, and brother of Hector, is in love with Cressida, daughter of Calchas a Trojan priest, who takes part with the Greeks. Pandarus, uncle of Cressida, encourages the suit of Troilus, and he and Cressida exchange vows of fidelity; she, however, proves inconstant, and is seen in her father's tent by Troilus in the act of giving a token of love he had presented her with, to the Grecian commander Diomedes. Hector sends a challenge, daring any of the Grecian warriors to meet him in combat, which is accepted by Ajax; the fight takes place, but is broken off by Hector, who embraces Ajax and is invited by the Greeks to visit their camp. Achilles, one of the Greek chieftains, has stood aloof from the conflict in consequence of a quarrel with Agamemnon, the general-in-chief of the Greeks, he, however, after Hector's combat with Ajax, provokes the Trojan warrior to challenge him. They meet on the field of battle, and Hector, having put aside his helmet, is surprised by Achilles and his myrmidons and slain. Dr. Johnson, speaking of this play, says, "It is more correctly written than most of Shakspere's compositions, but it is not one of those in which either the extent of his views, or elevation of his fancy, is fully displayed."

Act I.

Troilus's love for Cressida.

I tell thee I am mad
In Cressid's love: thou answer'st, She is fair;
Pour'st in the open ulcer of my heart
Her eyes, her hair, her cheek, her gait, her voice;
Handlest in thy discourse, O, that her hand,
In whose comparison all whites are ink,
Writing their own reproach; to whose soft seizure,
The cygnet's down is harsh, and spirit of sense
Hard as the palm of ploughman! This thou tell'st me,
As true thou tell'st me, when I say—I love her;
But, saying thus, instead of oil and balm,
Thou layest in every gash that love hath given me
The knife that made it.

Respect.

I ask, that I might waken reverence,
And bid the cheek be ready with a blush
Modest as morning when she coldly eyes
The youthful Phœbus.

Act III.

The potency of Love.

Even such a passion doth embrace my bosom:
My heart beats thicker than a feverish pulse;
And all my powers do their bestowing lose,
Like vassalage at unawares encount'ring
The eye of majesty.

Cressida's profession of Constancy.

If I be false, or swerve a hair from truth,
When time is old and hath forgot itself,

When waterdrops have worn the stones of Troy,
And blind oblivion swallow'd cities up,
And mighty states characterless are grated
To dusty nothing; yet let memory,
From false to false, among false maids in love,
Upbraid my falsehood! when they have said—as false
As air, as water, wind, or sandy earth,
As fox to lamb, as wolf to heifer's calf,
Pard to the hind, or stepdame to her son;
Yea, let them say, to stick the heart of falsehood,
As false as Cressid.

Honour.

Honour travels in a strait so narrow,
Where one but goes abreast: keep then the path:
For emulation hath a thousand sons,
That one by one pursue: if you give way,
Or hedge aside from the direct forthright,
Like to an enter'd tide, they all rush by,
And leave you hindmost.

Act IV.

Character of Troilus.

The youngest son of Priam, a true knight;
Not yet mature, yet matchless; firm of word:
Speaking in deeds, and deedless* in his tongue;
Not soon provoked, nor, being provoked, soon calm'd
His heart and hand both open and both free;
For what he has he gives, what thinks he shows:
Yet gives he not till judgment guides his bounty,
Nor dignifies an impair† thought with breath:
Manly as Hector, but more dangerous;

* Nct given to boasting. † Improper.

For Hector, in his blaze of wrath, subscribes*
To tender objects; but he, in heat of action,
Is more vindictive than jealous love.
They call him Troilus.

Hector in Battle.

I have, thou gallant Trojan, seen thee oft,
Labouring for destiny, make cruel way
Through ranks of Greekish youth: and I have seen
thee,
As hot as Perseus, spur thy Phrygian steed,
And seen thee scorning forfeits and subduements,
When thou hast hung thy advanced sword i' the air,
Not letting it decline on the declined,†
That I have said unto my standers by,
"Lo, Jupiter is yonder, dealing life!"
And I have seen thee pause, and take thy breath,
When that a ring of Greeks have hemm'd thee in,
Like an Olympian wrestling.

Achilles Surveying Hector.

Tell me, you heavens, in which part of his body
Shall I destroy him? Whether there, there, or there?
That I may give the local wound a name;
And make distinct the very breach whereout
Hector's great spirit flew: answer me heavens!

—ooo—

CORIOLANUS.

Caius Marcius, a noble Roman, surnamed Coriolanus, from a great victory obtained by him over the Volscians in Corioli, is un

* Gives way to. † Vanquished.

popular with the common people in Rome in consequence of his unbending austerity; he has, however, many firm friends, and is appointed Consul; the appointment, however, is revoked by the people, who are stirred up against Coriolanus by the tribunes Sicinius Velutus and Junius Brutus, who cause him to be banished from Rome. Indignant at the ingratitude of his countrymen, he joins the Volscians, and is received with open arms by their general, Tullus Aufidius, who divides his command with him. His countrymen, alarmed at the invasion of the Volscians, send to him to sue for peace, but he refuses to listen to them, till at length he is melted by the solicitations of his wife Virgilia and his mother Volumnia. Tullus Aufidius, jealous of the fame and influence which Coriolanus has obtained amongst the Volscians, conspires, with others against him, and he is assassinated by Aufidius and the conspirators. Dr. Johnson pronounces this to be "one of Shakspere's most amusing performances. The old man's bluntness," says he, "in Menenius; the lofty lady's dignity in Volumnia; the bridal modesty in Virgilia; the patrician and military haughtiness in Coriolanus; the plebeian malignity and tribunitian haughtiness in Brutus aud Sicinius, make a very pleasing and interesting varietv."

Act I.

Description of a Mob.

What would you have, you curs,
That like nor peace nor war? the one affrights you,
The other makes you proud. He that trusts you,
Where he should find you lions, finds you hares;
Where foxes, geese; you are no surer, no,
Than is the coal of fire upon the ice,
Or hailstone in the sun. Your virtue is
To make him worthy whose offence subdues him,
And curse that justice did it. Who deserves greatness,
Deserves your hate: and your affections are
A sick man's appetite, who desires most that

Which would increase his evil. He that depends
Upon your favours swims with fins of lead,
And hews down oaks with rushes. Hang ye! Trust ye?
With every minute you do change a mind;
And call him noble that was now your hate,
Him vile, that was your garland.

Volumnia's Patriotism.

Hear me profess sincerely:—had I a dozen sons,—each in my love alike, and none less dear than thine and my good Marcius,—I had rather had eleven die nobly for their country, than one voluptuously surfeit out of action.

Aufidius's Hate of Coriolanus.

Nor sleep, nor sanctuary,
Being naked, sick; nor fane, nor Capitol,
The prayers of priests, nor times of sacrifice,
Embarquements* all of fury, shall lift up
Their rotten privilege and custom 'gainst
My hate to Marcius: where I find him, were it
At home, upon my brother's guard,† even there,
Against the hospitable canon, would I
Wash my fierce hand in his heart.

Act II.

Prowess of Coriolanus.

Before him
He carries noise, and behind him he leaves tears;
Death, that dark spirit, in's nervy‡ arm doth lie;
Which being advanc'd, declines; and then men die.

* Embargoes. † My brother being his protector.
‡ Nervous, vigorous.

Cominius's Praise of Coriolanus to the Senators.

I shall lack voice: the deeds of Coriolanus
Should not be utter'd feebly.—It is held
That valour is the chiefest virtue, and
Most dignifies the haver:* if it be,
The man I speak of cannot in the world
Be singly counterpois'd. At sixteen years,
When Tarquin made a head for Rome, he fought
Beyond the mark of others: our then dictator,
Whom with all praise I point at, saw him fight,
When with his Amazonian chin† he drove
The bristled lips before him: he bestrid
An o'erpress'd Roman, and i' th' consul's view
Slew three opposers: Tarquin's self he met,
And struck him on his knee;‡ in that day's feats,
When he might act the woman in the scene,§
He proved best man i' the field, and for his meed
Was brow-bound with the oak. His pupil age
Man-enter'd thus, he waxed like a sea;
And, in the brunt of seventeen battles since,
He lurch'd‖ all swords o' the garland. For this last,
Before and in Corioli, let me say,
I cannot speak him home: he stopp'd the fliers;
And by his rare example made the coward
Turn terror into sport; as waves before
A vessel under sail, so men obey'd
And fell below his stem: his sword (death's stamp)
Where it did mark, it took; from face to foot
He was a thing of blood, whose every motion

* Possessor. † Beardless chin.
‡ Struck him down on his knee. § On account of his youth
‖ Won easily.

Was timed* with dying cries: alone he enter'd
The mortal gate o' the city, which he painted
With shunless destiny, aidless came off,
And with a sudden reinforcement struck
Corioli like a planet: now all's his:
When by and by the din of war 'gan pierce
His ready sense: then straight his doubled spirit
Requicken'd what in flesh was fatigate,†
And to the battle came he: where he did
Run reeking o'er the lives of men, as if
'T were a perpetual spoil: and, till we call'd
Both field and city ours, he never stood
To ease his breast with panting.

Popularity of Coriolanus.

I have seen
The dumb men throng to see him, and the blind
To hear him speak: the matrons flung their gloves,
Ladies and maids their scarfs and handkerchiefs,
Upon him as he pass'd: the nobles bended,
As to Jove's statue; and the commons made
A shower, and thunder, with their caps and shouts;
I never saw the like.

Act III.

Character of Coriolanus.

His nature is too noble for the world:
He would not flatter Neptune for his trident,
Or Jove for his power to thunder. His heart's his
mouth;
What his breast forges, that his tongue must vent;

* Every blow he struck was followed by dying cries.
† Fatigued.

And being angry, does forget that ever
He heard the name of death.

Coriolanus's Contempt for the Mob.

You common cry of curs! whose breath I hate
As reek* o' the rotten fens, whose loves I prize
As the dead carcases of unburied men
That do corrupt my air, I banish you;
And here remain with your uncertainty!
Let every feeble rumour shake your hearts!
Your enemies, with nodding of their plumes,
Fan you into despair! Have the power still
To banish your defenders; till, at length,
Your ignorance (which finds not till it feels),
Making not reservation of yourselves
(Still your own foes), deliver you, as most
Abated† captives, to some nation
That won you without blows. Despising
For you, the city, thus I turn my back:
There is a world elsewhere.

Act IV.

Fickleness of Friendship.

O world, thy slippery turns! Friends now fast sworn,
Whose double bosoms seem to wear one heart,
Whose hours, whose bed, whose meal, and exercise,
Are still together, who twin, as 'twere, in love
Unseparable, shall, within this hour,
On a dissension of a doit, break out
To bitterest enmity: so, fellest foes,

* Exhalation. † Vanquished.

Whose passions and whose plots have broke their sleep
To take the one the other, by some chance,
Some trick not worth an egg, shall grow dear friends,
And interjoin their issues.

Martial Friendship.

Let me twine
Mine arms about that body, where against
My grained ash a hundred times hath broke,
And scared the moon with splinters! Here I clip*
The anvil of my sword; and do contest
As hotly and as nobly with thy love,
As ever in ambitious strength I did
Contend against thy valour. Know thou first,
I lov'd the maid I married; never man
Sigh'd truer breath; but that I see thee here,
Thou noble thing! more dances my rapt heart,
Than when I first my wedded mistress saw
Bestride my threshold.

Act V.

A Favourable Time should be chosen to ask a Favour.

He was not taken well; he had not dined:
The veins unfill'd, our blood is cold, and then
We pout upon the morning, are unapt
To give or to forgive; but when we have stuff'd
These pipes and these conveyances of our blood
With wine and feeding, we have suppler souls
Than in our priest-like fasts: therefore I'll watch him,
Till he be dieted to my request,
And then I'll set upon him.

* Embrace

Inflexibility of Coriolanus to the Appeal of his Wife and Mother.

My wife comes foremost; then the honour'd mould
Wherein this trunk was fram'd, and in her hand
The grandchild to her blood. But, out affection!
All bond and privilege of nature, break!
Let it be virtuous to be obstinate.—
What is that curt'sey worth? or those doves' eyes,
Which can make gods forsworn?—I melt, and am not
Of stronger earth than others.—My mother bows;
As if Olympus to a molehill should
In supplication nod: and my young boy
Hath an aspect of intercession, which
Great nature cries, "Deny not."—Let the Volces
Plough Rome, and harrow Italy; I'll never
Be such a gosling to obey instinct; but stand,
As if a man were author of himself,
And knew no other kin.

Coriolanus' rekindled Love for his Wife

Like a dull actor now,
I have forgot my part, and I am out,
Even to a full disgrace. Best of my flesh.
Forgive my tyranny; but do not say,
For that, "Forgive our Romans."—O, a kiss
Long as my exile, sweet as my revenge!
Now, by the jealous queen of heaven, that kiss
I carried from thee, dear; and my true lip
Hath virgin'd it e'er since.—You gods, I prate
And the most noble mother of the world
Leave unsaluted: sink, my knee, i' the earth;
Of thy deep duty more impression show
Than that of common sons.

Coriolanus's Prayer for his Son.

The god of soldiers,
With the consent of supreme Jove, inform
Thy thoughts with nobleness; that thou mayst prove
To shame invulnerable, and stick i' the wars
Like a great sea-mark, standing every flaw,*
And saving those that eye thee!

Peace after a Siege.

Ne'er through an arch so hurried the blown tide,
As the recomforted through the gates. Why, hark you,
The trumpets, sackbuts, psalteries, and fifes,
Tabors, and cymbals, and the shouting Romans,
Make the sun dance.

Aufidius's Jealousy of Coriolanus.

Being banish'd for 't, he came unto my hearth;
Presented to my knife his throat: I took him;
Made him joint-servant with me; gave him way
In all his own desires; nay, let him choose
Out of my files, his projects to accomplish,
My best and freshest men; serv'd his designments
In mine own person; holp to reap the fame,
Which he did end all his; and took some pride
To do myself this wrong: till, at the last,
I seem'd his follower, not partner; and
He wag'd me with his countenance,† as if
I had been mercenary.

Coriolanus's furious Denunciation of Aufidius.

Measureless liar, thou hast made my heart
Too great for what contains it. Boy! O slave!—

* Storm. † Repaid me merely with good looks.

Pardon me, lords, 't is the first time that ever
I was forc'd to scold. Your judgments, my grave lords,
Must give this cur the lie: and his own notion
(Who wears my stripes impress'd on him that must bear
My beating to his grave), shall join to thrust
The lie unto him.

* * * * *

Cut me to pieces, Volces: men and lads,
Stain all your edges on me.—Boy! False hound!
If you have writ your annals true, 't is there,
That like an eagle in a dove-cote, I
Flutter'd your Volcians in Corioli:
Alone I did it.—Boy!

Contrition of Aufidius after the Assassination of Coriolanus.

My rage is gone,
And I am struck with sorrow.—Take him up:—
Help, three o' the chiefest soldiers; I'll be one.—
Beat thou the drum, that it speak mournfully:
Trail your steel pikes.—Though in this city he
Hath widowed and unchilded many a one,
Which to this hour bewail the injury,
Yet he shall have a noble memory.

—ooo—

ANTONY AND CLEOPATRA.

Mark Antony, joined in the Roman triumvirate with Octavius Cæsar and Lepidus, is passing his time in luxurious indolence in Egypt, when intelligence is brought to him of the death of his wife Fulvia, on which he repairs to Rome, where an altercation takes place between him and Cæsar; Lepidus interposes between the disputants, and their wranglings are healed by the marriage of Antony with Octavia, Cæsar's sister. The amity between the rival triumvirs is, however, but of brief duration, and war being declared between them, Antony is defeated at the battle of Actium. After this fatal engagement, through his ambassador Euphronius, he sues to Cæsar to be permitted to remain in Egypt, or, this not being granted, that he may reside as a private man at Athens. The conqueror refuses both petitions, and the strife is renewed. In a battle by land Antony is victorious, but his forces in a sea-fight are completely vanquished, and he ends his life by falling on his own sword. Cleopatra, Queen of Egypt, at whose court Antony has been residing, is taken prisoner by Cæsar; whilst a captive she obtains possession of an asp, a small venomous serpent, the bite of which, when applied to her breast, kills her, and the play concludes with an eloquent harangue from Cæsar. Speaking of this play, Dr. Johnson says it "keeps curiosity always busy and the passions always interested. The continual hurry of the action, the variety of incidents, and the quick succession of one passage to another, call the mind forwards without intermission, from the first act to the last."

Act I.

Antony's luxurious mode of Living.

You may see, Lepidus, and henceforth know,
It is not Cæsar's natural vice to hate
One great competitor. From Alexandria
This is the news: he fishes, drinks, and wastes
The lamps of night in revel; is not more manlike
Than Cleopatra; nor the queen of Ptolemy
More womanly than he: hardly gave audience, or
Vouchsaf'd to think he had partners. You shall find there
A man, who is the abstract of all faults
That all men follow.

Antony's Vices and Virtues.

I must not think, there are
Evils enough to darken all his goodness:
His faults, in him, seem as the spots of heaven,
More fiery by night's blackness; hereditary,
Rather than purchased; what he cannot change,
Than what he chooses.

Cleopatra's Love for Antony.

O Charmian,
Where think'st thou he is now? Stands he or sits he?
Or does he walk? or is he on his horse?
O happy horse, to bear the weight of Antony,
Do bravely, horse! for wot'st thou whom thou mov'st?
The demi-Atlas of this earth, the arm
And burgonet of men.—He's speaking now,
Or murmuring; "Where's my serpent of old Nile?"
For so he calls me.

Act II.

Description of Cleopatra sailing down the Cydnus.

The barge she sat in, like a burnish'd throne,
Burn'd on the water: the poop was beaten gold;
Purple the sails, and so perfumed, that
The winds were love-sick with them: the oars were silver;
Which to the tune of flutes kept stroke, and made
The water which they beat to follow faster,
As amorous of their strokes. For her own person,
It beggar'd all description; she did lie
In her pavilion (cloth of gold, of tissue),
O'er picturing that Venus, where we see,

The fancy outwork nature: on each side her,
Stood pretty dimpled boys, like smiling Cupids,
With diverse colour'd fans, whose wind did seem
To glow the delicate cheeks which they did cool,
And what they undid, did.*

* * * * *

Her gentlewomen, like the Nereides,
So many mermaids, tended her i' the eyes,
And made their bends adornings; at the helm
A seeming mermaid steers: the silken tackle
Swell with the touches of those flower-soft hands,
That rarely frame the office. From the barge
A strange invisible perfume hits the sense
Of the adjacent wharfs. The city cast
Her people out upon her; and Antony,
Enthroned in the market-place, did sit alone,
Whistling to the air; which, but for vacancy,
Had gone to gaze on Cleopatra too,
And make a gap in nature.

A Messenger with bad news unwelcome.

Though it be honest, it is never good
To bring bad news; give to a gracious message
A host of tongues; but let ill tidings tell
Themselves, when they be felt.

Act III.

The manner in which Octavia should have entered Rome.

Why have you stolen upon us thus? you come not
Like Cæsar's sister: the wife of Antony
Should have an army for an usher, and
The neighs of horse to tell of her approach,

* Increased the heat they were meant to cool.

Long ere she did appear; the trees by the way,
Should have borne men; and expectation fainted,
Longing for what it had not: nay, the dust
Should have ascended to the roof of heaven,
Rais'd by your populous troops: but you are come
A market-maid to Rome; and have prevented
The ostent* of our love, which left unshown
Is often left unlov'd: we should have met you
By sea and land; supplying every stage
With an augmented greeting.

Antony to his Attendants after his defeat.

Hark, the land bids me tread no more upon't,
It is asham'd to bear me! Friends, come hither,
I'm so lated† in the world, that I
Have lost my way for ever: I have a ship
Laden with gold; take that, divide it; fly
And make your peace with Cæsar.
I have fled myself; and have instructed cowards
To run, and show their shoulders. Friends, be-gone;
I have myself resolved upon a course,
Which has no need of you; be-gone:
My treasure's in the harbour, take it.—O,
I follow'd that I blush to look upon:
My very hairs do mutiny; for the white
Reprove the brown for rashness, and they them
For fear and doting. Friends, be-gone; you shall
Have letters from me to some friends, that will
Sweep your way for you. Pray you, look not sad
Nor make replies of loathness: take the hint
Which my despair proclaims; let that be left
Which leaves itself: to the sea-side straightway:

* Exhibition. † Behindhand.

I will possess you of that ship and treasure.
Leave me, I pray, a little : 'pray you, now :—
Nay, do so ; for, indeed, I have lost command.
Therefore I pray you :—I 'll see you by and by.

Act IV.

Antony taking Leave of his Servants.

Tend me to night ;
May be it is the period of your duty :
Haply, you shall not see me more ; or if,
A mangled shadow : perchance to-morrow
You'll serve another master. I look on you
As one that takes his leave. Mine honest friends,
I turn you not away ; but, like a master
Married to your good service, stay till death :
Tend me to-night two hours, I ask no more,
And the gods yield* you for 't !

Antony's Despondency.

O sun, thy uprise shall I see no more :
Fortune and Antony part here ; even here
Do we shake hands.—All come to this ;—the hearts
That spaniell'd me at heels, to whom I gave
Their wishes, do discandy, melt their sweets
On blossoming Cæsar ; and this pine is bark'd,
That overtopp'd them all. Betray'd I am :
O this false soul of Egypt ! this grave charm,
Whose eye beck'd forth my wars, and call'd them home,
Whose bosom was my crownet, my chief end,
Like a right gipsy, hath, at fast and loose,
Beguil'd me to the very heart of loss.

* Requite.

Description of Cleopatra's supposed Death.

Death of one person can be paid but once;
And that she has discharged: what thou wouldst do,
Is done unto thy hand: the last she spake
Was Antony! most noble Antony!
Then in the midst a tearing groan did break
The name of Antony; it was divided
Between her heart and lips: she render'd life,
Thy name so buried in her.

Cleopatra on the Death of Antony.

It were for me
To throw my sceptre at the injurious gods;
To tell them that this world did equal theirs,
Till they had stolen our jewel. All's but nought;
Patience is sottish; and impatience does
Become a dog that's mad; then is it sin,
To rush into the secret house of death,
Ere death dare come to us?—How do you, women?
What, what? good cheer! Why, how now, Charmian?
My noble girls!—Ah, women, women! look,
Our lamp is spent, it's out;—good sirs, take heart:—
We'll bury him; and then, what's brave, what's noble,
Let's do it after the high Roman fashion,
And make death proud to take us. Come, away;
This case of that huge spirit now is cold.

Act V.

Firm Resolution.

How poor an instrument
May do a noble deed! He brings me liberty.
My resolution's placed, I have nothing

Of woman in me: now from head to foot,
I am marble-constant: now the fleeting* moon
No planet is of mine.

Cleopatra's Speech on applying the Serpent to her breast.

Give me my robe, put on my crown; I have
Immortal longings in me: now no more
The juice of Egypt's grape shall moist this lip:
Yare, yare,† good Iras; quick—Methinks I hear
Antony call; I see him rouse himself
To praise my noble act: I hear him mock
The luck of Cæsar, which the gods give men
To excuse their after-wrath: Husband, I come:
Now to that name my courage prove my title!
I am fire and air; my other elements
I give to baser life.—So,—have you done?
Come then, and take the last warmth of my lips,
Farewell, kind Charmian;—Iris, long farewell.

Cæsar's Comments on the Death of Cleopatra.

Her physician tells me,
She hath pursu'd conclusions‡ infinite
Of easy ways to die. Take up her bed;
And bear her women from the monument:—
She shall be buried by her Antony:
No grave upon the earth shall clip§ in it
A pair so famous. High events as these
Strike those that make them; and their story is
No less in pity, than his glory which
Brought them to be lamented. Our army shall
In solemn show, attend this funeral;
And then to Rome. Come, Dolabella, see
High order in this great solemnity.

* Changeable. † Be quick.
‡ Tried experiments. § Enclose.

MERCHANT OF VENICE.

Shylock, a rich Jew of Venice, has advanced on loan three thousand ducats to Antonio, the Merchant of Venice, an agreement being signed by which, if the borrowed money be not repaid by a certain period, Shylock is to claim a pound of flesh to be cut from the merchant's body. Antonio, owing to sudden and unforeseen losses, forfeits the bond, and is cited before the Duke and magnificoes of Venice to pay the incurred penalty. The Duke tries to persuade Shylock to accept the money, which is now ready to be paid, but, influenced by a feeling of rancorous hatred, he insists on having the pound of flesh. In the meantime, Portia, a rich heiress, just married to Bassanio, an intimate friend of Antonio's, disguises herself as a doctor of laws, and attends the court where the Duke is sitting in judgment. The cause is left to Portia to arbitrate on; she admits the justice of Shylock's claim, but urges him to accept payment of the loan in money; this he refuses to do, and she then proceeds to pronounce sentence, explaining to the Jew that the bond gives him "no jot of blood," the words being "expressly a pound of flesh." Thus baffled, he agrees to take the money, but Portia further shows him that by the laws of Venice, he, being an alien, having sought the destruction of a citizen, has placed his life at the mercy of the Duke. The Duke pardons the Jew on condition that he turns Christian and "records a gift of all he dies possessed" to Lorenzo, a Christian gentleman, to whom his daughter Jessica is wedded. The loves of Bassanio and Portia, and Gratiano and Nerissa, form an agreeable episode, and the clown, Launcelot Gobbo, Shylock's servant, excites much amusement in the various scenes in which he appears.

Act I.

The true Value of the World.

I hold the world but as the world, Gratiano;
A stage where every man must play a part.

Cheerfulness.

Let me play the fool:
With mirth and laughter let old wrinkles come;
And let my liver rather heat with wine,
Than my heart cool with mortifying groans.
Why should a man, whose blood is warm within,
Sit like his grandsire cut in alabaster?
Sleep when he wakes? and creep into the jaundice
By being peevish?

Affected gravity.

I tell thee what, Antonio,—
I love thee, and it is my love that speaks;
There are a sort of men, whose visages
Do cream and mantle like a standing pond;
And do a wilful stillness entertain,
With purpose to be dress'd in an opinion
Of wisdom, gravity, profound conceit;
As who should say, "I am Sir Oracle,
And, when I ope my lips, let no dog bark!"
O, my Antonio, I do know of these,
That therefore only are reputed wise,
For saying nothing.

Loquacity.

Gratiano speaks an infinite deal of nothing, more than any man in all Venice: his reasons are as two grains of wheat hid in two bushels of chaff; you shall seek all day ere you find them; and when you have them, they are not worth the search.

Mediocrity.

For aught I see, they are as sick that surfeit with

too much, as they that starve with nothing: it is no mean happiness, therefore, to be seated in the mean; superfluity comes sooner by white hairs, but competency lives longer.

Speculation more easy than Practice.

If to do were as easy as to know what were good to do, chapels had been churches, and poor men's cottages princes' palaces. It is a good divine that follows his own instructions: I can easier teach twenty what were good to be done, than be one of the twenty to follow mine own teaching. The brain may devise laws for the blood; but a hot temper leaps over a cold decree; such a hare is madness the youth, to skip o'er the meshes of good counsel the cripple.

Shylock's Malice towards Antonio.

How like a fawning publican he looks!
I hate him, for he is a Christian:
But more for that, in low simplicity,
He lends out money gratis, and brings down
The rate of usance here with us in Venice.
If I can catch him once upon the hip,
I will feed fat the ancient grudge I bear him.
He hates our sacred nation, and he rails,
Even there where merchants most do congregate,
On me, my bargains, and my well won thrift,
Which he calls interest. Cursed be my tribe,
If I forgive him.

Hypocrisy.

Mark you this, Bassanio,
The devil can cite Scripture for his purpose.
An evil soul, producing holy witness,

Is like a villain with a smiling cheek;
A goodly apple rotten at the heart;
O, what a goodly outside falsehood hath!

Shylock's remonstrance with Antonio.

Signior Antonio, many a time and oft,
In the Rialto you have rated me
About my monies and my usances:
Still have I borne it with a patient shrug;
For sufferance is the badge of all our tribe;
You call me—misbeliever, cut-throat dog,
And spit upon my Jewish gaberdine,
And all for use of that which is mine own.
Well then, it now appears you need my help:
Go to then; you come to me, and you say,
"Shylock, we would have monies:" you say so;
You that did void your rheum upon my beard,
And foot me as you spurn a stranger cur
Over your threshold; monies is your suit;
What should I say to you? should I not say
"Hath a dog money? is it possible
A cur can lend three thousand ducats?" or
Shall I bend low, and in a bondman's key,
With 'bated breath, and whispering humbleness,
Say this,—
"Fair sir, you spit on me on Wednesday last:
You spurn'd me such a day; another time
You call'd me—dog; and for these courtesies
I'll lend you thus much monies?"

Act II.

Shylock's injunctions to his Daughter.

Lock up my doors; and when you hear the drum,
And the vile squeaking of the wry-neck'd fife,

Clamber not you up to the casements then,
Nor thrust your head into the public street,
To gaze on Christian fools with varnish'd faces:
But stop my house's ears, I mean my casements;
Let not the sound of shallow foppery enter
My sober house.

Portia's Suitors.

From the four corners of the earth they come,
To kiss this shrine, this mortal breathing saint.
The Hyrcanian deserts, and the vasty wilds
Of wide Arabia, are as through-fares now,
For princes to come view fair Portia:
The watery kingdom* whose ambitious head
Spits in the face of heaven, is no bar
To stop the foreign spirits; but they come,
As o'er a brook, to see fair Portia.

The Parting of Friends.

I saw Bassanio and Antonio part:
Bassanio told him he would make some speed
Of his return; he answered—"do not so,
Slubber† not business for my sake, Bassanio,
But stay the very riping of the time;
And for the Jew's bond, which he hath of me,
Let it not enter in your mind of love:
Be merry, and employ your chiefest thoughts
To courtship, and such fair ostents‡ of love
As shall conveniently become you there:"
And even there, his eye being big with tears,
Turning his face, he puts his hand behind him,

* The ocean.
† Do not slur over the business.
‡ Signs, marks.

And with affection wondrous sensible,
He wrung Bassanio's hand, and so they parted.

Honour should be conferred on Merit only.

For who shall go about
To cozen fortune, and be honourable
Without the stamp of merit! Let none presume
To wear an undeserved dignity!
O, that estates, degrees, and offices,
Were not derived corruptly! and that clear honour
Were purchased by the merit of the wearer!
How many then should cover, that stand bare?
How many be commanded, that command?
How much low peasantry would then be glean'd
From the true seed of honour? and how much honour
Pick'd from the chaff and ruin of the times,
To be new varnish'd?

Act III.

Shylock's Revenge.

If it will feed nothing else, it will feed my revenge. He hath disgraced me, and hindered me of half a million; laughed at my losses, mocked at my gains, scorned my nation, thwarted my bargains, cooled my friends, heated mine enemies; and what's his reason? I am a Jew. Hath not a Jew eyes? hath not a Jew hands, organs, dimensions, senses, affections, passions? fed with the same food, hurt with the same weapons, subject to the same diseases, healed by the same means, warmed and cooled by the same winter and summer, as a Christian is? if you prick us, do we not bleed? if you tickle us, do we not laugh? if you poison us, do we not die? and if you wrong us, shall we not revenge?

if we are like you in the rest, we will resemble you in that. If a Jew wrong a Christian, what is his humility? revenge: If a Christian wrong a Jew, what should his sufferance be by Christian example? why, revenge. The villany you teach me, I will execute: and it shall go hard, but I will better the instruction.

Shylock's Anguish at the loss of his Jewels.

Why there, there, there, there! a diamond gone, cost me two thousand ducats in Frankfort! The curse never fell upon our nation till now; I never felt it till now:—two thousand ducats in that; and other precious, precious jewels.—I would, my daughter were dead at my foot, and the jewels in her ear! 'would she were hears'd at my foot, and the ducats in her coffin! No news of them? Why, so:—and I know not what's spent in the search: Why, thou loss upon loss! the thief gone with so much, and so much to find the thief; and no satisfaction, no revenge: nor no ill luck stirring, but what lights o' my shoulders; no sighs, but o' my breathing; no tears, but o' my shedding.

Music.

Let music sound while he doth make his choice;
Then if he lose, he makes a swan-like end,
Fading in music; that the comparison
May stand more proper, my eye shall be the stream,
And wat'ry death-bed for him. He may win;
And what is music then? then music is
Even as the flourish when true subjects bow
To a new-crowned monarch: such it is,
As are those dulcet sounds in break of day,
That creep into the dreaming bridegroom's ear,
And summon him to marriage.

The Deceit of Appearances.

The world is still deceiv'd with ornament.
In law, what plea so tainted and corrupt,
But, being season'd with a gracious voice,
Obscures the show of evil? In religion,
What damned error, but some sober brow
Will bless it, and approve it with a text,
Hiding the grossness with fair ornament?
There is no vice so simple, but assumes
Some mark of virtue on its outward parts.
How many cowards, whose hearts are all as false
As stairs of sand, wear yet upon their chins
The beards of Hercules and frowning Mars;
Who, inward search'd have livers white as milk?
And these assume but valour's excrement,
To render them redoubted. Look on beauty,
And you shall see 'tis purchased by the weight;
Which therein works a miracle in nature,
Making them lightest that wear most of it:
So are those crisped snaky golden locks,
Which make such wanton gambols with the wind,
Upon supposed fairness, often known
To be the dowry of a second head,
The skull that bred them in the sepulchre.
Thus ornament is but the guiled* shore
To a most dangerous sea; the beauteous scarf
Veiling an Indian beauty; in a word,
The seeming truth which cunning times put on
To entrap the wisest.

Portia's Picture.

What find I here?
Fair Portia's counterfeit?† What demi-god

* Deceiving. † Portrait.

Hath come so near creation? Move these eyes?
Or whether, riding on the balls of mine,
Seem they in motion? Here are sever'd lips,
Parted with sugar breath; so sweet a bar
Should sunder such sweet friends: here in her hairs
The painter plays the spider; and hath woven
A golden mesh to entrap the hearts of men,
Faster than gnats in cobwebs: but her eyes,—
How could he see to do them? having made one,
Methinks, it should have power to steal both his,
And leave itself unfurnish'd.

Shylock's Malignity.

I'll have my bond; I will not hear thee speak;
I'll have my bond: and therefore speak no more.
I'll not be made a soft and dull-eyed fool,
To shake the head, relent, and sigh, and yield
To Christian intercessors.

Act IV.

Shylock's Reason for Revenge.

You'll ask me, why I rather choose to have
A weight of carrion flesh, than to receive
Three thousand ducats: I'll not answer that:
But, say, it is my humour; is it answer'd?
What if my house be troubled with a rat,
And I be pleased to give ten thousand ducats
To have it baned?* What, are you answer'd yet?

Mercy.

The quality of mercy is not strain'd;
It droppeth as the gentle rain from heaven

* Poisoned.

Upon the place beneath: it is twice bless'd;
It blesseth him that gives, and him that takes
'Tis mightiest in the mightiest: it becomes
The throned monarch better than his crown:
His sceptre shows the force of temporal power
The attribute to awe and majesty,
Wherein doth sit the dread and fear of kings;
But mercy is above this scepter'd sway,
It is enthroned in the hearts of kings;
It is an attribute to God himself;
And earthly power doth then show likest God's
When mercy seasons justice. Therefore, Jew,
Though justice be thy plea, consider this,—
That, in the course of justice, none of us
Should see salvation: we do pray for mercy;
And that same prayer doth teach us all to render
The deeds of mercy. I have spoke thus much,
To mitigate the justice of thy plea;
Which if thou follow, this strict court of Venice
Must needs give sentence 'gainst the merchant there.

Act V.

Moonlight.

How sweet the moonlight sleeps upon this bank!
Here will we sit, and let the sounds of music
Creep in our ears; soft stillness, and the night,
Become the touches of sweet harmony.
Sit, Jessica: look, how the floor of heaven
Is thick inlaid with patines* of bright gold;
There's not the smallest orb, which thou behold'st,
But in his motion like an angel sings,
Still quiring to the young-eyed cherubims:

* A small dish used in the sacramental service.

Such harmony is in immortal souls;
But, whilst this muddy vesture of decay
Doth grossly close it in, we cannot hear it.

Music.

Do but note a wild and wanton herd,
Or race of youthful and unhandled colts,
Fetching mad bounds, bellowing and neighing loud,
Which is the hot condition of their blood;
If they but hear perchance a trumpet sound,
Or any air of music touch their ears,
You shall perceive them make a mutual stand,
Their savage eyes turn'd to a modest gaze,
By the sweet power of music: therefore, the poet
Did feign that Orpheus drew trees, stones, and floods;
Since naught so stockish, hard and full of rage,
But music for the time doth change his nature.
The man that hath no music in himself,
Nor is not moved with concord of sweet sounds,
Is fit for treasons, stratagems, and spoils:
The motions of his spirit are dull as night,
And his affections dark as Erebus:
Let no such man be trusted.

A good deea.

How far that little candle throws his beams!
So shines a good deed in a naughty world.

Nothing good out of Season.

The crow doth sing as sweetly as the lark,
When neither is attended; and, I think
The nightingale, if she should sing by day,
When every goose is cackling, would be thought,
No better a musician than the wren.

How many things by season season'd are
To their right praise and true perfection!

—ooo—

A MIDSUMMER-NIGHT'S DREAM.

Hermia, daughter of Egeus, is in love with Lysander contrary to her father's will, he wishing her to marry Demetrius. An appeal is made by Egeus to Theseus, Duke of Athens, who condemns Hermia to death or perpetual celibacy except she marries the man of her father's choice. On hearing this sentence, Hermia and Lysander determine to escape beyond the sway of the Duke, and be married privately. Helena, who is in love with Demetrius, (who, however, does not return her love), informs him of the escape of the lovers, on which he pursues them, followed by Helena. In a wood near Athens, Oberon, king of the fairies, overhears a conversation between Helena and Demetrius, in which he rudely repulses her love. The fairy king instructs Puck, an attendant fairy, to squeeze the juice of a certain plant on the eyelids of Demetrius whilst he is asleep, by which he will be charmed into violent love for the first living object that meets his eyes when he awakes, it being presumed that Helena will be this object. Puck by mistake anoints the eyes of Lysander, whose waking eyes first light on Helena, to whom, in obedience to the charm, he at once transfers his affections. Oberon, discovering Puck's error, releases Lysander from the spell, thus restoring his love for Hermia, whilst Demetrius retains his newly awakened affection for Helena. The underplot, in which Titania the fairy queen figures prominently, adds greatly to the interest of the drama.

Act I.

A Father's Authority.

To you your father should be as a god;
One that compos'd your beauties; yea, and one

To whom you are but as a form in wax,
By him imprinted, and within his power
To leave the figure, or disfigure it.

Vexations of True Love.

For aught that ever I could read,
Could ever hear by tale or history,
The course of true love never did run smooth.

Assignation.

I swear to thee, by Cupid's strongest bow;
By his best arrow with the golden head;
By the simplicity of Venus' doves;
By that which knitteth souls, and prospers loves:
And by that fire which burn'd the Carthage queen,
When the false Trojan under sail was seen;
By all the vows that ever men have broke,
In number more than ever women spoke;—
In that same place thou hast appointed me,
To-morrow truly will I meet with thee.

The Moon.

When Phœbe doth behold
Her silver visage in the watery glass,
Decking with liquid pearl the bladed grass.

Love.

Things base and vile, holding no quantity,
Love can transpose to form and dignity.
Love looks not with the eyes, but with the mind;
And therefore is wing'd Cupid painted blind:
Nor hath love's mind of any judgment taste;
Wings, and no eyes, figure unheedy haste;
And therefore is love said to be a child,

Because in choice he is so oft beguiled.
As waggish boys in game themselves forswear,
So the boy love is perjured every where.

Act II.

The Fairy Puck.

I am that merry wanderer of the night,
I jest to Oberon, and make him smile,
When I a fat and bean-fed horse beguile,
Neighing in likeness of a filly foal:
And sometimes lurk I in a gossip's bowl,
In very likeness of a roasted crab;
And, when she drinks, against her lips I bob,
And on her withered dew-lap pour the ale.
The wisest aunt, telling the saddest tale,
Sometimes for three foot stool mistaketh me.

Fairy Jealousy, and the Effects of it described by Titania.

These are the forgeries of jealousy:
And never, since the middle summer's* spring,
Met we on hill, in dale, forest, or mead,
By paved fountain,† or by rushy brook,
Or on the beached margent of the sea
To dance our ringlets to the whistling wind,
But with thy brawls thou hast disturb'd our sport.
Therefore the winds, piping to us in vain,
As in revenge, have suck'd up from the sea
Contagious fogs; which, falling in the land,
Have every pelting‡ river made so proud,
That they have overborne their continents;§
The ox hath therefore stretch'd his yoke in vain,

* Midsummer.
† A pebbly stream.
‡ Petty, insignificant.
§ Their banks.

The ploughman lost his sweat; and the green corn
Hath rotted ere his youth attain'd a beard;
The fold stands empty in the drowned field,
And crows are fatted with the murrain flock;
The nine men's morris is filled up with mud,
And the quaint mazes in the wanton green,
For lack of tread, are undistinguishable;*
The human mortals want; their winter here,
No night is now with hymn or carol bless'd:
Therefore the moon, the governess of floods,
Pale in her anger, washes all the air,
That rheumatic diseases do abound:
And thorough this distemperature, we see
The seasons alter: hoary-headed frosts
Fall in the fresh lap of the crimson rose;
And on old Hyem's chin, and icy crown,
An odorous chaplet of sweet summer buds
Is, as in mockery, set: the spring, the summer,
The childing† autumn, angry winter, change
Their wonted liveries; and the 'mazed world,
By their increase, now knows not which is which.
And this same progeny of evils comes
From our debate, from our dissension;
We are their parents and original.

Love in Idleness.

Thou remember'st
Since once I sat upon a promontory,
And heard a mermaid, on a dolphin's back,
Uttering such dulcet and harmonious breath,
That the rude sea grew civil at her song;

* The "nine men's morris" was an old pastime played on the green turf.

† Autumn bringing forth flowers unnaturally.

And certain stars shot madly from their spheres,
To hear the sea-maid's music.
That very time I saw (but thou could'st not),
Flying between the cold moon and the earth,
Cupid all arm'd: a certain aim he took
At a fair vestal, throned by the west;
And loosed his love-shaft smartly from his bow,
As it should pierce a hundred thousand hearts:
But I might see young Cupid's fiery shaft
Quench'd in the chaste beams of the watery moon;
And the imperial votaress passed on,
In maiden-meditation, fancy-free.
Yet mark'd I where the bolt of Cupid fell:
It fell upon a little western flower,
Before, milk-white; now purple with love's wound,
And maidens call it love-in-idleness.

A Fairy Bank.

I know a bank where the wild thyme blows,
Where ox-lips and the nodding violet grows,
Quite over-canopied with luscious woodbine,
With sweet musk roses, and with eglantine:
There sleeps Titania, some time of the night,
Lull'd in these flowers with dances and delight.

Act III.

Fairy Courtesies.

Be kind and courteous to this gentleman;
Hop in his walks and gambol in his eyes:
Feed him with apricocks and dewberries,
With purple grapes, green figs, and mulberries;
The honey-bags steal from the humble-bees,
And, for night-tapers, crop their waxen thighs,

And light them at the fiery glow-worm's eyes,
To have my love to bed, and to arise;
And pluck the wings from painted butterflies,
To fan the moon-beams from his sleeping eyes:
Nod to him elves, and do him courtesies.

Female Friendship.

Is all the counsel that we two have shared,
The sister's vows, the hours that we have spent,
When we have chid the hasty-footed time
For parting us,—O, and is all forgot?
All school-days' friendship, childhood innocence?
We, Hermia, like two artificial gods,
Have with our needles created both one flower,
Both on one sampler, sitting on one cushion,
Both warbling of one song, both in one key;
As if our hands, our sides, voices, and minds,
Had been incorporate. So we grew together,
Like to a double cherry, seeming parted,
But yet a union in partition,
Two lovely berries moulded on one stem:
So, with two seeming bodies, but one heart;
Two of the first, like coats in heraldry,
Due but to one, and crowned with one crest.
And will you rent our ancient love asunder,
To join with men in scorning your poor friend?
It is not friendly, 'tis not maidenly:
Our sex, as well as I, may chide you for it,
Though I alone do feel the injury.

Daybreak.

Night's swift dragons cut the clouds full fast,
And yonder shines Aurora's harbinger;
At whose approach, ghosts, wandering here and there.
Troop home to churchyards.

Act IV.

The Dew in Flowers.

That same dew, which sometime on the buds
Was wont to swell, like round and orient pearls,
Stood now within the pretty flowret's eyes,
Like tears, that did their own disgrace bewail.

Hunting.

I was with Hercules and Cadmus once,
When in a wood of Crete they bay'd the bear
With hounds of Sparta: never did I hear
Such gallant chiding ;* for, besides the groves,
The skies, the fountains, every region near
Seem'd all one mutual cry: I never heard
So musical a discord, such sweet thunder.

Act V.

The Power of Imagination.

The poet's eye, in a fine frenzy rolling,
Doth glance from heaven to earth, from earth to heaven ;
And, as imagination bodies forth
The forms of things unknown, the poet's pen
Turns them to shapes, and gives to airy nothing
A local habitation and a name.

Modest Duty always acceptable.

Where I have come, great clerks have purposed
To greet me with premeditated welcomes ;
Where I have seen them shiver and look pale,
Make periods in the midst of sentences,

* Such cheerful sounds.

Throttle their practised accent in their fears,
And in conclusion, dumbly have broke off,
Not paying me a welcome. Trust me, sweet,
Out of this silence, yet, I pick'd a welcome;
And in the modesty of fearful duty
I read as much, as from the rattling tongue
Of saucy and audacious eloquence.

Time.

The iron tongue of midnight hath told twelve.

Night.

Now the hungry lion roars,
  And the wolf behowls the moon;
Whilst the heavy ploughman snores,
  All with weary task foredone.*
Now the wasted brands do glow,
  Whilst the scritch-owl, scritching loud,
Puts the wretch, that lies in woe,
  In remembrance of a shroud.
Now it is the time of night,
  That the graves all gaping wide,
Every one lets forth his sprite,
  In the church-way paths to glide.

—*ooo*—

MUCH ADO ABOUT NOTHING.

The scene opens in Messina, where Don Pedro, Prince of Arragon, arrives on a visit to Leonato, the governor of Messina. Here Claudio, a young lord of Florence, a friend of Don Pedro's, falls in love with Hero, daughter of Leonato, and they are engaged to

---

* Overcome with fatigue.

be married. At the church where the marriage is to be solemnized, Claudio, repenting of his promise, rudely rejects Hero, and retires with his friends. Overwhelmed with anguish at her lover's conduct, Hero swoons, and, by the advice of the friar who is present to perform the nuptial ceremony, she is reported to be dead. Claudio afterwards deeply regrets his conduct, and gladly accepts an offer of Leonato to marry his niece, whom he pronounces to be

"Almost the copy of his child that's dead."

The niece, to the great joy of Claudio, turns out to be Hero herself, who has in the interim remained in concealment. Don John, who has acted a villain's part throughout the play, flies from Messina, but is captured and brought back for punishment. The chief interest in the drama is, however, centred in Benedick, a young lord of Padua, who exclaims bitterly against marriage, and Beatrice, niece of Leonato, who, after constantly railing at each other, fall in love, and agree to be married. Much merriment is caused by the ignorance displayed by two city officers, Dogberry and Verges.

ACT II.

Friendship in Love.

FRIENDSHIP is constant in all other things,
Save in the office and affairs of love;
Therefore all hearts in love use their own tongues;
Let every eye negotiate for itself,
And trust no agent; for beauty is a witch,
Against whose charms faith melteth into blood.*

Benedick's Disparagement of Beatrice.

She speaks poniards, and every word stabs: if her breath were as terrible as her terminations, there were no living near her; she would infect to the north star. I would not marry her though she were endowed with all that Adam had left him before he transgressed: she

* Passion.

would have made Hercules have turned spit; yea, and have cleft his club to make the fire too.

Beatrice's Merry Disposition Described.

There's little of the melancholy element in her, my lord: she is never sad, but when she sleeps; and not ever sad then; for I have heard my daughter say, she hath often dreamt of unhappiness, and waked herself with laughing.

Benedick's Ridicule of Love.

I do much wonder that one man, seeing how much another man is a fool when he dedicates his behaviours to love, will, after he hath laughed at such shallow follies in others, become the argument of his own scorn, by falling in love: And such a man is Claudio. I have known when there was no music with him but the drum and the fife; and now he would rather hear the tabor and the pipe: I have known when he would have walked ten mile afoot to see a good armour; and now will he lie ten nights awake, carving the fashion of a new doublet. He was wont to speak plain, and to the purpose, like an honest man, and a soldier; and now is he turn'd orthographer; his words are a very fantastical banquet, just so many strange dishes. May I be so converted, and see with these eyes? I cannot tell; I think not: I will not be sworn, but love may transform me to an oyster; but I'll take my oath on it, till he have made an oyster of me, he shall never make me such a fool.

Balthazar's Song.

Sigh no more, ladies, sigh no more,
Men were deceivers ever;

One foot in sea, and one on shore;
To one thing constant never:
Then sigh not so,
But let them go,
And be you blithe and bonny;
Converting all your sounds of woe
Into, Hey nonny, nonny.
Sing no more ditties, sing no mo*
Of dumps so dull and heavy;
The fraud of men was ever so,
Since summer first was leavy,
Then sigh not so, etc.

Benedick the Bachelor's Recantation.

This can be no trick; the conference was sadly borne.—They have the truth of this from Hero. They seem to pity the lady; it seems her affections have their full bent. Love me! why it must be requited. I hear how I am censured: they say, I will bear myself proudly, if I perceive the love come from her; they say too, that she will rather die than give any sign of affection.—I did never think to marry:—I must not seem proud:—happy are they that hear their detractions, and can put them to mending. They say the lady is fair; 'tis a truth, I can bear them witness: and virtuous;—'tis so, I cannot reprove it: and wise, but for loving me;—by my troth, it is no addition to her wit;—nor no great argument of her folly, for I will be horribly in love with her.—I may chance have some odd quirks and remnants of wit broken on me, because I have railed so long against marriage:—but doth not the appetite alter? A man loves the meat in his youth, that he cannot endure in his age. Shall quips, and sentences, and these paper

* No longer.

bullets of the brain, awe a man from the career of his humour?

Act III.

Royal Favourites compared to Honeysuckles.

Bid her steal into the pleached bower,
Where honeysuckles ripen'd by the sun,
Forbid the sun to enter;—like favourites,
Made proud by princes, that advance their pride
Against that power that bred it.

Beatrice's disdainful manner described.

Disdain and scorn ride sparkling in her eyes,
Misprising* what they look on; and her wit
Values itself so highly, that to her
All matter else seems weak; she cannot love,
Nor take no shape nor project of affection,
She is so self-endeared,
I never yet saw man,
How wise, how noble, young, how rarely featured,
But she would spell him backward; if fair-faced,
She'd swear the gentleman should be her sister;
If black, why, nature, drawing of an antic,
Made a foul blot: if tall, a lance ill-headed;
If low, an agate very vilely cut:
If speaking, why a vane blown with all winds:
If silent, why a block moved with none.
So turns she every man the wrong side out;
And never gives to truth and virtue, that
Which simpleness and merit purchaseth.

* Undervaluing.

Beatrice's awakened love for Benedick.

What fire is in mine ears? Can this be true?
Stand I condemn'd for pride and scorn so much?
Contempt, farewell! and maiden pride adieu!
No glory lives behind the back of such.
And, Benedick, love on, I will requite thee;
Taming my wild heart to thy loving hand;
If thou dost love, my kindness shall incite thee
To bind our loves up in a holy band:
For others say, thou dost deserve; and I
Believe it better than reportingly.

Act IV.

Dissimulation.

O what authority and show of truth
Can cunning sin cover itself withal!

Innocence confirmed by the Countenance.

I have mark'd
A thousand blushing apparitions start
Into her face; a thousand innocent shames
In angel whiteness bear away those blushes;
And in her eye there hath appear'd a fire,
To burn the errors that these princes hold
Against her maiden truth.

Resolution.

I know not: if they speak but truth of her,
These hands shall tear her; if they wrong her honour,
The proudest of them shall well hear of it.
Time hath not yet so dried this blood of mine,
Nor age so eat up my invention,

Nor fortune made such havoc of my means,
Nor my bad life reft me so much of friends,
But they shall find, awaked in such a kind,
Both strength of limb, and policy of mind,
Ability in means, and choice of friends,
To quit me of them thoroughly.

The Desire of a beloved Object heightened by its Loss.

For it so falls out,
That what we have we prize not to the worth,
Whiles we enjoy it; but being lack'd and lost,
Why, then we rack* the value; then we find
The virtue, that possession would not show us
While it was ours:—so will it fare with Claudio
When he shall hear she died upon† his words,
The idea of her life shall sweetly creep
Into his study of imagination:
And every lovely organ of her life
Shall come apparell'd in more precious habit,
More moving delicate, and full of life,
Into the eye and prospect of his soul,
Than when she lived indeed.

Talking Braggarts.

Manhood is melted into courtesies, valour into compliment, and men are only turned into tongue, and trim ones too; he is now as valiant as Hercules, that only tells a lie, and swears it.

Act V.

Counsel ineffectual in Misfortune.

Men
Can counsel, and speak comfort to that grief

* Over-estimate. † In consequence of.

Which they themselves not feel; but, tasting it,
Their counsel turns to passion, which before
Would give preceptial medicine to rage,
Fetter strong madness in a silken thread,
Charm ach with air, and agony with words;
No, no; 'tis all men's office to speak patience
To those that wring under the load of sorrow;
But no man's virtue, nor sufficiency,
To be so moral, when he shall endure
The like himself.

Satire on the Stoic Philosophers.

I pray thee peace: I will be flesh and blood;
For there was never yet philosopher
That could endure the tooth-ach patiently:
However they have writ the style of gods,
And made a push* at chance and sufferance.

Empty Boasters.

What man! I know them, yea,
And what they weigh, even to the utmost scruple;
Scambling, out-facing, fashion-mong'ring boys,
That lie, and cog, and flout, deprave and slander,
Go anticly, and show outward hideousness,
And speak off half a dozen dangerous words,
How they might hurt their enemies, if they durst,
And this is all.

Daybreak.

The wolves have prey'd; and look, the gentle day,
Before the wheels of Phœbus, round about
Dapples the drowsy east with spots of gray.

* Defiance.

TAMING OF THE SHREW.

Baptista, a rich gentleman of Padua, has two daughters, Katharina and Bianca. For the hand of the latter, Gremio and Hortensio are suitors; Baptista, however, declines to assent to Bianca's marriage till her elder sister, Katharina, the Shrew, has obtained a husband. Lucentio, a gentleman of Pisa, arrives in Padua, and falls in love with Bianca, and, in order to urge his suit, he disguises himself as a schoolmaster, and undertakes to become her instructor. In this assumed character he avows his passion, and after telling her that he is Lucentio, woos and marries her. Petruchio, a gentleman of Verona, has, in the meantime, with the consent of Baptista, proffered his love to Katharina, and, after an uncouth courtship, they are married. The chief action of the play consists in the efforts made by Petruchio to curb the wild temper of his wife; in this he is at length completely successful, and she becomes a model of obedience. The play concludes with an animated speech from Katharina on the duties of wives to their husbands.

Induction.

Hounds.

Thy hounds shall make the welkin answer them,
And fetch shrill echoes from the hollow earth.

Painting.

Dost thou love pictures? we will fetch thee straight
Adonis painted by a running brook:
And Cytherea all in sedges hid:
Which seem to move and wanton with her breath.
Even as the waving sedges play with wind.

Act I.

Woman's Tongue.

Think you, a little din can daunt mine ears?
Have I not in my time heard lions roar?
Have I not heard the sea, puff'd up with winds,
Rage like an angry boar, chafed with sweat?
Have I not heard great ordnance in the field,
And heaven's artillery thunder in the skies?
Have I not in a pitched battl heard
Loud 'larums, neighing steeds, and trumpets' clang?
And do you tell me of a woman's tongue;
That gives not half so great a blow to the ear,
As will a chestnut in a farmer's fire?

Act II.

Petruchio's uncouth mode of wooing.

I will attend her here
And woo her with some spirit when she comes.
Say, that she rail; Why, then I'll tell her plain,
She sings as sweetly as a nightingale:
Say, that she frown; I'll say, she looks as clear
As morning roses newly wash'd with dew:
Say, she be mute, and will not speak a word,
Then I'll commend her volubility,
And say, she uttereth piercing eloquence:
If she do bid me pack, I'll give her thanks,
As though she bid me stay by her a week;
If she deny to wed, I'll crave the day
When I shall ask the bans, and when be married.

Petruchio's Mock Flattery of Katharina.

I find you passing gentle.
'Twas told me you were rough, and coy, and sullen,

And now I find report a very liar;
For thou art pleasant, gamesome, passing courteous;
But slow in speech, yet sweet as spring-time flowers.
Thou canst not frown, thou canst not look askance,
Nor bite the lip, as angry wenches will;
Nor hast thou pleasure to be cross in talk;
But thou with mildness entertain'st thy wooers,
With gentle conference, soft and affable.
Why does the world report that Kate doth limp?
O slanderous world! Kate, like the hazel-twig,
Is straight and slender; and as brown in hue
As hazel-nuts, and sweeter than the kernels.

Act IV.

The Mind alone Valuable.

For 'tis the mind that makes the body rich:
And as the sun breaks through the darkest clouds,
So honour peereth* in the meanest habit.
What! is the jay more precious than the lark,
Because his feathers are more beautiful?
Or is the adder better than the eel,
Because his painted skin contents the eyes?
O, no, good Kate: neither art thou the worse
For this poor furniture and mean array.

Act V.

The Wife's Duty to her Husband.

Fie, fie! unknit that threatening unkind brow;
And dart not scornful glances from those eyes,
To wound thy lord, thy king, thy governor:
It blots thy beauty, as frost bites the meads:

* Appeareth.

Confounds thy fame, as whirlwinds shake fair buds;
And in no sense is meet, or amiable.
A woman moved is like a fountain troubled,
Muddy, ill-seeming, thick, bereft of beauty;
And, while it is so, none so dry or thirsty
Will deign to sip or touch one drop of it.
Thy husband is thy lord, thy life, thy keeper,
Thy head, thy sovereign; one that cares for thee,
And for thy maintenance; commits his body
To painful labour, both by sea and land;
To watch the night in storms, the day in cold,
While thou liest warm at home, secure and safe;
And craves no other tribute at thy hands,
But love, fair looks, and true obedience:—
Too little payment for so great a debt.
Such duty as the subject owes the prince,
Even such a woman oweth to her husband:
And, when she's froward, peevish, sullen, sour,
And not obedient to his honest will,
What is she but a foul contending rebel,
And graceless traitor to her loving lord?—
I am ashamed that women are so simple
To offer war where they should kneel for peace;
Or seek for rule, supremacy, and sway,
When they are bound to serve, love, and obey.
Why are our bodies soft, and weak, and smooth,
Unapt to toil and trouble in the world,
But that our soft conditions and our hearts
Should well agree with our external parts?

ALL'S WELL THAT ENDS WELL.

Helena, a favoured attendant on the Countess of Roussillon, is secretly in love with Bertram, son of the countess, he being ignorant of her attachment to him. The play opens with the departure of Bertram for France, the king of which country is suffering from a malady, which is pronounced by his physicians to be incurable. Helena's father, who has been dead six months, was a physician of eminence; and she, possessing a knowledge of the virtues of some of his prescriptions, follows Bertram to the Court of France, anxious to try the effect of her father's prescriptions on the king. She obtains his majesty's consent to make the trial and restores him to health, claiming as her reward the hand of Bertram, who is commanded by the French king to marry Helena forthwith. Much against his inclination, Bertram assents to the marriage, and immediately after the ceremony orders his newly-wedded wife to return to his mother at Roussillon, whilst he himself departs for the wars, and, attended by Parolles, a vain and empty braggart, who figures conspicuously in the play, he joins the army of the Duke of Florence. Helena, in disguise, proceeds to Florence in search of Bertram; without making herself known to him, she follows him home to Roussillon, where, to the great satisfaction of his mother and the King of France, he accepts her as his wife. Dr. Johnson says—"This play has many delightful scenes, though not sufficiently probable, and some happy characters, though not new, nor produced by any deep knowledge of human nature."

Act I.

Advice.

Be thou blest, Bertram! and succeed thy father
In manners, as in shape! thy blood and virtue,
Contend for empire in thee; and thy goodness
Share with thy birth-right! Love all, trust a few,
Do wrong to none: be able for thine enemy

Rather in power, than use; and keep thy friend
Under thy own life's key: be check'd for silence,
But never tax'd for speech.

Too ambitious Love.

I am undone; there is no living, none,
If Bertram be away. It were all one
That I should love a bright particular star,
And think to wed it, he is so above me:
In his bright radiance and collateral light
Must I be comforted, not in his sphere.
The ambition in my love thus plagues itself:
The hind that would be mated by the lion,
Must die for love. 'Twas pretty, though a plague,
To see him every hour; to sit and draw
His arched brows, his hawking eye, his curls,
In our heart's table;* heart, too capable
Of every line and trick † of his sweet favour: ‡
But now he's gone, and my idolatrous fancy
Must sanctify his relics.

Helena's description of Parolles.

I know him a notorious liar,
Think him a great way fool, solely a coward:
Yet these fix'd evils sit so fit in him,
That they take place, when virtue's steely bones
Look bleak in the cold wind.

The remedy of Evils exists in Ourselves.

Our remedies oft in ourselves do lie,
Which we ascribe to heaven: the fated sky

* The tablet or surface on which a picture is painted, used here for the picture itself.

† Peculiarity of feature. ‡ Countenance

Gives us free scope; only doth backward pull,
Our slow designs, when we ourselves are dull.

Character of a noble Courtier.

In his youth
He had the wit, which I can well observe
To-day in our young lords; but they may jest
Till their own scorn return to them unnoted,
Ere they can hide their levity in honour.
So like a courtier, contempt nor bitterness
Were in his pride or sharpness; if they were,
His equal had awaked them; and his honour,
Clock to itself, knew the true minute when
Exception bid him speak, and at this time,
His tongue obey'd his hand:* who were below him
He used as creatures of another place:
And bow'd his eminent top to their low ranks,
Making them proud of his humility,
In their poor praise he humbled; such a man
Might be a copy to these younger times.

Humility.

The Count Rousillon cannot be my brother:
I am from humble, he from honour'd name;
No note upon my parents, his all noble:
My master, my dear lord he is; and I
His servant live, and will his vassal die.

Helena's Hopeless Love for Bertram.

Then, I confess,
Here on my knee, before high heaven and you,
That before you, and next unto high heaven,

* Hand of a clock; the word clock in a previous line being used metaphorically.

I love your son:—
My friends were poor, but honest; so 's my love.
Be not offended; for it hurts not him,
That he is lov'd of me: I follow him not
By any token of presumptuous suit;
Nor would I have him, till I do deserve him;
Yet never know how that desert should be.
I know I love in vain, strive against hope;
Yet, in this captious and intenible sieve,*
I still pour in the waters of my love,
And lack not to lose still: thus, Indian like,
Religious in mine error, I adore
The sun, that looks upon his worshipper,
But knows of him no more.

Act II.

Honour due to Personal Virtue, not to Birth.

From lowest place when virtuous things proceed,
The place is dignified by the doer's deed:
Where great additions† swell, and virtue none,
It is a dropsied honour: good alone
Is good, without a name; vileness is so:‡
The property by what it is should go,
Not by the title. She is young, wise, fair;
In these to nature she 's immediate heir;
And these breed honour; that is honour's scorn,
Which challenges itself as honour's born,
And is not like the sire: Honours best thrive,

* Captious and intenible sieve—able to receive, but not to retain.

† Titles.

‡ Good is good in itself, and so is vileness vile, without reference to worldly considerations.

When rather from our acts we them derive
Than our fore-goers: the mere world's a slave,
Debauch'd on every tomb; on every grave,
A lying trophy, and as oft is dumb,
Where dust and damn'd oblivion is the tomb
Of honour'd bones indeed.

Act III.

Self-accusation of too great Love.

Poor lord! is't I
That chase thee from thy country, and expose
Those tender limbs of thine to the event
Of the non-sparing war? and is it I
That drive thee from the sportive court, where thou
Was shot at with fair eyes, to be the mark
Of smoky muskets? O you leaden messengers,
That ride upon the violent speed of fire,
Fly with false aim; move the still-piercing air,
That sings with piercing, do not touch my lord!
Whoever shoots at him, I set him there;
Whoever charges on his forward breast,
I am the caitiff that do hold him to it;
And, though I kill him not, I am the cause
His death was so effected: better 'twere
I met the ravin* lion when he roar'd
With sharp constraint of hunger: better 'twere
That all the miseries which nature owes
Were mine at once: No, come thou home, Roussillon,
Whence honour but of danger wins a scar,
As oft it loses all; I will be gone:
My being here it is that holds thee hence:
Shall I stay here to do't? no, no, although

* Voracious.

The air of paradise did fan the house,
And angels officed all: I will be gone;
That pitiful rumour may report my flight,
To consolate thine ear.

Act IV.

Life Chequered.

The web of our life is of a mingled yarn, good and ill together: our virtues would be proud if our faults whipped them not; and our crimes would despair if they were not cherished by our virtues.

A Cowardly Braggart.

Yet am I thankful: if my heart were great,
'T would burst at this: captain I'll be no more!
But I will eat and drink, and sleep as soft
As captain shall: simply the thing I am
Shall make me live. Who knows himself a braggart,
Let him fear this; for it will come to pass
That every braggart shall be found an ass.
Rust, sword! cool, blushes! and, Parolles, live
Safest in shame! being fool'd, by foolery thrive!
There's place, and means, for every man alive.

Act V.

Praise of a Lost Object.

Praising what is lost,
Makes the remembrance dear.

Against Delay.

Let's take the instant by the forward top;
For we are old, and on our quick'st decrees

The inaudible and noiseless foot of time
Steals ere we can effect them.

Excuse for Unreasonable Dislike.

At first
I stuck my choice upon her, ere my heart
Durst make too bold a herald of my tongue:
Where the impression of mine eye infixing,
Contempt his scornful perspective did lend me,
Which warp'd the line of every other favour;
Scorn'd a fair colour, or express'd it stolen;
Extended or contracted all proportions
To a most hideous object: thence it came,
That she, whom all men praised, and whom myself,
Since I have lost, have loved, was in mine eye
The dust that did offend it.

—ooo—

AS YOU LIKE IT.

The play commences with a quarrel between the brothers Oliver and Orlando, sons of the deceased Sir Rowland de Bois, after which Orlando engages in a bout of wrestling with Charles, a noted wrestler, whom he overthrows. Rosalind and Celia, who are cousins, and inseparable friends, witness the combat, and the former falls in love with Orlando. The reigning Duke Frederick, father of Celia, has usurped the government and banished his brother, the rightful duke and father of Rosalind, from his dominions. The exiled duke retires with Jaques, a cynical lord, and other courtiers, to the forest of Arden, where he is followed by Rosalind and Celia, who are accompanied by Touchstone, a clownish servitor. Orlando, attended by Adam, an old and faithful servant, encounters in the forest the banished Duke and his friends; here also he meets with Rosalind, and several love scenes occur between them. In the end, the chief characters being assembled together, Hymen enters and joins the hands of Rosalind and Orlando, and Celia and Oliver. At this juncture Jaques de Bois, another son of Sir Rowland, arrives, and brings intelligence that the usurping Duke Frederick has resolved to bequeath his crown to his brother and retire into solitude, and the comedy thus concludes. Much amusement is created by the clown Touchstone, who marries Audrey, a country girl whom he has met in the forest. Dr. Johnson says of this comedy: "The fable is wild and pleasing; the character of Jaques is natural and well preserved; the comic dialogue is very sprightly, with less mixture of low buffoonery than in some other plays, and the graver part is elegant and harmonious."

Act I.

Modesty and Courage in Youth.

I beseech you, punish me not with your hard thoughts, wherein I confess me much guilty, to deny so fair and excellent ladies anything. But let your fair eyes and gentle wishes go with me to my trial: wherein if I be foiled, there is but one shamed that was never gracious; if killed, but one dead that is willing to be so: I shall do my friends no wrong, for I have none to lament me; the world no injury, for in it I have nothing; only in the world I fill up a place, which may be better supplied when I have made it empty.

Play-fellows.

We still have slept together,
Rose at an instant, learn'd, play'd, eat together:
And wheresoe'er we went, like Juno's swans,
Still we went coupled, and inseparable.

Act II.

Solitude preferred to a Court Life, and the Advantages of Adversity.

Now, my co-mates, and brothers in exile,
Hath not old custom made this life more sweet
Than that of painted pomp? Are not these woods
More free from peril than the envious court?
Here feel we but the penalty of Adam,
The seasons' difference; as the icy fang,
And churlish chiding of the winter's wind;
Which, when it bites and blows upon my body,
Even till I shrink with cold, I smile, and say,
This is no flattery: these are counsellors
That feelingly persuade me what I am.
Sweet are the uses of adversity;
Which, like the toad, ugly and venomous,
Wears yet a precious jewel in his head;
And this our life, exempt from public haunt,
Finds tongues in trees, books in the running brooks,
Sermons in stones, and good in every thing.

Reflections on a wounded Stag.

Duke. Come, shall we go and kill us venison?
And yet it irks me, the poor dappled fools,—
Being native burghers of this desert city,—
Should, in their own confines, with forked heads*
Have their round haunches gored.
Lord. Indeed, my lord,
The melancholy Jaques grieves at that;
And, in that kind, swears you do more usurp
Than doth your brother that hath banish'd you.
To-day, my lord of Amiens, and myself,

* The heads of arrows barbed.

Did steal behind him, as he lay along
Under an oak, whose antique root peeps out
Upon the brook that brawls along this wood;
To the which place a poor sequester'd stag,
That from the hunter's aim had ta'en a hurt,
Did come to languish: and, indeed, my lord,
The wretched animal heaved forth such groans,
That their discharge did stretch his leathern coat
Almost to bursting; and the big round tears
Coursed one another down his innocent nose
In piteous chase; and thus the hairy fool,
Much marked of the melancholy Jaques,
Stood on the extremest verge of the swift brook,
Augmenting it with tears.
DUKE. But what said Jaques?
Did he not moralize this spectacle?
LORD. O, yes, into a thousand similes.
First, for his weeping in the needless stream;
"Poor deer," quoth he, "thou mak'st a testament
As worldlings do, giving thy sum of more
To that which had too much." Then, being alone,
Left and abandon'd of his velvet friends;
"'Tis right," quoth he, "thus misery doth part
The flux of company." Anon, a careless herd,
Full of the pasture, jumps along by him,
And never stays to greet him: "Ay," quoth Jaques,
"Sweep on you fat and greasy citizens;
'T is just the fashion: Wherefore do you look
Upon that poor and broken bankrupt there?"

Gratitude in an Old Servant.

I have five hundred crowns,
The thrifty hire I saved under your father,
Which I did store to be my foster-nurse,

When service should in my old limbs lie lame,
And unregarded age in corners thrown;
Take that: and He that doth the ravens feed,
Yea, providently caters for the sparrow,
Be comfort to my age! Here is the gold;
All this I give you: Let me be your servant:
Though I look old, yet I am strong and lusty:
For in my youth I never did apply
Hot and rebellious liquors to my blood.

A Lover described.

O, thou didst then ne'er love so heartily;
If thou remember'st not the slightest folly
That ever love did make thee run into,
Thou hast not loved:
Or if thou hast not sat as I do now,
Wearing thy hearer in thy mistress' praise,
Thou hast not loved:
Or if thou hast not broke from company
Abruptly, as my passion now makes me,
Thou hast not loved.

Jaques' description of a Fool.

A fool, a fool!——I met a fool i' the forest,
A motley fool;—a miserable world!—
As I do live by food, I met a fool;
Who laid him down and bask'd him in the sun,
And rail'd on lady Fortune in good terms,
In good set terms,—and yet a motley fool.
"Good-morrow, fool," quoth I; "No, sir," quoth he,
"Call me not fool, till heaven hath sent me fortune:"
And then he drew a dial from his poke;
And looking on it with lack lustre eye,

Says, very wisely, "It is ten o'clock:
Thus may we see," quoth he, "how the world wags;
'T is but an hour ago, since it was nine;
And after an hour more, 'twill be eleven;
And so, from hour to hour, we ripe, and ripe,
And then, from hour to hour, we rot, and rot,
And thereby hangs a tale!" When I did hear
The motley fool thus moral on the time,
My lungs began to crow like chanticleer,
That fools should be so deep-contemplative;
And I did laugh sans intermission,
An hour by his dial.—O noble fool!
A worthy fool! Motley's the only wear.*

A Fool's Liberty of Speech.

I must have liberty
Withal, as large a charter as the wind,
To blow on him I please: for so fools have:
And they that are most galled with my folly
They most must laugh: And why, sir, must they so?
The *why* is plain as way to parish church:
He, that a fool doth very wisely hit,
Doth very foolishly, although he smart,
Not to seem senseless of the bob;† if not,
The wise man's folly is anatomised
Even by the squand'ring glances of the fool.

A gentle Petition.

But whate'er you are,
That in this desert inaccessible,

* Alluding to the parti-coloured garment worn by the ancient jester.

† Bob—hit, blow.

Under the shade of melancholy boughs,
Lose and neglect the creeping hours of time;
If ever you have look'd on better days,
If ever been where bells have knoll'd to church:
If ever sat at any good man's feast;
If ever from your eye-lids wiped a tear,
And know what 'tis to pity and be pitied,
Let gentleness my strong enforcement be.

The Seven Ages of Man.

All the world's a stage,
And all the men and women merely players;
They have their exits and their entrances;
And one man in his time plays many parts,
His acts being seven ages. At first the infant,
Mewling and puking in the nurse's arms;
And then, the whining school-boy, with his satchel,
And shining morning face, creeping like snail
Unwillingly to school; and then, the lover;
Sighing like furnace, with a woful ballad
Made to his mistress' eye-brow. Then a soldier;
Full of strange oaths, and bearded like the pard,
Jealous in honour, sudden and quick in quarrel,
Seeking the bubble reputation
Even in the cannon's mouth: And then, the justice;
In fair round belly, with good capon lined,
With eyes severe, and beard of formal cut,
Full of wise saws and modern instances;
And so he plays his part: The sixth age shifts
Into the lean and slipper'd pantaloon:
With spectacles on nose, and pouch on side;
His youthful hose well sav'd, a world too wide
For his shrunk shank; and his big manly voice,
Turning again toward childish treble, pipes

And whistles in his sound: Last scene of all,
That ends this strange eventful history,
Is second childishness, and mere oblivion:
Sans teeth, sans eyes, sans taste, sans everything.

Ingratitude. A Song.

Blow, blow, thou winter wind,
Thou art not so unkind
As man's ingratitude;
Thy tooth is not so keen,
Because thou art not seen,
Although thy breath be rude.
Heigh, ho! sing heigh ho! unto the green holly:
Most friendship is feigning, most loving mere folly:
Then heigh, ho, the holly!
This life is most jolly.

Freeze, freeze, thou bitter sky,
That dost not bite so nigh
As benefits forgot:
Though thou the waters warp,
Thy sting is not so sharp
As friend remember'd not.
Heigh, ho! sing heigh ho! etc.

Act III.

A Shepherd's Philosophy.

I know the more one sickens, the worse at ease he is; and that he that wants money, means, and content, is without three good friends:—That the property of rain is to wet, and fire to burn: That good pasture makes fat sheep: and that a great cause of the night is lack of the sun; That he, that hath learned no wit by nature nor art, may complain of good breeding,* or comes of a very dull kindred.

Character of an Honest and Simple Shepherd.

Sir, I am a true labourer; I earn that I eat, get that I wear; owe no man hate, envy no man's happiness; glad of other men's good, content with my harm;† and the greatest of my pride is to see my ewes graze, and my lambs suck.

Humorous Description of a Lover.

A lean cheek; which you have not: a blue eye, and sunken; which you have not: an unquestionable spirit; which you have not: a beard neglected; which you have not:—(but I pardon you for that; for, simply, your having in beard is a younger brother's revenue):—Then your hose should be ungartered, your bonnet unbanded, your sleeve unbuttoned, your shoe untied, and everything about you demonstrating a careless desolation. But you are no such man: you are rather point-device‡ in your accoutrements; as loving yourself, than seeming the lover of any other.

Real Passion Dissembled.

Think not I love him, though I ask for him;
'Tis but a peevish boy:—yet he talks well;—
But what care I for words? yet words do well,
When he that speaks them pleases those that hear.
It is a pretty youth:—not very pretty:—
But, sure, he's proud; and yet his pride becomes him.
He'll make a proper man: the best thing in him
Is his complexion; and faster than his tongue

* The want of good breeding.

† Content with my own misfortunes. ‡ Over careful.

Did make offence, his eye did heal it up.
He is not tall; yet for his years he's tall:
His leg is but so-so; and yet 'tis well:
There was a pretty redness in his lip:
A little riper and more lusty red
Than that mix'd in his cheek; 'twas just the differ-
ence
Betwixt the constant red and mingled damask.
There be some women, Silvius, had they mark'd him
In parcels as I did, would have gone near
To fall in love with him: but, for my part,
I love him not, nor hate him not; and yet
I have more cause to hate him than to love him;
For what had he to do to chide at me?
He said, mine eyes were black, and my hair black;
And, now I am remember'd, scorn'd at me:
I marvel why I answer'd not again:
But that's all one; omittance is no quittance.

Act IV.

Jaques' Description of Melancholy.

I have neither the scholar's melancholy, which is emulation: nor the musician's, which is fantastical; nor the courtier's, which is proud; nor the soldier's, which is ambitious; nor the lawyer's, which is politic; nor the lady's, which is nice;* nor the lover's, which is all these.

Marriage alters the Temper.

Men are April when they woo, December when they wed; maids are May when they are maids, but the sky changes when they are wives. I will be more jealous

* Assumed, feigned.

of thee than a Barbary cock-pigeon over his hen; more clamorous than a parrot against rain; more new-fangled than an ape; more giddy in my desires than a monkey; I will weep for nothing, like Diana in the fountain, and I will do that when you are disposed to be merry.

Oliver's Exposure to Danger whilst Sleeping.

Under an oak, whose boughs were moss'd with age,
And high top bald with dry antiquity,
A wretched ragged man, o'ergrown with hair,
Lay sleeping on his back; about his neck
A green and gilded snake had wreath'd itself,
Who with her head, nimble in threats, approach'd
The opening of his mouth; but suddenly
Seeing Orlando, it unlink'd itself,
And with indented glides did slip away
Into a bush: under which bush's shade
A lioness with udders all drawn dry,
Lay couching, head on ground, with cat-like watch,
When that sleeping man should stir: for 'tis
The royal disposition of that beast
To prey on nothing that doth seem as dead.

Act V.

Humorous Epilogue spoken by Rosalind.

It is not the fashion to see the lady the epilogue: but it is no more unhandsome than to see the lord the prologue. If it be true that "good wine needs no bush," 'tis true that a good play needs no epilogue: Yet to good wine they do use good bushes; and good plays prove the better by the help of good epilogues. What a case am I in then, that am neither a good epilogue, nor cannot insinuate with you in the behalf of a good play! I am not furnished* like a beggar, therefore to beg will not become me: my way is, to conjure you; and I'll begin with the women. I charge you, O women, for the love you bear to men, to like as much of this play as please you: and I charge you, O men, for the love you bear to women (as I perceive by your simpering none of you hate them), that between you and the women the play may please. If I were a woman, I would kiss as many of you as had beards that pleased me, complexions that liked me, and breaths that I defied not: and, I am sure, as many as have good beards, or good faces, or sweet breaths, will, for my kind offer, when I make curt'sy, bid me farewell.

—*ooo*—

COMEDY OF ERRORS.

The chief incidents in this comedy arise out of the close similitude between the two brothers Antipholus of Ephesus and Antipholus of Syracuse, who, with their attendants, Dromio of Ephesus and Dromio of Syracuse, also twins, and bearing the same exact likeness to each other, have been shipwrecked in their infancy; Antipholus of Ephesus, with his attendant, being separated in the wreck from his brother and his attendant. Twenty-five years have elapsed, and the brothers meet at Ephesus, where, owing to the resemblance each bears to the other, numerous amusing mistakes occur. At last Ægeon and Æmilia, the father and mother of the Antipholus twins, who have also been separated in the wreck, meet each other, and their long-lost children at Ephesus, and the play concludes with the pardon of Ægeon by the Duke of Ephesus, for unwittingly breaking a recently enacted

---

* Clothed.

law. Mr. Steevens, the learned commentator on Shakspere, remarks, that this comedy "exhibits more intricacy of plot than distinction of character; and that attention is not actively engaged, since every one can tell how the denouement will be effected."

Act II.

Man's Pre-eminence.

There's nothing situate under Heaven's eye
But hath its bound, in earth, in sea, in sky;
The beasts, the fishes, and the winged fowls,
Are their males' subjects, and at their controls:
Men, more divine, the masters of all these,
Lords of the wide world, and wild watery seas,
Endued with intellectual sense and souls,
Of more pre-eminence than fish and fowls,
Are masters to their females, and their lords:
Then let your will attend on their accords.

Patience more easily taught than practised.

Patience, unmoved, no marvel though she pause,
They can be meek that have no other cause.
A wretched soul, bruised with adversity,
We bid be quiet when we hear it cry;
But were we burden'd with like weight of pain,
As much, or more, we should ourselves complain.

Defamation.

I see the jewel, best enamelled,
Will lose his beauty; and though gold 'bides still,
That others touch, yet often touching will
Wear gold; and so no man, that hath a name,
But falsehood and corruption doth it shame.

Act IV.

Description of a Cruel Master.

I have served him from the hour of my nativity to this instant, and have nothing at his hands for my service but blows. When I am cold, he heats me with beating; when I am warm, he cools me with beating: I am waked with it when I sleep; raised with it when I sit; driven out of doors with it when I go from home; welcomed home with it when I return; nay, I bear it on my shoulders as a beggar wont* her brat; and, I think, when he hath lamed me, I shall beg with it from door to door.

Act V.

Description of a Fortune-teller.

A hungry lean-faced villain
A mere anatomy, a mountebank,
A thread-bare juggler, and a fortune-teller:
A needy hollow-eyed, sharp-looking wretch,
A living dead man: this pernicious slave,
Forsooth, took on him as a conjurer;
And, gazing in mine eyes, feeling my pulse,
And with no face, as 'twere, outfacing me,
Cries out I was possess'd.

Old Age.

Though now this grained† face of mine be hid
In sap-consuming winter's drizzled snow,
And all the conduits of my blood froze up;
Yet hath my night of life some memory,
My wasting lamp some fading glimmer left,
My dull deaf ears a little use to hear:

* Is accustomed to carry. † Wrinkled, furrowed.

All these old witnesses (I cannot err)
Tell me, thou art my son Antipholus.

—ooo—

LOVE'S LABOUR'S LOST.

Biron, Longaville, and Dumain, lords of the Court of Navarre, together with Ferdinand, King of Navarre, agree to spend three years in entire seclusion from female society, and to devote their time to the pursuit of knowledge. No sooner have they decided on this than the Princess of France, attended by three of her ladies, Rosaline, Maria, and Katharine, arrives at Navarre, in embassy, respecting the restitution of the province of Aquitain to her sick and bed-ridden father. Notwithstanding the misanthropical resolution he has made, the king grants audience to the princess, and falls in love with her, whilst his three courtiers become enamoured with Rosaline, Maria, and Katharine. After much good-humoured raillery from the ladies, the gentlemen repent of their cynical resolve, and each of them is promised the hand of the lady of his heart, at the end of a year, during which period a penance of retirement from the world is imposed by the princess and her friends on their lovers. This comedy is said to have been played before Queen Elizabeth at the Christmas of 1597. Dr. Johnson says, "There are many passages in it mean, childish, and vulgar; but there are scattered through the whole many sparks of genius; nor is there any play that has more evident marks of the hand of Shakspere."

Act I.

Self-Denial.

Brave conquerors! for so you are,
That war against your own affections,
And the huge army of the world's desires.

Vanity of Pleasures.

Why all delights are vain ; but that most vain,
Which, with pain purchased, doth inherit pain.

On Study.

Study is like the heaven's glorious sun,
That will not be deep search'd with saucy looks :
Small have continual plodders ever won,
Save base authority from other's books :
These earthly godfathers of heaven's lights,
That give a name to every fixed star,
Have no more profit of their shining nights,
Than those that walk, and wot not what they are :
Too much to know, is to know naught but fame ;
And every godfather can give a name.

A conceited Courtier.

A man in all the world's new fashion planted,
That hath a mint of phrases in his brain :
One, whom the music of his own vain tongue
Doth ravish, like enchanting harmony ;
A man of compliments, whom right and wrong
Have chose as umpire of their mutiny ;
This child of fancy, that Armado hight,*
For interim to our studies, shall relate,
In high-born words, the worth of many a knight
From tawny Spain, lost in the world's debate.

Act II.

Beauty.

My beauty, though but mean,
Needs not the painted flourish of your praise ;

* Named.

Beauty is bought by judgment of the eye,
Not utter'd by base sale of chapmen's tongues.*

Biron's Mirthfulness described.

A merrier man,
Within the limit of becoming mirth,
I never spent an hour's talk withal:
His eye begets occasion for his wit;
For every object that the one doth catch,
The other turns to a mirth-moving jest;
Which his fair tongue (conceit's expositor)
Delivers in such apt and gracious words,
That aged ears play truant at his tales,
And younger hearings are quite ravished;
So sweet and voluble in his discourse.

Act IV.

Sonnet.

Did not the heavenly rhetoric of thine eye
('Gainst whom the world cannot hold argument)
Persuade my heart to this false perjury?
Vows, for thee broke, deserve not punishment.
A woman I foreswore; but, I will prove,
Thou being a goddess, I foreswore not thee:
My vow was earthly, thou a heavenly love;
Thy grace being gain'd, cures all disgrace in me:
Vows are but breath, and breath a vapour is;
Then thou, fair sun, which on my earth dost shine,
Exhal'st this vapour vow; in thee it is:
If broken, then, it is no fault of mine;
If by me broke. What fool is not so wise,
To lose an oath to win a paradise?

* Chapman, a dealer or seller.

The Power of Love.

But love, first learned in a lady's eyes,
Lives not alone immured in the brain ;
But, with the motion of all elements,
Courses as swift as thought in every power ;
And gives to every power a double power,
Above their functions and their offices.
It adds a precious seeing to the eye :
A lover's eyes will gaze an eagle blind ;
A lover's ear will hear the lowest sound,
When the suspicious head of theft is stopp'd ;
Love's feeling is more soft and sensible
Than are the tender horns of cockled snails ;
Love's tongue proves dainty Bacchus gross in taste ;
For valour, is not love a Hercules,
Still climbing trees in the Hesperides ?
Subtle as sphinx ; as sweet and musical
As bright Apollo's lute, strung with his hair ;
And, when love speaks, the voice of all the gods
Makes heaven drowsy with the harmony.
Never durst poet touch a pen to write
Until his ink were temper'd with love's sighs :
O, then his lines would ravage savage ears,
And plant in tyrants mild humility.

Woman's Eyes.

From woman's eyes this doctrine I derive
They sparkle still the right Promethean fire ;
They are the books, the arts, the academes,
That show, contain, and nourish all the world.

MEASURE FOR MEASURE.

Vincentio, Duke of Vienna, announces his intention to leave his dominions and travel in Poland. Taking leave of his friends, he deputes Angelo, assisted by Escalus (both of them lords of his court), to govern in his absence. Instead, however, of taking his departure, the Duke disguises himself as a friar, and remains in Vienna, being desirous of ascertaining how justice is administered when he is an absentee. No sooner has he disappeared from the court than Angelo, reviving an obsolete law, commits Claudio, a young gentleman in love with Juliet, to prison, and inhumanly condemns him to death. Isabella, Claudio's sister, a lady of exalted character, who is about to enter a nunnery, becomes a suppliant to Angelo for her brother's life; she, however, sues in vain, and Claudio is left for execution. An interview between the brother and sister takes place in the prison, and their conversation is overheard by the Duke, who thus is made aware of the harsh manner in which Angelo is overstraining the laws. At length the Duke throws off his disguise, and condemns Angelo to death, whom he, however, subsequently pardons at the intercession of Isabella. Claudio is released and marries Juliet, and the Duke himself, charmed with the nobility of character and piety of Isabella, offers her his hand. Dr. Johnson, speaking of "Measure for Measure," says: "The light or comic part is very natural and pleasing; but the grave scenes (a few passages excepted), have more labour than elegance; the plot is rather intricate than artful."

Act I.

Virtue given to be Exerted.

Heaven doth with us as we with torches do;
Not light them for themselves: for if our virtues
Did not go forth of us, 'twere all alike
As if we had them not. Spirits are not finely touch'd,

But to fine issues: nor nature never lends
The smallest scruple of her excellence;
But, like a thrifty goddess, she determines
Herself the glory of a creditor,
Both thanks and use.*

Eloquence and Beauty.

In her youth
There is a prone† and speechless dialect,
Such as moves men; beside, she hath prosperous art
When she will play with reason and discourse,
And well she can persuade.

Angelo's Character as a Governor described.

Lord Angelo is precise;
Stands at a guard with envy; scarce confesses
That his blood flows, or that his appetite
Is more to bread than stone: hence shall we see,
If power change purpose, what our seemers be.

Resolution.

Our doubts are traitors,
And make us lose the good we oft might win,
By fearing to attempt.

Act II.

Mercy.

No ceremony that to great ones 'longs,
Not the king's crown, nor the deputed sword,
The marshal's truncheon, nor the judge's robe,
Become them with one half so good a grace
As mercy does.

* Interest of money. † Facile, ready.

The Duty of Forgiveness.

Alas! alas!
Why, all the souls that were, were forfeit once,
And he that might the vantage best have took
Found out the remedy. How would you be,
If He, which is the top of judgment, should
But judge you as you are? O, think on that;
And mercy then will breathe within your lips,
Like man new made.

The Abuse of Power.

O, it is excellent
To have a giant's strength: but it is tyrannous
To use it like a giant.

The Abuse of Authority.

Could great men thunder
As Jove himself does, Jove would ne'er be quiet,
For every pelting,* petty officer,
Would use his heaven for thunder; nothing but thunder—
Merciful Heaven!
Thou rather, with thy sharp and sulphurous bolt,
Splitt'st the unwedgeable and gnarled oak,
Than the soft myrtle: O, but man, proud man!
Drest in a little brief authority:
Most ignorant of what he's most assured,
His glassy essence,—like an angry ape,
Plays such fantastic tricks before high heaven,
As make the angels weep.

The Privilege of Authority.

That in the captain's but a choleric word,
Which in the soldier is flat blasphemy.

* Mean, despicable.

Act III.

Hope.

The miserable have no other medicine,
But only hope.

The Vanity of Life.

Reason thus with life,—
If I do lose thee, I do lose a thing
That none but fools would keep; a breath thou art
(Servile to all the skyey influences.)
That dost this habitation, where thou keep'st,
Hourly afflict: merely, thou art death's fool;
For him thou labourest by thy flight to shun,
And yet runs't toward him still: thou art not noble;
For all the accommodations that thou bear'st
Are nursed by baseness: thou art by no means valiant;
For thou dost fear the soft and tender fork
Of a poor worm: thy best of rest is sleep,
And that thou oft provok'st, yet grossly fear'st
Thy death, which is no more: thou art not thyself;
For thou exist'st on many a thousand grains
That issue out of dust: happy thou art not;
For what thou hast not, still thou strivest to get;
And what thou hast, forget'st: thou art not certain;
For thy complexion shifts to strange effects,*
After the moon: if thou art rich, thou art poor;
For, like an ass, whose back with ingots bows,
Thou bear'st thy heavy riches but a journey,
And death unloads thee: friend hast thou none;
For thine own bowels, which do call thee sire,
The mere effusion of thy proper loins,
Do curse the gout, serpigo,† and the rheum,

* Affections. † A Leprous disease.

For ending thee no sooner: thou hast nor youth nor age:
But, as it were, an after-dinner's sleep,
Dreaming on both: for all thy blessed youth
Becomes as aged, and doth beg the arms
Of palsied eld;* and when thou art old and rich,
Thou hast neither heat, affection, limb, nor beauty,
To make thy riches pleasant. What's yet in this
That bears the name of life. Yet in this life
Lie hid more thousand deaths: yet death we fear,
That makes these odds all even.

The Terrors of Death chiefly in Apprehension.

O, I do fear thee, Claudio; and I quake
Lest thou a feverous life shouldst entertain,
And six or seven winters more respect
Than a perpetual honour. Darest thou die?
The sense of death is most in apprehension;
And the poor beetle that we tread upon,
In corporal sufferance finds a pang as great
As when a giant dies.

The Fear of Death.

Ay, but to die, and go we know not where;
To lie in cold obstruction, and to rot;
This sensible warm motion to become
A kneaded clod; and the delighted spirit
To bathe in fiery floods, or to reside
In thrilling regions of thick-ribb'd ice;
To be imprison'd in the viewless † winds.
And blown with restless violence about
The pendent world; or to be worse than worst
Of those, that lawless and incertain thoughts
Imagine howling!—'tis too horrible!

* Old age. † Invisible.

The weariest and most loathed worldly life
That age, ache, penury, and imprisonment
Can lay on nature, is a paradise
To what we fear of death.

Virtue and Goodness.

Virtue is bold, and goodness never fearful.

—ooo—

CYMBELINE.

Leonatus Posthumus has secretly married Imogen, daughter of Cymbeline, King of Britain, and his deceased queen. Cymbeline marries a second wife, who is a widow, having a son named Cloten, whom they design as a husband for Imogen. The king, incensed at the discovery of his daughter's marriage, orders her to be confined in the palace, whilst Posthumus is banished, and departs for Rome, where he takes up his abode in the house of his friend Philario. Belarius, a lord of Britain, in former years belonging to the court, has been unjustly banished, and retires into the mountains of Wales, taking with him Guiderius and Arviragus, the two infant sons of the king, whom he brings up as his own children. In the meantime war breaks out between the Romans and the Britons and a battle ensues, in which the former are at first successful, but Belarius and his two foster-sons, being joined by Posthumus, who has returned to Britain, rally their soldiers, and obtain the victory. Belarius, to the great joy of Cymbeline, restores to him his long-lost sons, and Imogen and Posthumus receive pardon for their surreptitious marriage. The queen, who has been, amongst other crimes, guilty of plotting against her husband's life, dies confessing her wickedness, and her son Cloten is slain by Guiderius in single combat. Iachimo, an Italian who has behaved treacherously to Posthumus, confesses his offences, and is forgiven, and the play concludes with a declaration of peace with the Romans.

Act II.

Imogen reading in bed.

Mine eyes are weak :—
Fold down the leaf where I have left : to bed :
Take not away the taper, leave it burning ;
And if thou canst awake by four o' the clock,
I pr'ythee, call me. Sleep hath seized me wholly.
To your protection, I commend me, gods !
From fairies, and the tempters of the night,
Guard me, beseech ye !

Imogen sleeping.

'T is her breathing that
Perfumes the chamber thus : the flame o' the taper
Bows towards her, and would underpeep her lids,
To see the enclosed lights, now canopied
Under these windows, white and azure, laced
With blue, of heaven's own tinct.*

* * * * *

On her left breast
A mole cinque-spotted, like the crimson drops
I' the bottom of a cowslip.

Song.

Hark ! hark ! the lark at heaven's gate sings,
And Phœbus 'gins arise,
His steeds to water at those springs
On chalic'd flowers that lies ;
And winking Mary-buds begin
To ope their golden eyes ;
With every thing that pretty bin ;
My lady sweet, arise ;
Arise, arise.

* The blue veins intersecting the white skin.

Gold.

'Tis gold
Which makes the true man kill'd, and saves the thief;
Nay, sometime, hangs both thief and true man: what
Can it not do, and undo?

Act III.

Impatience of Imogen to meet her husband Posthumus.

O, for a horse with wings!—Hear'st thou, Pisanio,
He is at Milford-Haven: read, and tell me
How far 'tis thither. If one of mean affairs
May plod it in a week, why may not I
Glide thither in a day?—Then, true Pisanio,
(Who long'st, like me, to see thy lord; who long'st—
O, let me 'bate,—but not like me:—yet long'st—
But in a fainter kind;—O, not like me;
For mine's beyond beyond), say, and speak thick*
(Love's counsellor should fill the bores of hearing,
To the smothering of the sense), how far it is
To this same blessed Milford; and, by the way,
Tell me how Wales was made so happy, as
To inherit such a haven. But, first of all,
How we may steal from hence; and, for the gap
That we shall make in time, from our hence-going,
And our return, to excuse.

Belarius' Description of his Banishment.

Two villains, whose false oaths prevail'd
Before my perfect honour, swore to Cymbeline,
I was confederate with the Romans: so,
Follow'd my banishment; and, this twenty years,

* Rapidly.

This rock and these demesnes have been my world.
Where I have liv'd at honest freedom; paid
More pious debts to heaven, than in all
The fore-end of my time.—But, up to the mountains;
This is not hunters' language:—He, that strikes
The venison first, shall be the lord o' the feast;
To him the other two shall minister:
And we will fear no poison, which attends
In place of greater state.

The Force of Nature.

How hard it is to hide the sparks of nature!
These boys know little they are sons to the king;
Nor Cymbeline dreams that they are alive.
They think they are mine: and though train'd up thus meanly
I' the cave, wherein they bow, their thoughts do hit
The roofs of palaces; and nature prompts them,
In simple and low things, to prince it much
Beyond the trick of others. This Polydore,—
The heir of Cymbeline and Britain, whom
The king his father called Guiderius—Jove!
When on my three-foot stool I sit, and tell
The warlike feats I have done, his spirits fly out
Into my story: say,—"Thus mine enemy fell;
And thus I set my foot on his neck;" even then
The princely blood flows in his cheek, he sweats,
Strains his young nerves, and puts himself in posture
That acts my words. The younger brother, Cadwal,
(Once Arviragus), in as like a figure,
Strikes life into my speech, and shows much more
His own conceiving.

Slander.

No, 'tis slander;
Whose edge is sharper than the sword: whose tongue
Outvenoms all the worms of Nile; whose breath
Rides on the posting winds, and doth belie
All corners of the world: kings, queens, and states,
Maids, matrons, nay, the secrets of the grave
This viperous slander enters.

Labour.

Weariness
Can snore upon the flint, when restive
Finds the down pillow hard.

Act IV.

In-born Royalty.

O thou goddess,
Thou divine nature, how thyself thou blazon'st
In these two princely boys! They are as gentle
As zephyrs, blowing below the violet,
Not wagging his sweet head: and yet as rough,
Their royal blood enchafed, as the rudest wind,
That by the top doth take the mountain pine,
And make him stoop to the vale. 'Tis wonderful,
That an invisible instinct should frame them,
To royalty unlearn'd; honour untaught:
Civility not seen from other; valour,
That wildly grows in them, but yields a crop
As if it had been sow'd.

Funeral Dirge.

Fear no more the heat o' the sun,
Nor the furious winter's rages;

Thou thy worldly task hast done,
  Home art gone, and ta'en thy wages;
Golden lads and girls all must
As chimney sweepers, come to dust.

Fear no more the frown o' the great,
  Thou are past the tyrant's stroke,
Care no more to clothe and eat;
  To thee the reed is as the oak:
The sceptre, learning, physic, must
All follow this, and come to dust.

Fear no more the lightning flash,
  Nor the all-dreaded thunder stone:
Fear not slander, censure rash;
  Thou hast finish'd joy and moan:
All lovers young, all lovers must
Consign to thee, and come to dust.

No exorciser harm thee!
Nor no witchcraft charm thee!
Ghost unlaid forbear thee!
Nothing ill come near thee!
Quiet consummation have;
And renowned be thy grave!

Act V.

A Routed Army.

No blame be to you, sir; for all was lost,
But that the heavens fought: the king himself
Of his wings destitute, the army broken,
And but the backs of Britons seen, all flying

Through a straight lane ; the enemy, full-hearted,
Lolling the tongue with slaughtering, having work
More plentiful than tools to do 't, struck down
Some mortally, some slightly touch'd, some falling
Merely through fear ; that the straight pass was damm'd
With dead men, hurt behind, and cowards living
To die with lengthen'd shame.

—ooo—

OTHELLO.

Othello, a valiant Moor, has won the affections of Desdemona, the daughter of Brabantio, a senator of Venice, and married her, unknown to her father. On hearing of the marriage, Brabantio is greatly irritated, and summons Othello before the Duke and Senators, where the Moor justifies his conduct, and is sent to Cyprus to command the Venetian forces against the Turks, who have despatched a fleet against Cyprus. Othello arrives at Cyprus, where Desdemona, by previous arrangement, follows him. Here Iago, who is a villain of the deepest dye, plots with Roderigo, a foolish Venetian, against Othello and his lieutenant Cassio. In the meantime, Othello, incited to the act by Iago, murders Desdemona, and stabs himself, falling dead by her side. Iago, who completes his career of crime by stabbing his wife Emilia, is condemned to the torture, as a punishment for his wicked actions. Of this tragedy, Dr. Johnson remarks, "The fiery openness of Othello; magnanimous, artless, and credulous; boundless in his confidence, ardent in his affections, inflexible in his resolution, and obdurate in his revenge; the soft simplicity of Desdemona, confident of merit, and conscious of innocence; the cool malignity of Iago, silent in his resentment, subtle in his designs, and studious at once of his interest and his vengeance, are such proofs of Shakspere's skill in human nature, as I suppose it is vain to seek in any modern writer."

Act I.

Iago's Dispraise of Honesty.

We cannot all be masters, nor all masters
Cannot be truly followed. You shall mark
Many a duteous and knee-crooking knave,
That, doting on his own obsequious bondage,
Wears out his time, much like his master's ass,
For naught but provender; and when he's old, cashier'd:
Whip me such honest knaves. Others there are
Who, trimm'd in forms and visages of duty,
Keep yet their hearts attending on themselves,
And, throwing but shows of service on their lords,
Do well thrive by them, and, when they have lined
their coats,
Do themselves homage: these fellows have some soul,
And such a one do I profess myself.
For, sir,
It is as sure as you are Roderigo,
Were I the Moor, I would not be Iago:
In following him, I follow but myself;
Heaven is my judge, not I for love and duty,
But seeming so, for my peculiar end:
For when my outward action doth demonstrate
The native act and figure of my heart
In compliment extern,* 'tis not long after
But I will wear my heart upon my sleeve
For daws to peck at: I am not what I am.

Love the sole inducement for Othello to marry

For know, Iago,
But that I love the gentle Desdemona,
I would not my unhoused free condition

* In merely external civility.

Put into circumscription and confine
For the sea's worth.

Othello's Relation to the Senate of his wooing Desdemona.

Most potent, grave, and reverend signiors,
My very noble and approved good masters,
That I have ta'en away this old man's daughter,
It is most true; true, I have married her:
The very head and front of my offending
Hath this extent, no more. Rude am I in my speech,
And little bless'd with the set phrase of peace;
For since these arms of mine had seven years' pith,
Till now some nine moons wasted, they have used
Their dearest action in the tented field;
And little of this great world can I speak,
More than pertains to feats of broil and battle;
And therefore little shall I grace my cause
In speaking for myself; yet, by your gracious patience,
I will a round unvarnish'd tale deliver
Of my whole course of love: what drugs, what charms,
What conjuration, and what mighty magic
(For such proceeding I am charged withal)
I won his daughter with.

* * * * * *

Her father lov'd me: oft invited me;
Still question'd me the story of my life,
From year to year; the battles, sieges, fortunes,
That I have pass'd.
I ran it through, even from my boyish days,
To the very moment that he bade me tell it.
Wherein I spoke of most disastrous chances,
Of moving accidents by flood and field;
Of hair-breadth 'scapes i' the imminent deadly breach
Of being taken by the insolent foe.

And sold to slavery; of my redemption thence,
And portance* in my travel's history.
Wherein of antres vast, and deserts idle,†
Rough quarries, rocks, and hills whose heads touch heaven,
It was my hint to speak, such was the process;
And of the Cannibals that each other eat,
The Anthropophagi, and men whose heads
Do grow beneath their shoulders.
These things to hear,
Would Desdemona seriously incline:
But still the house affairs would draw her thence,
Which ever as she could with haste despatch,
She'd come again, and with a greedy ear
Devour up my discourse: which I observing,
Took once a pliant hour, and found good means
To draw from her a prayer of earnest heart,
That I would all my pilgrimage dilate,
Whereof by parcels she had something heard,
But not intentively:‡ I did consent,
And often did beguile her of her tears,
When I did speak of some distressful stroke
That my youth suffer'd. My story being done,
She gave me for my pains a world of sighs:
She swore,—in faith, 'twas strange, 'twas passing strange;
'Twas pitiful, 'twas wondrous pitiful:
She wish'd she had not heard it: yet she wish'd
That heaven had made her such a man: she thank'd me;
And bade me, if I had a friend that lov'd her,

* Behaviour. † Idle is used to signify barren.
‡ Intention and attention were once synonymous. Attentively.

I should but teach him how to tell my story,
And that would woo her. Upon this hint I spake:
She lov'd me for the dangers I had pass'd;
And I lov'd her that she did pity them.
This only is the witchcraft I have used.

Act II.

Othello's joy at Desdemona's arrival at Cyprus.

O my soul's joy!
If after every tempest come such calms,
May the winds blow till they have waken'd death!
And let the labouring bark climb hills of seas
Olympus-high, and duck again as low
As hell's from heaven! If it were now to die,
'T were now to be most happy; for, I fear,
My soul hath her content so absolute,
That not another comfort like to this
Succeeds in unknown fate.

Act III.

Othello's passionate love for Desdemona.

Excellent wretch!* Perdition catch my soul,
But I do love thee! and when I love thee not,
Chaos is come again.

Othello's mistaken estimate of Iago's character.

I know thou art full of love and honesty,
And weigh'st thy words before thou giv'st them breath,—
Therefore these stops of thine fright me the more:
For such things, in a false disloyal knave,
Are tricks of custom; but, in a man that's just,

* Used here as a term of endearment.

They are close denotements, working from the heart,
That passion cannot rule.

Reputation.

Good name, in man and woman, dear my lord,
Is the immediate jewel of their souls;
Who steals my purse, steals trash; 't is something, nothing;
'T was mine, 't is his, and has been slave to thousands;
But he, that filches from me my good name,
Robs me of that which not enriches him,
And makes me poor indeed.

Jealousy.

Trifles, light as air,
Are, to the jealous, confirmations strong
As proofs of Holy Writ.

Othello's Farewell Speech.

O now, for ever,
Farewell the tranquil mind! farewell content!
Farewell the plumed troop, and the big wars,
That make ambition virtue! O, farewell!
Farewell the neighing steed, and the shrill trump,
The spirit-stirring drum, the ear-piercing fife,
The royal banner; and all quality,
Pride, pomp, and circumstance of glorious war!
And O you mortal engines, whose rude throats
The immortal Jove's dread clamours counterfeit,
Farewell! Othello's occupation's gone!

Iago's Hypocrisy.

O wretched fool,
That liv'st to make thine honesty a vice!—

O monstrous world! Take note, take note, O world,
To be direct and honest is not safe.—
I thank you for this profit; and, from hence,
I'll love no friend, since love breeds such offence.

Othello's Story of the Handkerchief.

That handkerchief
Did an Egyptian to my mother give;
She was a charmer,* and could almost read
The thoughts of people. She told her, while she kept it,
'T would make her amiable, and subdue my father
Entirely to her love; but if she lost it,
Or made a gift of it, my father's eye
Should hold her loathly, and his spirits should hunt
After new fancies. She, dying, gave it me;
And bid me, when my fate would have me wive,
To give it her. I did so: and take heed of't,
Make it a darling like your precious eye,
To lose or give't away, were such perdition,
As nothing else could match.

* * * * *

'Tis true; there's magic in the web of it:
A sibyl, that had number'd in the world
The sun to make two hundred compasses,
In her prophetic fury sew'd the work:
The worms were hallow'd that did breed the silk;
And it was dyed in mummy, which the skilful
Conserv'd of maidens' hearts.

A Lover's Computation of Time.

What! keep a week away? seven days and nights?
Eight score eight hours? and lover's absent hours,

* An Enchantress.

More tedious than the dial eight score times?
O weary reckoning!

Act IV.

Othello's Disordered Mind described.

The lethargy must have his quiet course;
If not, he foams at mouth; and, by and by,
Breaks out to savage madness. Look, he stirs:
Do you withdraw yourself a little while,
He will recover straight; when he is gone,
I would on great occasion speak with you.

Woman's Tears.

If that the earth could teem with woman's tears,
Each drop she falls would prove a crocodile.

Scene between Othello and Desdemona.

Desdemona. Alas, the heavy day!—Why do you weep?
Am I the occasion of these tears, my lord?
If, haply, you my father do suspect,
An instrument of this your calling back,
Lay not your blame on me; if you have lost him,
Why, I have lost him too.
Othello. Had it pleas'd Heaven
To try me with affliction; had he rain'd
All kinds of sores and shames on my bare head;
Steep'd me in poverty to the very lips;
Given to captivity me and my utmost hopes;
I should have found in some part of my soul
A drop of patience: but, alas! to make me
A fixed figure, for the hand of scorn
To point his slow unmoving finger at,—

Yet I could bear that too ; well, very well:
But there, where I have garner'd up my heart ;
Where either I must live, or bear no life ;
The fountain from the which my current runs,
Or else dries up ; to be discarded thence !
Or keep it as a cistern for foul toads
To knot and gender in !—Turn thy complexion there !
Patience, thou young and rose-lipp'd cherubim ;
Ay, there, look grim as hell !

Emilia's Indignation against Slanderers.

I will be hang'd, if some eternal villain,
Some busy and insinuating rogue,
Some cogging cozening slave, to get some office,
Hath not devis'd this slander ; I'll be hanged else.

* * * * *

The Moor's abus'd by some most villanous knave,
Some base notorious knave, some scurvy fellow :—
O heaven, that such companions * thou'dst unfold,
And put in every honest hand a whip,
To lash the rascals naked through the world,
Even from the east to the west !

Desdemona's Presentiment of her Death.

My mother had a maid call'd—Barbara ;
She was in love; and he, she lov'd, prov'd mad,
And did forsake her : she had a song of—" willow,"
An old thing 'twas, but it express'd her fortune,
And she died singing it : That song, to-night,
Will not go from my mind ; I have much to do,
But to go hang my head all at one side,
And sing it like poor Barbara.

* Fellows.

Act V.

Othello's Scene with Desdemona in the Bed-chamber before he kills her.

It is the cause, it is the cause, my soul,—
Let me not name it to you, you chaste stars!—
It is the cause.—Yet I'll not shed her blood:
Nor scar that whiter skin of hers than snow,
And smooth as monumental alabaster.
Yet she must die, else she'll betray more men.
Put out the light, and then—put out the light!
If I quench thee, thou flaming minister,
I can again thy former light restore,
Should I repent me: but once put out thine,
Thou cunning'st pattern of excelling nature,
I know not where is that Promethean heat,
That can thy light relume. When I have pluck'd thy rose,
I cannot give it vital growth again,
It needs must wither:—I'll smell it on the tree.—
[*Kissing her.*
O balmy breath, that dost almost persuade
Justice to break her sword!—One more, one more.—
Be thus when thou art dead, and I will kill thee,
And love thee after.—One more, and this the last:
So sweet was ne'er so fatal. I must weep,
But they are cruel tears: this sorrow's heavenly:
It strikes where it doth love.

Othello's Perplexity after the Murder.

Yes!—'tis Emilia:—by and by. She's dead.
'Tis like she comes to speak of Cassio's death;
The noise was high.—Ha! no more moving?

Still as the grave. Shall she come in? Were't good?
I think she stirs again:—No.—What's the best?
If she come in, she'll sure speak to my wife:
My wife! my wife! what wife?—I have no wife:
O, insupportable! O heavy hour!
Methinks it should be now a huge eclipse
Of sun and moon: and that the affrighted globe
Should yawn at alteration.

Othello's Love for Desdemona.

If heaven would make me such another world
Of one entire and perfect chrysolite,*
I'd not have sold her for it.

Othello's Remorse.

Behold! I have a weapon;
A better never did itself sustain
Upon a soldier's thigh: I have seen the day,
That, with this little arm, and this good sword,
I have made my way through more impediments
Than twenty times your stop.—But, O vain boast!
Who can control his fate? 'tis not so now.—
Be not afraid, though you do see me weapon'd;
Here is my journey's end, here is my butt,
And very sea-mark of my utmost sail.
Do you go back dismay'd? 'tis a lost fear;
Man but a rush against Othello's breast,
And he retires! where should Othello go?—
Now, how dost thou look now? O ill-starr'd wench!
Pale as thy smock! when we shall meet at compt,†
This look of thine will hurl my soul from heaven,
And fiends will snatch at it.

* A precious stone. † At our account hereafter

Othello's Speech before he Kills himself.

Soft you ; a word or two before you go.
I have done the state some service, and they know it ;
No more of that. I pray you, in your letters,
When you shall these unlucky deeds relate,
Speak of me as I am ; nothing extenuate,
Nor set down aught in malice : then must you speak
Of one, that loved not wisely, but too well :
Of one not easily jealous, but, being wrought,
Perplex'd in the extreme ; of one, whose hand,
Like the base Judean, threw a pearl away,
Richer than all his tribe ; of one whose subdu'd eyes,
Albeit unus'd to the melting mood,
Drop tears as fast as the Arabian trees
Their medicinal gum. Set you down this :
And say besides,—that in Aleppo once,
Where a malignant and a turban'd Turk
Beat a Venetian, and traduc'd the state,
I took by the throat the circumcised dog,
And smote him—thus. [*Stabs himself.*

Ludovico's Denunciation of Iago.

O Spartan dog,
More fell than anguish, hunger, or the sea !
Look on the tragic loading of this bed ;
This is thy work—the object poisons sight ;—
Let it be hid.—Gratiano, keep the house,
And seize upon the fortunes of the Moor,
For they succeed to you.—To you, lord governor,
Remains the censure of this hellish villain ;
The time, the place, the torture,—O enforce it !
Myself will straight aboard ; and, to the state,
This heavy act with heavy heart relate.

ROMEO AND JULIET.

A deadly feud exists between the noble families of Capulet and Montague, who reside in Verona. Romeo, son of Montague, and Juliet, daughter of Capulet, become violently enamoured with each other, and are privately married, unknown to their friends, by Laurence, a Franciscan friar. Shortly after their marriage, Tybalt, one of the Capulet faction, in a street brawl, kills Mercutio, and is himself killed by Romeo. For this Romeo is exiled by the Prince of Verona, and retires to Mantua. Capulet and his wife, ignorant of their daughter's marriage, have resolved to unite her to Paris, a young nobleman of Verona. To avoid this marriage, Juliet takes a drug provided for her by Friar Laurence, which produces a death-like lethargy. Her friends, supposing her to be dead, inter her in the tomb of the Capulets. It is intended by the friar that Romeo shall be advised of these events, so that he may be present when Juliet wakes, and take her away to Mantua. By an error, however, Romeo hears that Juliet is dead, on which he procures poison, and enters the monument in which she is entombed; here he meets Paris, who provokes him to fight, and is killed. Romeo then takes the poison. No sooner is he dead than Juliet wakes from her lethargy, and finding her husband dead by her side, stabs herself; and the play concludes with the reconciliation of the Capulets and Montagues.

Act I.

The Prince of Verona's Charge to Capulet and Montague.

Rebellious subjects, enemies to peace,
Profaners of this neighbour-stained steel,—
Will they not hear ?—what ho ! you men, you beasts,—
That quench the fire of your pernicious rage
With purple fountains issuing from your veins,
On pain of torture, from those bloody hands
Throw your mistemper'd weapons to the ground,

And hear the sentence of your moved prince.
Three civil brawls, bred of an airy word,
By thee, old Capulet and Montague,
Have thrice disturb'd the quiet of our streets,
And made Verona's ancient citizens
Cast by their grave beseeming ornaments,
To wield old partizans, in hands as old,
Canker'd with peace to part your canker'd hate:
If ever you disturb our streets again,
Your lives shall pay the forfeit of the peace.
For this time, all the rest depart away:
You, Capulet, shall go along with me;
And, Montague, come you this afternoon,
To know our further pleasure in this case,
To old Free-town, our common judgment-place.
Once more, on pain of death, all men depart.

Romeo's Melancholy.

Madam, an hour before the worshipp'd sun
Peer'd forth the golden window of the east,
A troubled mind drave me to walk abroad;
Where,—underneath the grove of sycamore,
That westward rooteth from the city's side,—
So early walking did I see your son:
Towards him I made; but he was 'ware of me,
And stole into the covert of the wood:
I, measuring his affections by my own,—
That most are busied when they are most alone,—
Pursued my humour, not pursuing his,
And gladly shunn'd who gladly fled from me.

* * * * *

Many a morning hath he there been seen,
With tears augmenting the fresh morning's dew,
Adding to clouds more clouds with his deep sighs:

But all so soon as the all-cheering sun
Should in the furthest east begin to draw
The shady curtains from Aurora's bed,
Away from light steals home my heavy son,
And private in his chamber pens himself;
Shuts up his windows, locks fair daylight out,
And makes himself an artificial night:
Black and portentous must this humour prove,
Unless good counsel may the cause remove.

Love.

Love is a smoke rais'd with the fume of sighs,
Being purg'd, a fire sparkling in lover's eyes:
Being vex'd, a sea nourish'd with lover's tears:
What is it else? a madness most discreet,
A choking gall, and a preserving sweet.

Capulet's Description of Juliet's Youth.

My child is yet a stranger in the world,
She hath not seen the change of fourteen years;
Let two more summers wither in their pride,
Ere we may think her ripe to be a bride.

Capulet's Consent to the Suit of Paris.

The earth hath swallow'd all my hopes but she,
She is the hopeful lady of my earth:
But woo her, gentle Paris, get her heart,
My will to her consent is but a part;
An she agree, within her scope of choice
Lies my consent and fair according voice.
This night I hold an old accustom'd feast,
Whereto I have invited many a guest,
Such as I love; and you, among the store,
One more, most welcome, makes my number more.

At my poor house, look to behold this night
Earth-treading stars, that make dark heaven light:
Such comfort as do lusty young men feel
When well-apparell'd April on the heel
Of limping winter treads, even such delight
Among fresh female buds shall you this night
Inherit at my house; hear all, all see,
And like her most whose merit most shall be.

Lady Capulet's Eulogy on Paris.

What say you? can you love the gentleman?
This night you shall behold him at our feast:
Read o'er the volume of young Paris' face,
And find delight writ there with beauty's pen;
Examine every married lineament,
And see how one another lends content;
And what obscur'd in this fair volume lies,
Find written in the margin of his eyes.
This precious book of love, this unbound lover,
To beautify him only lacks a cover:
The fish lives in the sea; and 'tis much pride
For fair without the fair within to hide:
That book in many's eyes doth share the glory,
That in gold clasps locks in the golden story;
So shall you share all that he doth possess,
By having him, making yourself no less.

Mercutio's Speech on Dreams.

O, then, I see, queen Mab hath been with you.
She is the fairies' midwife; and she comes
In shape no bigger than an agate stone
On the forefinger of an alderman,
Drawn with a team of little atomies*

* Atoms.

Athwart men's noses as they lie asleep:
Her waggon spokes made of long spinner's legs;
The cover, of the wings of grasshoppers;
The traces of the smallest spider's web;
The collars, of the moonshine's wat'ry beams:
Her whip, of cricket's bone; the lash, of film;
Her waggoner, a small gray-coated gnat,
Not half so big as a round little worm
Prick'd from the lazy finger of a maid:
Her chariot is an empty hazel nut,
Made by the joiner squirrel, or old grub,
Time out of mind the fairies' coachmakers.
And in this state she gallops night by night
Through lovers' brains, and then they dream of love:
On courtiers' knees, that dream on court'sies straight:
O'er lawyers' fingers, who straight dream on fees:
O'er ladies' lips, who straight on kisses dream;
Which oft the angry Mab with blisters plagues,
Because their breaths with sweetmeats tainted are.
Sometimes she gallops o'er a courtier's nose,
And then dreams he of smelling out a suit;*
And sometimes comes she with a tithe-pig's tail,
Tickling a parson's nose as 'a lies asleep,
Then dreams he of another benefice:
Sometimes she driveth o'er a soldier's neck,
And then dreams he of cutting foreign throats,
Of breaches, ambuscadoes, Spanish blades,
Of healths five fathom deep; and then anon
Drums in his ear; at which he starts, and wakes;
And, being thus frighted, swears a prayer or two,
And sleeps again. This is that very Mab,
That plats the manes of horses in the night;

* A position at court.

And bakes the elf-locks* in foul sluttish hairs,
Which, once untangled, much misfortune bodes.

* * * * *

I talk of dreams:
Which are the children of an idle brain,
Begot of nothing but vain fantasy;
Which is as thin of substance as the air;
And more inconstant than the wind, who woos
Even now, the frozen bosom of the north,
And, being anger'd, puffs away from thence,
Turning his face to the dew-dropping south.

Description of a Beauty.

O, she doth teach the torches to burn bright!
Her beauty hangs upon the cheek of night
Like a rich jewel in an Ethiop's ear:
Beauty too rich for use, for earth too dear!
So shows a snowy dove trooping with crows,
As yonder lady o'er her fellows shows.

Capulet's Favourable Opinion of Romeo.

He bears him like a portly gentleman;
And, to say truth, Verona brags of him,
To be a virtuous and well-govern'd youth:
I would not for the wealth of all this town,
Here in my house, do him disparagement:
Therefore be patient, take no note of him,
It is my will; the which if thou respect,
Show a fair presence, and put off these frowns,
An ill-beseeming semblance for a feast.

Romeo and Juliet at the Ball.

ROMEO. If I profane with my unworthy hand
This holy shrine, the gentle fine is this,—

* *i.e.*, Fairy locks, locks of hair clotted and tangled in the night.

My lips, two blushing pilgrims, ready stand
To smooth that rough touch with a tender kiss.
JULIET. Good pilgrim, you do wrong your hand too much,
Which mannerly devotion shows in this:
For saints have hands that pilgrims' hands do touch,
And palm to palm is holy palmers' kiss.
ROMEO. Have not saints lips, and holy palmers too?
JULIET. Ay, pilgrim, lips that they must use in prayer.
ROMEO. O then, dear saint, let lips do what hands do;
They pray, grant thou, lest faith turn to despair.
JULIET. Saints do not move, though grant for prayers' sake.
ROMEO. Then move not, while my prayer's effect I take.
Thus from my lips, by yours, my sin is purg'd.
JULIET. Then have my lips the sin that they have took.
ROMEO. Sin from my lips? O trespass sweetly urg'd!
Give me my sin again.
JULIET. You kiss by the book.

ACT II.

The Garden Scene.

ROMEO. He jests at scars that never felt a wound.—
But, soft! what light through yonder window breaks;
It is the east, and Juliet is the sun!—
Arise, fair sun, and kill the envious moon,
Who is already sick and pale with grief,
That thou her maid art far more fair than she:
Be not her maid, since she is envious:
Her vestal livery is but sick and green,
And none but fools do wear it; cast it off.—

It is my lady; O, it is my love:
O, that she knew she were!—
She speaks, yet she says nothing; what of that?
Her eye discourses, I will answer it.—
I am too bold, 'tis not to me she speaks:
Two of the fairest stars in all the heaven,
Having some business, do entreat her eyes
To twinkle in their spheres till they return.
What if her eyes were there, they in her head:
The brightness of her cheek would shame those stars,
As daylight doth a lamp; her eye in heaven
Would through the airy region stream so bright,
That birds would sing, and think it were not night.
See, how she leans her cheek upon her hand,
O, that I were a glove upon that hand,
That I might touch that cheek.

JULIET. Ah me!

ROMEO. She speaks:—
O, speak again, bright angel! for thou art
As glorious to this night, being o'er my head,
As is a winged messenger of heaven
Unto the white up-turned wond'ring eyes
Of mortals, that fall back to gaze on him,
When he bestrides the lazy-pacing clouds,
And sails upon the bosom of the air.

JULIET. O Romeo, Romeo! wherefore art thou Romeo?
Deny thy father, and refuse thy name:
Or, if thou wilt not, be but my sworn love,
And I'll no longer be a Capulet.

ROMEO. Shall I hear more, or shall I speak at this?

JULIET. 'Tis but thy name that is my enemy.
Thou art thyself though,* not a Montague.

* Juliet estimates him for his own good qualities, regardless of her dislike for his family.

What's Montague? it is nor hand, nor foot,
Nor arm, nor face, nor any other part
Belonging to a man. O, be some other name!
What's in a name? that which we call a rose
By any other name would smell as sweet:
So Romeo would, were he not Romeo call'd,
Retain that dear perfection which he owes,*
Without that title:—Romeo, doff† thy name:
And for that name, which is no part of thee,
Take all myself.

ROMEO. I take thee at thy word:
Call me but love, and I'll be new baptiz'd;
Henceforth I never will be Romeo.

JULIET. What man art thou, that, thus bescreen'd in night,
So stumblest on my counsel?

ROMEO. By a name
I know not how to tell thee who I am:
My name, dear saint, is hateful to myself,
Because it is an enemy to thee;
Had I it written, I would tear the word.

JULIET. My ears have not yet drunk a hundred words
Of that tongue's utterance, yet I know the sound:
Art thou not Romeo, and a Montague?

ROMEO. Neither, fair saint, if either thee dislike.

JULIET. How camest thou hither, tell me? and wherefore?
The orchard walls are high, and hard to climb;
And the place death, considering who thou art,
If any of my kinsmen find thee here.

ROMEO. With love's light wings did I o'erperch these walls;
For stony limits cannot hold love out:

* Possesses. † Put aside

And what love can do, that dares love attempt,
Therefore thy kinsmen are no stop to me.

JULIET. If they do see thee, they will murder thee.

ROMEO. Alack! there lies more peril in thine eye
Than twenty of their swords; look thou but sweet,
And I am proof against their enmity.

JULIET. I would not for the world they saw thee here.

ROMEO. I have night's cloak to hide me from their sight;
And, but thou love me,* let them find me here:
My life were better ended by their hate,
Than death prorogued, wanting of thy love.

JULIET. By whose direction found'st thou out this place?

ROMEO. By love, who first did prompt me to inquire:
He lent me counsel, and I lent him eyes.
I am no pilot; yet, wert thou as far
As that vast shore wash'd with the furthest sea,
I would adventure for such merchandise.

JULIET. Thou know'st the mask of night is on my face:
Else would a maiden blush bepaint my cheek,
For that which thou hast heard me speak to-night.
Fain would I dwell on form, fain, fain deny
What I have spoke: but farewell compliment!†
Dost thou love me? I know thou wilt say, Ay:
And I will take thy word; yet, if thou swear'st,
Thou may'st prove false; at lovers' perjuries,
They say Jove laughs. O, gentle Romeo,
If thou dost love, pronounce it faithfully:
Or if thou think'st I am too quickly won,
I'll frown and be perverse, and say thee nay,
So thou wilt woo; but else not for the world.
In truth, fair Montague, I am too fond;

* Except you love me. † False delicacy.

And therefore thou may'st think my 'haviour light.
But trust me, gentleman, I'll prove more true
Than those that have more cunning to be strange.*
I should have been more strange, I must confess,
But that thou overheard'st, ere I was 'ware,
My true love's passion : therefore pardon me ;
And not impute this yielding to light love,
Which the dark night hath so discovered.

ROMEO. Lady, by yonder blessed moon I swear,
That tips with silver all these fruit-tree tops.

JULIET. O, swear not by the moon, the inconstant moon,
That monthly changes in her circled orb,
Lest that thy love prove likewise variable.

ROMEO. What shall I swear by?

JULIET. Do not swear at all,
Or, if thou wilt, swear by thy gracious self,
Which is the god of my idolatry,
And I'll believe thee.

ROMEO. If my heart's dear love—

JULIET. Well, do not swear : although I joy in thee,
I have no joy of this contract to-night ;
It is too rash, too unadvis'd, too sudden :
Too like the lightning, which doth cease to be
Ere one can say, It lightens. Sweet, good night!
This bud of love, by summer's ripening breath,
May prove a beauteous flower when next we meet.
Good night, good night! as sweet repose and rest
Come to thy heart, as that within my breast!

ROMEO. O, wilt thou leave me so unsatisfied?

JULIET. What satisfaction canst thou have to night?

ROMEO. The exchange of thy love's faithful vow for mine.

* Bashful.

JULIET. I gave thee mine before thou didst request it:
And yet I would it were to give again.
ROMEO. Wouldst thou withdraw it? for what purpose, love?
JULIET. But to be frank, and give it thee again.
And yet I wish but for the thing I have:
My bounty is as boundless as the sea,
My love as deep; the more I give to thee,
The more I have, for both are infinite.

* * * * *

ROMEO. Sleep dwell upon thine eyes, peace in thy breast!—
Would I were sleep and peace, so sweet to rest.

The Dawn of Day.

The grey-ey'd morn smiles on the frowning night,
Checkering the eastern clouds with streaks of light;
And flecked* darkness like a drunkard reels
From forth day's path-way, made by Titan's† wheels.

Early Rising.

What early tongue so sweet saluteth me?—
Young son, it argues a distemper'd head,
So soon to bid good morrow to thy bed:
Care keeps his watch in every old man's eye,
And where care lodges, sleep will never lie;
But where unbruised youth, with unstuff'd brain
Doth couch his limbs, there golden sleep doth reign:
Therefore thy earliness doth me assure,
Thou art up-rous'd by some distemp'rature;
Or, if not so, then here I hit it right—
Our Romeo hath not been in bed to-night.

* Dappled, spotted. † Titan, used for the sun

Mercutio's Description of Romeo in Love.

Alas, poor Romeo, he is already dead; stabbed with a white wench's black eye; shot through the ear with a love-song; the very pin* of his heart cleft with the blind bow-boy's butt-shaft.†

Love's Heralds.

Love's heralds should be thoughts,
Which ten times faster glide than the sun's beams,
Driving back shadows over low'ring hills:
Therefore do nimble-pinion'd doves draw love,
And therefore hath the wind-swift Cupid wings.

Violent Delights not Lasting.

These violent delights have violent ends,
And in their triumph die: like fire and powder,
Which, as they kiss, consume.

Lovers light of Foot.

O, so light a foot
Will ne'er wear out the everlasting flint:
A lover may bestride the gossamers
That idle in the wanton summer air,
And yet not fall; so light is vanity.

Act III.

Mercutio's description of a Brawler.

Thou! why thou wilt quarrel with a man that hath a hair more, or a hair less, in his beard, than thou hast. Thou wilt quarrel with a man for cracking nuts,

* Pin of his heart, that is the centre. † Cupid's arrow.

having no other reason but because thou hast hazel eyes. What eye but such an eye, would spy out such a quarrel? Thy head is as full of quarrels as an egg is full of meat; and yet thy head hath been beaten as addle as an egg for quarrelling. Thou hast quarrelled with a man for coughing in the street, because he hath wakened thy dog that hath lain asleep in the sun. Didst thou not fall out with a tailor for wearing his new doublet before Easter? with another, for tying his new shoes with old ribbon? and yet thou wilt tutor me from quarrelling.

Juliet's impatience for Romeo.

Come, night!—Come, Romeo! come, thou day in night!
For thou wilt lie upon the wings of night
Whiter than new snow on a raven's back.—
Come, gentle night; come, loving, black-brow'd night,
Give me my Romeo: and, when he shall die,
Take him and cut him out in little stars,
And he will make the face of heaven so fine,
That all the world will be in love with night,
And pay no worship to the garish sun.

Romeo's Banishment.

FRIAR LAURENCE. A gentler judgment vanish'd from his lips,
Not body's death, but body's banishment.
ROMEO. Ha! banishment? be merciful, say death:
For exile hath more terror in his look,
Much more than death: do not say banishment.
FRIAR. Hence from Verona art thou banished:
Be patient, for the world is broad and wide.
ROMEO. There is no world without Verona walls,

But purgatory, torture, hell itself.
Hence-banished, is banish'd from the world,
And world's exile is death ;—then banishment,
Is death mis-term'd ; calling death banishment,
Thou cutt'st my head off with a golden axe,
And smil'st upon the stroke that murders me.
FRIAR. O deadly sin ! O rude unthankfulness !
Thy fault our law calls death ; but the kind prince,
Taking thy part, hath rush'd aside the law,
And turn'd that black word death to banishment,
This is dear mercy, and thou seest it not.
ROMEO. 'Tis torture, and not mercy ; heaven is here,
Where Juliet lives ; and every cat, and dog,
And little mouse, every unworthy thing,
Live here in heaven, and may look on her,
But Romeo may not.—More validity
More honourable state, more courtship lives
In carrion flies than Romeo : they may seize
On the white wonder of dear Juliet's hand,
And steal immortal blessings from her lips ;
Who, even in pure and vestal modesty,
Still blush, as thinking their own kisses sin ;
But Romeo may not ; he is banish'd :
Flies may do this, when I from this must fly ;
They are free men, but I am banished.
And say'st thou yet that exile is not death ?
Had'st thou no poison mix'd, no sharp-ground knife,
No sudden mean of death, though ne'er so mean,
But—banished—to kill me ; banished ?
O friar, the damned use that word in hell ;
Howlings attend it : how hast thou the heart,
Being a divine, a ghostly confessor,
A sin-absolver, and my friend professed,
To mangle me with that word—banishment ?

FRIAR. Thou fond madman, hear me but speak a word.

ROMEO. O thou wilt speak again of banishment.

FRIAR. I'll give thee armour to keep off that word :
Adversity's sweet milk, philosophy,
To comfort thee, though thou art banished.

ROMEO. Yet banished !—Hang up philosophy !
Unless philosophy can make a Juliet,
Displant a town, reverse a prince's doom :
It helps not, it prevails not ; talk no more.

FRIAR. O then I see that madmen have no ears.

ROMEO. How should they, when that wise men have no eyes?

FRIAR. Let me dispute with thee of thy estate.

ROMEO. Thou canst not speak of what thou dost not feel.
Wert thou as young as I, Juliet thy love,
An hour but married, Tybalt murdered,
Doting like me, and like me banished,
Then mightst thou speak, then mightst thou tear thy hair,
And fall upon the ground as I do now,
Taking the measure of an unmade grave.

Reluctance of Lovers to part.

JULIET. Wilt thou be gone? It is not yet near day.
It was the nightingale, and not the lark,
That pierced the fearful hollow of thine ear ;
Nightly she sings on yon pomegranate tree :
Believe me, love, it was the nightingale.

ROMEO. It was the lark, the herald of the morn,
No nightingale : look, love, what envious streaks
Do lace the severing clouds in yonder east ;
Night's candles are burnt out, and jocund day

Stands tiptoe on the misty mountain tops:
I must be gone and live, or stay and die.
JULIET. Yon light is not daylight, I know it, I:
It is some meteor that the sun exhales,
To be to thee this night a torch-bearer,
And light thee on thy way to Mantua;
Therefore stay yet, thou need'st not to be gone.
ROMEO. Let me be ta'en, let me be put to death;
I am content, so thou will have it so.
I'll say, yon grey is not the morning's eye,
'Tis but the pale reflex of Cynthia's brow;
Nor that is not the lark, whose notes do beat
The vaulty heaven so high above our heads:
I have more care to stay than will to go;—
Come, death, and welcome! Juliet wills it so,—
How is't, my soul? let's talk, it is not day.
JULIET. It is, it is, hie hence, be gone, away;
It is the lark that sings so out of tune,
Straining harsh discords, and unpleasing sharps.
Some say, the lark makes sweet division;
This doth not so, for she divideth us:
Some say, the lark and loathed toad change eyes,
O, now I would they had chang'd voices too!
Since arm from arm that voice doth us affray,
Hunting thee hence with hunts-up to the day.
O, now be gone; more light and light it grows.

Capulet's Anger at Juliet's Refusal to Marry Paris.

It makes me mad: Day, night, late, early,
At home, abroad, alone, in company,
Waking or sleeping, still my care hath been
To have her match'd: and having now provided
A gentleman of princely parentage,
Of fair demesnes, youthful, and nobly train'd,

Stuff'd (as they say) with honourable parts,
Proportion'd as one's heart could wish a man,—
And then to have a wretched puling fool,
A whining mammet, in her fortune's tender,
To answer—*I'll not wed,—I cannot love,*
I am too young,—I pray you pardon me;—
But, an you will not wed, I'll pardon you:
Graze where you will, you shall not house with me;
Look to't, think on't, I do not use to jest.
Thursday is near; lay hand on heart, advise;
An you be mine, I'll give you to my friend;
An you be not, hang, beg, starve, die i' the streets,
For, by my soul, I'll ne'er acknowledge thee,
Nor what is mine shall never do thee good:
Trust to't, bethink you, I'll not be forsworn.

Juliet's Anguish at the Thought of her Marriage with Paris.

Is there no pity sitting in the clouds,
That sees into the bottom of my grief?
O, sweet my mother, cast me not away!
Delay this marriage for a month, a week;
Or, if you do not, make the bridal bed
In that dim monument were Tybalt lies.

The Nurse's Description of Paris.

Romeo's a dishclout to him; an eagle, madam,
Hath not so green, so quick, so fair an eye,
As Paris hath. Beshrew my very heart,
I think you are happy in this second match,
For it excels your first.

Act IV.

Juliet's Appeal to Friar Laurence, to prevent her Marriage with Paris.

Juliet. Tell me not, friar, that thou hear'st of this,
Unless thou tell me how I may prevent it:
If, in thy wisdom, thou canst give no help,
Do thou but call my resolution wise,
And with this knife I'll help it presently.
God join'd my heart and Romeo's, thou our hands:
And ere this hand, by thee to Romeo seal'd,
Shall be the label to another deed,
Or my true heart with treacherous revolt
Turn to another, this shall slay them both:
Therefore, out of thy long-experienc'd time,
Give me some present counsel; or, behold,
'Twixt my extremes and me this bloody knife
Shall play the umpire; arbitrating that
Which the commission of thy years and art
Could to no issue of true honour bring.
Be not so long to speak; I long to die,
If what thou speak'st speak not of remedy.

Friar. Hold, daughter; I do spy a kind of hope,
Which craves as desperate an execution
As that is desperate which we would prevent.
If, rather than to marry county Paris,
Thou hast the strength of will to slay thyself;
Then is it likely, thou wilt undertake
A thing like death to chide away this shame,
That cop'st with death himself to scape from it;
And, if thou dar'st, I'll give thee remedy.

Juliet. O bid me leap, rather than marry Paris,
From off the battlements of yonder tower;
Or walk in thievish ways; or bid me lurk

Where serpents are; chain me with roaring bears;
Or shut me nightly in a charnel-house,
O'er-cover'd quite with dead men's rattling bones,
With reeky shanks, and yellow chapless sculls;
Or bid me go into a new-made grave,
And hide me with a dead man in his shroud;
Things that, to hear them told, have made me tremble:
And I will do it without fear or doubt,
To live an unstain'd wife to my sweet love.

FRIAR. Hold, then; go home, be merry, give consent
To marry Paris; Wednesday is to-morrow;
To-morrow night look that thou lie alone,
Let not thy nurse lie with thee in thy chamber:
Take thou this phial, being then in bed,
And this distilled liquor drink thou off:
When presently, through all thy veins shall run
A cold and drowsy humour, which shall seize
Each vital spirit; for no pulse shall keep
His natural progress, but surcease to beat:
No warmth, no breath, shall testify thou liv'st;
The roses in thy lips and cheeks shall fade
To paly ashes; thy eyes' windows fall,
Like death when he shuts up the day of life;
Each part, depriv'd of supple government,
Shall stiff, and stark, and cold appear like death:
And in this borrow'd likeness of shrunk death
Thou shalt remain full two and forty hours,
And then awake as from a pleasant sleep.
Now when the bridegroom in the morning comes
To rouse thee from thy bed, there art thou dead:
Then (as the manner of our country is),
In thy best robes uncover'd on the bier,
Thou shalt be borne to that same ancient vault,

Where all the kindred of the Capulets lie.
In the meantime, against thou shalt awake,
Shall Romeo by my letters know our drift;
And hither shall he come: and he and I
Will watch thy waking, and that very night
Shall Romeo bear thee hence to Mantua.
And this shall free thee from this present shame;
If no unconstant toy, nor womanish fear,
Abate thy valour in the acting it.

Juliet's Soliloquy on Drinking the Potion.

Farewell!—God knows when we shall meet again.
I have a faint cold fear thrills through my veins,
That almost freezes up the heat of life:
I'll call them back again to comfort me;—
Nurse!—What should she do here?
My dismal scene I needs must act alone.—
Come, phial.—
What if this mixture do not work at all?
Shall I be married then to-morrow morning?
No, no;—this shall forbid it:—lie thou there.—
[*Laying down a dagger.*
What if it be a poison, which the friar
Subtly hath minister'd to have me dead;
Lest in this marriage he should be dishonour'd,
Because he married me before to Romeo?
I fear it is: and yet, methinks, it should not,
For he hath still been tried a holy man:
I will not entertain so bad a thought.—
How, if when I am laid into the tomb,
I wake before the time that Romeo
Come to redeem me? there's a fearful point!
Shall I not then be stifled in the vault,
To whose foul mouth no healthsome air breathes in,

And there die strangled ere my Romeo comes?
Or, if I live, is it not very like,
The horrible conceit of death and night,
Together with the terror of the place,—
As in a vault, an ancient receptacle,
Where, for these many hundred years, the bones
Of all my buried ancestors are pack'd;
Where bloody Tybalt, yet but green in earth,
Lies fest'ring in his shroud; where, as they say,
At some hours in the night, spirits resort;—
Alack, alack! is it not like, that I,
So early waking,—what with loathsome smells;
And shrieks like mandrakes torn out of the earth,
That living mortals, hearing them, run mad.
O! if I wake, shall I not be distraught,
Environed with all these hideous fears?
And madly play with my forefathers' joints?
And pluck the mangled Tybalt from his shroud?
And, in this rage, with some great kinsman's bone,
As with a club, dash out my desperate brains?
O, look! methinks I see my cousin's ghost
Seeking out Romeo, that did spit his body
Upon a rapier's point.—Stay, Tybalt, stay!
Romeo, I come! this do I drink to thee.

Juliet after taking the Potion.

Out, alas! she's cold;
Her blood is settled; and her joints are stiff;
Life and these lips have long been separated:
Death lies on her, like an untimely frost
Upon the sweetest flower of all the field.

Joy changed to Grief.

All things that we ordained festival,
Turn from their office to black funeral:

Our instruments to melancholy bells;
Our wedding cheer to a sad burial feast:
Our solemn hymns to sullen dirges change:
Our bridal flowers serve for a buried corse.
And all things change them to the contrary.

Act V.

Dreams.

If I may trust the flattering eye of sleep,
My dreams presage some joyful news at hand:
My bosom's lord sits lightly in his throne;
And, all this day, an unaccustom'd spirit
Lifts me above the ground with cheerful thoughts.
I dreamt my lady came and found me dead;
(Strange dream! that gives a dead man leave to think,
And breath'd such life with kisses in my lips,
That I reviv'd, and was an emperor.
Ah me! how sweet is love itself possess'd,
When but love's shadows are so rich in joy?

Romeo's conference with the Apothecary.

Romeo. O, mischief, thou art swift
To enter in the thoughts of desperate men!
I do remember an apothecary,—
And hereabouts he dwells,—whom late I noted
In tatter'd weeds, with o'erwhelming brow,
Culling of simples,* meagre were his looks,
Sharp misery had worn him to the bones:
And in his needy shop a tortoise hung,
An alligator stuff'd, and other skins
Of ill-shaped fishes; and about his shelves
A beggarly account of empty boxes,

* Picking out herbs

Green earthen pots, bladders, and musty seeds,
Remnants of packthread, and old cakes of roses,
Were thinly scatter'd to make up a show.
Noting this penury, to myself I said,—
And if a man did need a poison now,
Whose sale is present death in Mantua,
Here lives a caitiff wretch would sell it him.
O, this same thought did but fore-run my need;
And this same needy man must sell it me.
As I remember, this should be the house:
Being holiday, the beggar's shop is shut.—
What, ho! apothecary!

APOTHECARY. Who calls so loud?

ROMEO. Come hither, man.—I see that thou art poor,
Hold, there is forty ducats: let me have
A dram of poison; such soon-speeding geer*
As will disperse itself through all the veins,
That the life-weary taker may fall dead;
And that the trunk may be discharg'd of breath
As violently as hasty powder fir'd
Doth hurry from the fatal cannon's womb.

APOTHECARY. Such mortal drugs I have; but Mantua's law
Is death to any he that utters them.

ROMEO. Art thou so bare, and full of wretchedness,
And fear'st to die? famine is in thy cheeks,
Need and oppression starveth in thy eyes,
Upon thy back hangs ragged misery;
The world is not thy friend, nor the world's law:
The world affords no law to make thee rich;
Then be not poor, but break it, and take this.

APOTHECARY. My poverty, but not my will, consents.

* Such swiftly acting poison.

Romeo. I pay thy poverty, and not thy will.
Apothecary. Put this in any liquid thing you will,
And drink it off; and, if you had the strength
Of twenty men, it would despatch you straight.
Romeo. There is thy gold, worse poison to men's souls,
Doing more murders in this loathsome world
Than these poor compounds that thou mayst not sell:
I sell thee poison, thou hast sold me none.
Farewell; buy food, and get thyself in flesh.
Come, cordial, and not poison; go with me
To Juliet's grave, for there must I use thee.

Romeo and Paris at the Tomb.

Romeo. Thou detestable maw, thou womb of death,
Gorg'd with the dearest morsel of the earth,
Thus I enforce thy rotten jaws to open,
[*Breaking open the door of the Monument.*
And, in despite, I'll cram thee with more food!
Paris. This is that banish'd haughty Montague,
That murder'd my love's cousin;—with which grief,
It is supposed the fair creature died,—
And here is come to do some villanous shame
To the dead bodies: I will apprehend him.—
[*Advances.*
Stop thy unhallow'd toil, vile Montague;
Can vengeance be pursu'd farther than death?
Condemned villain, I do apprehend thee:
Obey, and go with me; for thou must die.
Romeo. I must, indeed; and therefore came I hither.
Good gentle youth, tempt not a desperate man,
Fly hence, and leave me;—think upon these gone;
Let them affright thee.—I beseech thee, youth,

Heap not another sin upon my head,
By urging me to fury!—O, begone!
By heaven, I love thee better than myself:
For I come hither arm'd against myself:
Stay not, begone;—live, and hereafter say—
A madman's mercy bade thee run away.

PARIS. I do defy thy conjurations,
And do attach thee as a felon here.

ROMEO. Wilt thou provoke me; then have at thee, boy. [*They fight.*

* * * * *

PARIS. O, I am slain! If thou be merciful,
Open the tomb, lay me with Juliet. [*Dies.*

ROMEO. In faith, I will:—Let me peruse this face;—
Mercutio's kinsman, noble county Paris:—
What said my man, when my betossed soul
Did not attend him as we rode? I think
He told me, Paris should have married Juliet:
Said he not so? or did I dream it so?
Or am I mad, hearing him talk of Juliet,
To think it was so?—O, give me thy hand,
One writ with me in sour misfortune's book?
I'll bury thee in a triumphant grave,—
A grave? O, no; a lantern, slaughtered youth,
For here lies Juliet, and her beauty makes
This vault a feasting presence full of light.
Death, lie thou there, by a dead man interr'd.
[*Laying Paris in the Monument.*
How oft when men are at the point of death
Have they been merry? which their keepers call
A lightning before death: O, how may I
Call this a lightning?—O, my love! my wife!
Death, that hath suck'd the honey of thy breath,

Hath had no power yet upon thy beauty :
Thou art not conquer'd ; beauty's ensign yet
Is crimson in thy lips, and in thy cheeks,
And death's pale flag is not advanced there.—
Tybalt, liest thou there in thy bloody sheet ?
O, what more favour can I do to thee,
Than with that hand that cut thy youth in twain,
To sunder his that was thine enemy ?
Forgive me, cousin ?—Ah, dear Juliet,
Why art thou yet so fair ? Shall I believe
That unsubstantial Death is amorous ;
And that the lean abhorred monster keeps
Thee here in dark to be his paramour ?
For fear of that, I will still stay with thee ;
And never from this palace of dim night
Depart again ; here, here will I remain
With worms that are thy chambermaids ; O here
Will I set up my everlasting rest ;
And shake the yoke of inauspicious stars
From this world-wearied flesh.—Eyes, look your last !
Arms, take your last embrace ! and lips, O you
The doors of breath, seal with a righteous kiss
A dateless bargain to engrossing death ?—
Come, bitter conduct, come unsavoury guide !
Thou desperate pilot, now at once run on
The dashing rocks thy sea-sick weary bark !
Here's to my love !—[*Drinks the poison.*] O, true
apothecary !
Thy drugs are quick.—Thus with a kiss I die. [*Dies.*

Friar Laurence's Explanation to the Prince of Verona.

I will be brief, for my short date of breath
Is not so long as is a tedious tale.
Romeo, there dead, was husband to that Juliet ;

And she, there dead, that Romeo's faithful wife:
I married them; and their stolen marriage-day
Was Tybalt's doomsday, whose untimely death
Banish'd the new-made bridegroom from this city
For whom, and not for Tybalt, Juliet pin'd.
You—to remove that siege * of grief from her,—
Betroth'd, and would have married her perforce,
To county Paris:—Then comes she to me;
And, with wild looks, bid me devise some means
To rid her from this second marriage,
Or, in my cell there would she kill herself.
Then gave I her, so tutor'd by my art,
A sleeping potion; which so took effect
As I intended, for it wrought on her
The form of death: meantime I writ to Romeo,
That he should hither come as this dire night,
To help to take her from her borrow'd grave,
Being the time the potion's force should cease.
But he which bore my letter, Friar John,
Was staid by accident; and yesternight
Return'd my letter back: Then all alone,
At the prefixed hour of her waking,
Came I to take her from her kindred's vault;
Meaning to keep her closely at my cell,
Till I conveniently could send to Romeo:
But when I came (some minute ere the time
Of her awakening), here untimely lay
The noble Paris, and true Romeo, dead.
She wakes; and I entreated her come forth,
And bear this work of heaven with patience:
But then a noise did scare me from the tomb;
And she too desperate, would not go with me,
But (as it seems) did violence on herself.

* That source of grief.

All this I know; and to the marriage
Her nurse is privy: And, if aught in this
Miscarried by my fault, let my old life
Be sacrificed some hour before his time,
Unto the rigour of severest law.

—ooo—

KING JOHN.

The play commences with the arrival at the court of England of Chatillon, ambassador from the French king, who demands King John's abdication in favour of Prince Arthur. This is refused, and war is immediately declared between England and France. The two armies meet before the walls of Angiers, where a marriage is arranged between Lewis, the dauphin of France, and Blanch, niece of King John; thus an alliance is cemented between the French King Philip and John. At this juncture Cardinal Pandulph, the Pope's legate, arrives, to urge on King John the appointment of Stephen Langton to the see of Canterbury. This the king declines to accede to, telling Pandulph that

> No Italian priest
> Shall tithe or toll in his dominions.

On which Pandulph declares him excommunicated, and induces the French king to declare war against him. In a battle which ensues, Prince Arthur is taken and sent to England, under the charge of Hubert, who has been ordered by John to kill the prince by burning out his eyes. Hubert, overcome by the prayers of Prince Arthur, will not execute the command given him; but the prince, in making an effort to escape from Northampton Castle, where he is confined, falls from the walls and is killed. The war continuing, the French land in England, and in a battle which ensues, King John, in accordance with a message he receives from Faulconbridge, leaves the field and retires to Swinstead

Abbey, where he dies, poison having been administered to him by a monk, and the play concludes with a defiant appeal on behalf of England from Faulconbridge.

Act I.

King John's Defiance to the French Ambassador.

Be thou as lightning in the eyes of France ;
For, ere thou canst report I will be there,
The thunder of my cannon shall be heard.
So hence ! Be thou the trumpet of our wrath,
And sullen presage of your own decay.

Faulconbridge's Speech on New Titles.

Good den, Sir Richard,—God-a-mercy, fellow ;*
And if his name be George, I'll call him Peter :
For new-made honour doth forget men's names ;
'Tis too respective, and too sociable,
For your conversion.† Now your traveller,—
He and his tooth-pick at my worship's mess :
And when my knightly stomach is sufficed,
Why then I suck my teeth and catechize
My picked man of countries.‡——*My dear sir*
(Thus, leaning on mine elbow, I begin),
I shall beseech you—That is question now ;
And then comes answer like an A B C-book ;
O sir, says answer, *at your best command ;*
At your employment : at your service, sir :—
No, sir, says question, *I, sweet sir, at yours :*
And so, ere answer knows what question would,
(Saving in dialogue of compliment ;
And talking of the Alps and Apennines,

* Good e'en, good evening. † Advanced position in life.
‡ Picked man of countries ; that is, one who has travelled much.

The Pyrenean, and the river Po),
It draws towards supper in conclusion so.
But this is worshipful society,
And fits the mounting spirit like myself.

Act II.

Description of England.

That pale, that white-faced shore,
Whose foot spurns back the ocean's roaring tides,
And coops from other lands her islanders,
Even till that England, hedg'd in with the main,
That water-walled bulwark, still secure
And confident from foreign purposes,
Even till that utmost corner of the west
Salute thee for her king.

Description of an English Army.

All the unsettled humours of the land,—
Rash, inconsiderate, fiery voluntaries,
With ladies' faces, and fierce dragons' spleens,—
Have sold their fortunes at their native homes,
Bearing their birthrights proudly on their backs,
To make a hazard of new fortunes here.
In brief, a braver choice of dauntless spirits,
Than now the English bottoms have waft o'er,
Did never float upon the swelling tide,
To do offence and scath* in Christendom.
The interruption of their churlish drums
Cuts off more circumstance: they are at hand.

* Injury.

Courage.

By how much unexpected, by so much
We must awake endeavour for defence;
For courage mounteth with occasion.

A Boaster.

What cracker is this same, that deafs our ears
With this abundance of superfluous breath?

Description of Victory by the French.

You men of Angiers, open wide your gates,
And let young Arthur, Duke of Bretagne, in;
Who, by the hand of France, this day hath made
Much work for tears in many an English mother,
Whose sons lie scattered on the bleeding ground:
Many a widow's husband grovelling lies,
Coldly embracing the discolour'd earth;
And victory, with little loss, doth play
Upon the dancing banners of the French;
Who are at hand, triumphantly display'd,
To enter conquerors.

Description of Victory by the English.

Rejoice, you men of Angiers, ring your bells;
King John, your king and England's, doth approach,
Commander of this hot malicious day!
Their armours, that march'd hence so silver bright,
Hither return all gilt with Frenchman's blood;
There stuck no plume in any English crest,
That is removed by a staff of France;
Our colours do return in those same hands
That did display them when we first march'd forth;
And, like a jolly troop of huntsmen, come

Our lusty English, all with purpled hands,
Dyed in the dying slaughter of their foes.

A complete Lady.

If lusty love should go in quest of beauty,
Where should he find it fairer than in Blanch?
If zealous love should go in search of virtue,
Where should he find it purer than in Blanch?
If love ambitious sought a match of birth,
Whose veins bound richer blood than lady Blanch?

Beauty.

In her eye I find
A wonder, or a wondrous miracle,
The shadow of myself form'd in her eye;
Which, being but the shadow of your son,
Becomes a sun, and makes your son a shadow:
I do protest I never lov'd myself,
Till now infixed I beheld myself,
Drawn in the flattering table of her eye.

Obedience.

My uncle's will, in this respect, is mine.
If he see aught in you, that makes him like,
That any thing he sees, which moves his liking,
I can with ease translate it to my will;
Or, if you will (to speak more properly),
I will enforce it easily to my love.

Act III.

A Woman's fears.

Thou shalt be punish'd for thus frighting me,
For I am sick, and capable* of fears;

* Susceptible.

Oppress'd with wrongs, and therefore full of fears;
A widow, husbandless, subject to fears;
A woman, naturally born to fears;
And though thou now confess, thou didst but jest,
With my vex'd spirits, I cannot take a truce,
But they will quake and tremble all this day.

Signs of Grief.

What dost thou mean by shaking of thy head?
Why dost thou look so sadly on my son?
What means that hand upon that breast of thine?
Why holds thine eye that lamentable rheum,
Like a proud river peering o'er his bounds?
Be these sad signs confirmers of thy words?
Then speak again; not all thy former tale,
But this one word, whether thy tale be true.

A Mother's fondness for her Child.

If thou, that bidst me be content, wert grim,
Ugly, and sland'rous,
Full of unpleasing blots, and sightless* stains,
Lame, foolish, crooked, swart, prodigious,
Patch'd with foul moles, and eye-offending marks,
I would not care, I then would be content;
For then I should not love thee; no, nor thou
Become thy great birth, nor deserve a crown.
But thou art fair; and at thy birth dear boy!
Nature and fortune join'd to make thee great:
Of nature's gifts thou may'st with lilies boast,
And with the half-blown rose.

Grief.

I will instruct my sorrows to be proud;
For grief is proud and makes his owner stout.

* Ugly.

Constance's reproaches to the Archduke of Austria.

O Lymoges! O Austria thou dost shame
That bloody spoil: thou slave, thou wretch, thou coward;
Thou little valiant, great in villany!
Thou ever strong upon the stronger side!
Thou Fortune's champion that dost never fight
But when her humorous ladyship is by
To teach thee safety; thou art perjured, too,
And sooth'st up greatness. What a fool art thou,
A ramping fool; to brag, and stamp, and swear,
Upon my party! Thou cold-blooded slave,
Hast thou not spoke like thunder on my side?
Been sworn my soldier? bidding me depend
Upon thy stars, thy fortune, and thy strength?
And dost thou now fall over to my foes?
Thou wear a lion's hide! doff* it for shame,
And hang a calf's skin on those recreant limbs.

King John's Conspiracy with Hubert to Murder Prince Arthur.

KING JOHN. Come hither, Hubert, O my gentle Hubert,
We owe thee much; within this wall of flesh
There is a soul, counts thee her creditor,
And with advantage means to pay thy love:
And, my good friend, thy voluntary oath
Lives in this bosom, dearly cherished,
Give me thy hand. I had a thing to say,—
But I will fit it with some better time.
By heaven, Hubert, I am almost asham'd
To say what good respect I have of thee.

* Put it off.

HUBERT. I am much bounden to your majesty.

KING JOHN. Good friend, thou hast no cause to say so yet:
But thou shalt have; and creep time ne'er so slow,
Yet it shall come, for me to do thee good.
I had a thing to say,—But let it go:
The sun is in the heaven, and the proud day,
Attended with the pleasures of the world,
Is all too wanton, and too full of gauds,*
To give me audience:—If the midnight bell
Did, with his iron tongue and brazen mouth,
Sound one unto the drowsy race of night;
If this same were a church-yard where we stand,
And thou possessed with a thousand wrongs;
Or if that surly spirit, melancholy,
Had bak'd thy blood, and made it heavy, thick;
(Which, else, runs tickling up and down the veins,
Making that idiot, laughter, keep men's eyes,
And strain their cheeks to idle merriment,
A passion hateful to my purposes);
Or if that thou could'st see me without eyes,
Hear me without thine ears, and make reply
Without a tongue, using conceit alone,
Without eyes, ears, and harmful sound of words;
Then, in despite of brooded watchful day,
I would into thy bosom pour my thoughts:
But ah, I will not:—Yet I love thee well;
And by my troth, I think thou lov'st me well.

HUBERT. So well, that what you bid me undertake,
Though that my death were adjunct to my act,
By heaven, I'd do 't.

KING JOHN. Do not I know, thou would'st?
Good Hubert, Hubert, Hubert, throw thine eye

* Gaiety.

On yon young boy: I'll tell thee what, my friend—
He is a very serpent in my way;
And wheresoe'er this foot of mine doth tread,
He lies before me: Dost thou understand me?
Thou art his keeper.
HUBERT. And I will keep him so,
That he shall not offend your majesty.
KING JOHN. Death.
HUBERT. My lord?
KING JOHN. A grave.
HUBERT. He shall not live.
KING JOHN. Enough.
I could be merry now: Hubert, I love thee;
Well, I'll not say what I intend for thee.

Constance's Apostrophe to Death.

Death, death, O amiable lovely death!
Thou odoriferous stench! sound rottenness!
Arise forth from the couch of lasting night,
Thou hate and terror to prosperity,
And I will kiss thy detestable bones:
And put my eye-balls in thy vaulty brows:
And ring these fingers with thy household worms!
And stop this gap of breath with fulsome dust,
And be a carrion monster like thyself;
Come, grin on me; and I will think thou smil'st,
And buss thee as thy wife! Misery's love,
O, come to me!

A Mother's Despair.

I am not mad: this hair I tear, is mine;
My name is Constance; I was Geffrey's wife:
Young Arthur is my son, and he is lost:
I am not mad:—I would to heaven I were!

For then, 'tis like I should forget myself:
O, if I could, what grief should I forget!—
Preach some philosophy to make me mad,
And thou shalt be canoniz'd, cardinal;
For, being not mad, but sensible of grief,
My reasonable part produces reason
How I may be deliver'd of these woes,
And teaches me to kill or hang myself:
If I were mad, I should forget my son:
Or madly think a babe of clouts were he;
I am not mad; too well too well I feel
The different plague of each calamity.

A Mother's distress for the loss of her Child.

Father cardinal, I have heard you say,
That we shall see, and know our friends in heaven:
If that be true, I shall see my boy again;
For, since the birth of Cain the first male child,
To him that did but yesterday suspire,*
There was not such a gracious† creature born.
But now will canker sorrow eat my bud,
And chase the native beauty from his cheek,
And he will look as hollow as a ghost;
As dim and meagre as an ague's fit;
And so he'll die; and, rising so again
When I shall meet him in the court of heaven
I shall not know him; therefore never, never,
Must I behold my pretty Arthur more.

Grief.

Grief fills the room up of my absent child,
Lies in his bed, walks up and down with me;
Puts on his pretty looks, repeats his words,

* Breathe. † Comely, handsome.

Remembers me of all his gracious parts.
Stuffs out his vacant garments with his form;
Then have I reason to be fond of grief.

Despondency.

There's nothing in this world can make me joy;
Life is as tedious as a twice-told tale,
Vexing the dull ear of a drowsy man.

Strength of a Disease when on the point of cure.

Before the curing of a strong disease,
Even in the instant of repair and health,
The fit is strongest; evils, that take leave,
On their departure most of all show evil.

Danger clings to any Support.

He that stands upon a slippery place,
Makes nice of no vile hold to stay him up.

Act IV.

Scene between Hubert and Prince Arthur.

ARTHUR. Mercy on me!
Methinks nobody should be sad but I.
Yet I remember, when I was in France,
Young gentlemen would be as sad as night,
Only for wantonness. By my christendom,
So I were out of prison, and kept sheep,
I should be as merry as the day is long;
And so I would be here, but that I doubt
My uncle practises more harm to me.
He is afraid of me, and I of him.
Is it my fault that I was Geffrey's son?
No, indeed, it's not; and I would to heaven
I were your son, so you would love me, Hubert.

HUBERT. If I talk to him, with his innocent prate
He will awake my mercy, which lies dead.
Therefore, I will be sudden and despatch.
ARTHUR. Are you sick, Hubert? You look pale to-day;
In sooth I would you were a little sick,
That I might sit all night and watch with you.
I warrant I love you more than you do me.
HUBERT. His words do take possession of my bosom.
Read here, young Arthur. How now, foolish rheum!
Turning dispiteous torture out of door!
I must be brief, lest resolution drop
Out at mine eyes, in tender womanish tears.
Can you not read it? Is it not fair writ?
ARTHUR. Too, fairly, Hubert, for so foul effect.
Must you with hot irons burn out both mine eyes?
HUBERT. Young boy, I must.
ARTHUR. And will you?
HUBERT. And I will.
ARTHUR. Have you the heart? When your head did but ache,
I knit my handkerchief about your brows,
(The best I had—a princess wrought it me),
And I did never ask it you again;
And with my hand at midnight held your head;
And, like the watchful minutes to the hour,
Still and anon cheer'd up the heavy time;
Saying, What lack you? and Where lies your grief?
Or, What good love may I perform for you?
Many a poor man's son would have lain still
And ne'er have spoke a loving word to you;
But you at your sick service had a prince.
Nay, you may think my love was crafty love,
And call it cunning. Do, an if you will.

If Heaven be pleas'd that you must use me ill,
Why then you must. Will you put out mine eyes?
These eyes that never did, nor never shall,
So much as frown on you?
HUBERT. I have sworn to do it;
And with hot irons must I burn them out.
ARTHUR. Ah, none but in this iron age would do it!
The iron of itself, though heat red-hot,
Approaching near these eyes, would drink my tears,
And quench his fiery indignation,
Even in the matter of mine innocence:
Nay, after that, consume away in rust,
But for containing fire to harm mine eye.
Are you more stubborn hard than hammer'd iron?
And if an angel should have come to me,
And told me Hubert should put out mine eyes,
I would not have believ'd no tongue but Hubert's.

* * * * * *

HUBERT. Come, boy, prepare yourself.
ARTHUR. Is there no remedy?
HUBERT. None, but to lose your eyes.
ARTHUR. O heaven!—that there were but a mote in your's,
A grain, a dust, a gnat, a wand'ring hair,
Any annoyance in that precious sense!
Then, feeling what small things are boist'rous there,
Your vile intent must needs seem horrible.
HUBERT. Is this your promise? go to, hold your tongue.
ARTHUR. Hubert, the utterance of a brace of tongues
Must needs want pleading for a pair of eyes:
Let me not hold my tongue; let me not, Hubert!
Or, Hubert, if you will, cut out my tongue,
So I may keep mine eyes; O spare mine eyes;

Though to no use, but still to look on you!
Lo, by my troth, the instrument is cold,
And would not harm me.
HUBERT. I can heat it, boy.
ARTHUR. No, in good sooth; the fire is dead with grief
(Being create for comfort) to be us'd
In undeserv'd extremes: See else yourself;
There is no malice in this burning coal;
The breath of heaven hath blown his spirit out,
And strew'd repentant ashes on his head.
HUBERT. But with my breath I can revive it, boy.
ARTHUR. And if you do, you will but make it blush,
And glow with shame of your proceedings, Hubert:
Nay, it perchance will sparkle in your eyes;
And, like a dog that is compell'd to fight,
Snatch at his master that doth tarre* him on.
All things, that you should use to do me wrong,
Deny their office: only you do lack
That mercy, which fierce fire, and iron, extends,
Creatures of note, for mercy-lacking uses.
HUBERT. Well, see to live; I will not touch thine eyes
For all the treasure that thine uncle owes:
Yet am I sworn, and I did purpose, boy,
With this same very iron to burn them out.
ARTHUR. O now you look like Hubert! all this while
You were disguised.
HUBERT. Peace: no more. Adieu;
Your uncle must not know but you are dead:
I'll fill these dogged spies with false reports.
And, pretty child, sleep doubtless and secure,

* Urge him on.

That Hubert, for the wealth of all the world,
Will not offend thee.

Perfection needs no Addition.

To gild refined gold, to paint the lily,
To throw a perfume on the violet,
To smooth the ice, or add another hue
Unto the rainbow, or with taper-light
To seek the beauteous eye of heaven to garnish,
Is wasteful and ridiculous excess.

* * * * * *

In this, the antique and well-noted face
Of plain old form is much disfigured:
And, like a shifted wind unto a sail,
It makes the course of thoughts to fetch about:
Startles and frights consideration;
Makes sound opinion sick, and truth suspected,
For putting on so new a fashion'd robe.

The Countenance of an Assassin.

This is the man should do the bloody deed;
He showed his warrant to a friend of mine;
The image of a wicked heinous fault
Lives in his eye; that close aspect of his
Does show the mood of a much troubled breast.

A struggling Conscience.

The colour of the king doth come and go,
Between his purpose and his conscience,
Like heralds 'twixt two dreadful battles set:
His passion is so ripe it needs must break.

News-tellers.

Old men and beldams, in the streets
Do prophesy upon it dangerously;

Young Arthur's death is common in their mouths:
And when they talk of him they shake their heads,
And whisper one another in the ear;
And he, that speaks, doth gripe the hearer's wrist;
Whilst he, that hears, makes fearful action,
With wrinkled brows, with nods, with rolling eyes.
I saw a smith stand with his hammer thus,
The whilst his iron did on the anvil cool,
With open mouth swallowing a tailor's news:
Who, with his shears and measure in his hand,
Standing on slippers (which his nimble haste
Had falsely thrust upon contrary feet),
Told of a many thousand warlike French,
That were embattled and rank'd in Kent:
Another lean unwash'd artificer
Cuts off his tale, and talks of Arthur's death.

The wicked commands of Kings too promptly executed

It is the curse of kings to be attended
By slaves that take their humours for a warrant
To break within the bloody house of life;
And, on the winking of authority,
To understand a law; to know the meaning
Of dangerous majesty, when perchance, it frowns
More upon humour than advised respect.

A Murderer's look and readiness to execute a bad deed.

How oft the sight of means to do ill deeds,
Makes deeds ill done! Hadst not thou been by,
A fellow by the hand of nature mark'd,
Quoted, and sign'd, to do a deed of shame,
This murder had not come into my mind.
But, taking note of thy abhorr'd aspect,—
Finding thee fit for bloody villany,

Apt, liable, to be employ'd in danger,
I faintly broke with thee of Arthur's death ;
And thou, to be endeared to a king,
Made it no conscience to destroy a prince.
* * * * *
Hadst thou but shook thy head, or made a pause,
When I spake darkly what I purposed ;
Or turn'd an eye of doubt upon my face,
As bid me tell my tale in express words ;
Deep shame had struck me dumb, made me break off,
And those thy fears might have wrought fears in me.

Hypocrisy.

Trust not those cunning waters of his eyes
For villany is not without such rheum ;
And he long traded in it makes it seem
Like rivers of remorse and innocency.

Despair.

If thou didst but consent,
To this most cruel act, do but despair,
And if thou want'st a cord, the smallest thread
That ever spider twisted from her womb
Will serve to strangle thee ; a rush will be
A beam to hang thee on ; or wouldst thou drown thyself,
Put but a little water in a spoon,
And it shall be as all the ocean,
Enough to stifle such a villain up.

Act V.

Faulconbridge's Appeal to King John on the Invasion of the French.

But wherefore do you droop ? Why look you sad ?
Be great in act, as you have been in thought ;

Let not the world see fear and sad distrust
Govern the motion of a kingly eye.
Be stirring as the time; be fire with fire;
Threaten the threat'ner, and outface the brow
Of bragging horror: so shall inferior eyes,
That borrow their behaviours from the great,
Grow great by your example, and put on
The dauntless spirit of resolution,
Away: and glister like the god of war,
When he intendeth to become the field:
Show boldness and aspiring confidence.
What, shall they seek the lion in his den,
And fright him there? And make him tremble there?
O, let it not be said! Forage, and run
To meet displeasure further from the doors,
And grapple with him, ere he come so nigh.

A Man's Tears.

Let me wipe off this honourable dew,
That silvery doth progress on thy cheeks;
My heart hath melted at a lady's tears,
Being an ordinary inundation;
But this effusion of such manly drops,
This shower, blown up by tempest of the soul,
Startles mine eyes, and makes me more amaz'd
Than had I seen the vaulty top of heaven
Figur'd quite o'er with burning meteors.
Lift up thy brow, renowned Salisbury,
And with a great heart heave away this storm:
Commend these waters to those baby eyes,
That never saw the giant world enrag'd;
Nor met with fortune other than at feasts,
Full warm of blood, of mirth, of gossiping.

Faulconbridge's Disparagement of the French Army.

Now hear our English king :
For thus his royalty doth speak in me.
He is prepar'd ; and reason, too, he should :
This apish and unmannerly approach,
This harness'd mask, and unadvised revel,
This unhair'd* sauciness, and boyish troops,
The king doth smile at, and is well prepar'd
To whip this dwarfish war, these pigmy arms,
From out the circle of his territories.
That hand which had the strength, even at your door,
To cudgel you, and make you take the hatch ;
To dive, like buckets, in concealed wells ;
To crouch in litter of your stable planks ;
To lie, like pawns, lock'd up in chests and trunks ;
To hug with swine ; to seek sweet safety out
In vaults and prisons ; and to thrill, and shake,
Even at the crying of your nation's crow,†
Thinking his voice an armed Englishman ;—
Shall that victorious hand be feebled here,
That in your chambers gave you chastisement ?
No : know, the gallant monarch is in arms,
And, like an eagle, o'er his aiery towers,
To souse annoyance that comes near his nest.

Faulconbridge's Defiance of the Dauphin.

Do but start
An echo with the clamour of thy drum,
And even at hand a drum is ready brac'd,
That shall reverberate all as loud as thine ;

* Unbearded, alluding to the youth of the Dauphin.
† The crowing of a cock.

Sound but another, and another shall,
As loud as thine, rattle the welkin's ear,
And mock the deep-mouth'd thunder.

The Approach of Death.

It is too late; the life of all his blood
Is touch'd corruptibly; and his pure brain
(Which some suppose the soul's frail dwelling-house)
Doth by the idle comments that it makes,
Foretell the ending of mortality.

King John's Death by Poison.

Ay, marry, now my soul hath elbow-room;
It would not out at windows, nor at doors.
There is so hot a summer in my bosom,
That all my bowels crumble up to dust:
I am a scribbled form, drawn with a pen
Upon a parchment; and against this fire
Do I shrink up.

* * * * *

Poison'd—ill-fare;—dead, forsook, cast off:
And none of you will bid the winter come,
To thrust his icy fingers in my maw;
Nor let my kingdom's rivers take their course
Through my burn'd bosom; nor entreat the north
To make his bleak winds kiss my parched lips,
And comfort me with cold.

England Invincible if Unanimous.

This England never did, nor never shall,
Lie at the proud foot of a conqueror,
But when it first did help to wound itself.
Now these her princes are come home again,
Come the three corners of the world in arms,

And we shall shock them: Naught shall make us rue,
If England to itself do rest but true.

—ooo—

KING RICHARD II.

This historical play describes the dethronement and death of the monarch whose name it bears. Richard, on the death of John of Gaunt, Duke of Lancaster, appropriates to himself the lands of the deceased nobleman, to enable him to prosecute a war in Ireland, for which country he takes his departure. In the king's absence, Bolingbroke (son of John of Gaunt), who had been banished, returns to England, and levying an army, hastens to meet the king on his return from Ireland. Finding his nobles falling away from him, and his soldiers deserting his standard, the king accompanies Bolingbroke to London, and there resigns his crown to him. The dethroned monarch is imprisoned in Pomfret Castle, where he is assassinated by Sir Pierce of Exton, and the play concludes with the reproval of Exton by Bolingbroke, who resolves himself to make a pilgrimage to the Holy Land, to expiate his cruelty towards the unfortunate King Richard. Dr. Johnson says of this tragedy—"It is not finished at last with that happy force of some others of Shakspere's tragedies; nor can it be said much to affect the passions, or enlarge the understanding"

Act I

Reputation.

The purest treasure mortal times afford
Is—spotless reputation; that away,
Men are but gilded loam, or painted clay.

Cowardice.

That which in mean men we entitle—patience,
Is pale cold cowardice in noble breasts.

Banishment.

All places, that the eye of heaven visits,
Are to a wise man ports and happy havens:
Teach thy necessity to reason thus;
There is no virtue like necessity.
Think not, the king did banish thee;
But thou the king; woe doth the heavier sit,
Where it perceives it is but faintly borne.
Go, say—I sent thee forth to purchase honour,
And not—the king exiled thee: or suppose,
Devouring pestilence hangs in our air,
And thou art flying to a fresher clime.
Look, what thy soul holds dear, imagine it
To lie that way thou go'st, not whence thou com'st;
Suppose the singing birds musicians;
The grass whereon thou tread'st, the presence strew'd
The flowers, fair ladies; and thy steps no more
Than a delightful measure, or a dance:
For gnarling* sorrow hath less power to bite
The man that mocks at it, and sets it light.

Imagination Ineffectual to Moderate Afflictions.

O, who can hold a fire in his hand
By thinking on the frosty Caucasus?
Or cloy the hungry edge of appetite
By bare imagination of a feast!
Or wallow naked in December's snow,
By thinking on fantastic summer's heat?

* Grumbling, snarling.

O, no! the apprehension of the good,
Gives but the greater feeling to the worse:
Fell sorrow's tooth does never rankle more,
Than when it bites, but lanceth not the sore.

Popularity.

Ourself, and Bushy, Bagot here, and Green,
Observed his courtship to the common people:—
How he did seem to dive into their hearts,
With humble and familiar courtesy;
What reverence he did throw away on slaves;
Wooing poor craftsmen with the craft of smiles,
And patient underbearing of his fortune,
As 'twere, to banish their affects with him.
Off goes his bonnet to an oyster-wench;
A brace of draymen bid—God speed him well,
And had the tribute of his supple knee,
With—"Thanks my countrymen, my loving friends;"
—As were our England in reversion his,
And he our subjects next degree in hope.

Act II.

England described.

This royal throne of kings, this scepter'd isle,
This earth of majesty, this seat of Mars,
This other Eden, demi-paradise;
This fortress, built by nature for herself,
Against infection and the hand of war;
This happy breed of men, this little world;
This precious stone set in the silver sea,
Which serves it in the office of a wall,
Or as a moat defensive to a house,
Against the envy of less happier lands,

This blessed plot, this earth, this realm, this England.
*   *   *   *   *

England bound in with the triumphant sea;
Whose rocky shore beats back the envious siege
Of watery Neptune, is now bound in with shame,
With inky blots and rotten parchment bonds;
That England, that was wont to conquer others,
Hath made a shameful conquest of itself.

Grief.

Each substance of a grief hath twenty shadows,
Which show like grief itself, but are not so;
For sorrow's eye, glazed with blinding tears,
Divides one thing entire to many objects;
Like perspectives, which rightly gazed upon,
Show nothing but confusion; eyed awry,
Distinguish form.

Hope Deceitful.

I will despair, and be at enmity
With cozening hope; he is a flatterer,
A parasite, a keeper back of death,
Who gently would dissolve the bands of life,
Which false hope lingers in extremity.

Prognostics of War.

The bay-trees in our country are all wither'd,
And meteors fright the fixed stars of heaven:
The pale-faced moon looks bloody on the earth,
And lean look'd prophets whisper fearful change;
Rich men look sad, and ruffians dance and leap.

Act III.

Richard's Apostrophe to England.

I weep for joy
To stand upon my kingdom once again.
Dear earth, I do salute thee with my hand,
Though rebels wound thee with their horses' hoofs;
As a long parted mother with her child
Plays fondly with her tears, and smiles in meeting;
So weeping, smiling, greet I thee, my earth,
And do thee favour with my royal hands.
Feed not thy sovereign's foe, my gentle earth,
Nor with thy sweets comfort his ravenous sense;
But let thy spiders, that suck up thy venom,
And heavy-gaited toads, lie in their way,
Doing annoyance to the treacherous feet,
Which with usurping steps do trample thee.
Yield stinging nettles to mine enemies;
And when they from thy bosom pluck a flower,
Guard it, I pray thee, with a lurking adder,
Whose double tongue may with a mortal touch
Throw death upon thy sovereign's enemies;
Mock not my senseless conjuration, lords;
This earth shall have a feeling, and these stones
Prove armed soldiers, ere her native king
Shall falter under foul rebellious arms.

Sun-rising after a dark Night.

Know'st thou not,
That when the searching eye of heaven is hid
Behind the globe, and lights the lower world,
Then thieves and robbers range abroad unseen,
In murders, and in outrage, bloody here;
But when, from under this terrestrial ball,

He fires the proud tops of the eastern pines,
And darts his light through every guilty hole,
Then murders, treasons, and detested sins,
The cloak of night being pluck'd from off their backs,
Stand bare and naked, trembling at themselves?

The Sanctity of a King.

Not all the water in the rough rude sea
Can wash the balm from an anointed king:
The breath of worldly men cannot depose
The deputy elected by the Lord.
For every man that Bolingbroke hath press'd
To lift shrewd steel against our golden crown,
God for his Richard hath in heavenly pay
A glorious angel; then, if angels fight,
Weak men must fall; for Heaven still guards the right.

The Power of Majesty.

Am I not king?
Awake, thou sluggard majesty! thou sleep'st.
Is not the king's name forty thousand names?
Arm, arm, my name!—A puny subject strikes
At thy great glory. Look not to the ground,
Ye favourites of a king; are we not high?
High be our thoughts.

The Vanity of Power, and Misery of a King.

No matter where; of comfort no man speak:
Let's talk of graves, of worms and epitaphs;
Make dust our paper, and with rainy eyes
Write sorrow on the bosom of the earth.
Let's choose executors, and talk of wills;
And yet not so,—for what can we bequeath,
Save our deposed bodies to the ground?

Our lands, our lives and all are Bolingbroke's,
And nothing can we call our own but death,
And that small model of the barren earth
Which serves as paste and cover to our bones.
For heaven's sake let us sit upon the ground,
And tell sad stories of the death of kings:—
How some have been deposed, some slain in war:
Some haunted by the ghosts they have deposed:
Some poison'd by their wives; some sleeping kill'd;
All murder'd:—for within the hollow crown
That rounds the mortal temples of a king
Keeps Death his court: and there the antic sits,
Scoffing his state, and grinning at his pomp;
Allowing him a breath, a little scene,
To monarchise, be fear'd, and kill with looks;
Infusing him with self and vain conceit,—
As if this flesh, which walls about our life,
Were brass impregnable; and humour'd thus,
Comes at the last, and with a little pin
Bores through his castle wall, and—farewell king!
Cover your heads, and mock not flesh and blood
With solemn reverence; throw away respect,
Tradition, form, and ceremonious duty,
For you have but mistook me all this while:
I live with bread like you, feel want, taste grief,
Need friends: subjected thus,
How can you say to me I am a king?

Sunrise.

See, see, King Richard doth himself appear,
As doth the blushing discontented sun
From out the fiery portal of the east;
When he perceives the envious clouds are bent

To dim his glory, and to stain the track
Of his bright passage to the occident.

Richard's Humility.

What must the king do now? Must he submit?
The king shall do it. Must he be depos'd?
The king shall be contented. Must he lose
The name of king? O' God's name, let it go.
I'll give my jewels for a set of beads;
My gorgeous palace for a hermitage;
My gay apparel for an alms-man's gown;
My figur'd goblets for a dish of wood;
My sceptre for a palmer's walking-staff;
My subjects for a pair of carved saints;
And my large kingdom for a little grave,
A little little grave—an obscure grave:
Or I'll be buried in the king's highway,
Some way of common trade, where subjects' feet
May hourly trample on their sovereign's head:
For on my heart they tread now whilst I live;
And, buried once, why not upon my head?

Act IV.

The Emptiness of Royalty.

Alack, why am I sent for to a king,
Before I have shook off the regal thoughts
Wherewith I reign'd? I hardly yet have learn'd
To insinuate, flatter, bow, and bend my knee:—
Give sorrow leave awhile to tutor me
To this submission. Yet I well remember
The favours* of these men: were they not mine?
Did they not sometime cry, all hail! to me?

* The countenances.

So Judas did to Christ; but he, in twelve,
Found truth in all, but one; I in twelve thousand, none.
God save the king!—Will no man say amen?
Am I both priest and clerk? well then, amen.
God save the king! although I be not he;
And yet, amen, if heaven do think him me.

Richard's Resignation of his Crown.

Now mark me how I will undo myself:
I give this heavy weight from off my head,
And this unwieldly sceptre from my hand,
The pride of kingly sway from out my heart;
With mine own tears I wash away my balm,—
With mine own hands I give away my crown,—
With mine own tongue deny my sacred state,—
With mine own breath release all duteous oaths:
All pomp and majesty I do forswear:
My manors, rents, revenues, I forego;
My acts, decrees, and statutes, I deny:
God pardon all oaths that are broke to me!
God keep all vows unbroke are made to thee!
Make me, that nothing have, with nothing griev'd;
And thou with all pleas'd, that hast all achiev'd!
Long mayst thou live in Richard's seat to sit,
And soon lie Richard in an earthly pit!
God save King Henry, unking'd Richard says,
And send him many years of sunshine days!

Act V.

Melancholy Stories.

In winter's tedious nights, sit by the fire
With good old folks; and let them tell thee tales

Of woeful ages, long ago betid: *
And ere thou bid good night, to quit their grief,
Tell thou the lamentable fall of me,
And send the hearers weeping to their beds.

Bolingbroke coming into London.

Then, as I said, the duke, great Bolingbroke,—
Mounted upon a hot and fiery steed,
Which his aspiring rider seem'd to know,—
With slow, but stately pace, kept on his course,
While all tongues cried—God save thee, Bolingbroke
You would have thought the very windows spake,
So many greedy looks of young and old
Through casements darted their desiring eyes
Upon his visage; and that all the walls,
With painted imagery, had said at once,—
Jesu preserve thee! welcome, Bolingbroke!
Whilst he, from one side to the other turning,
Bare-headed, lower than his proud steed's neck,
Bespake them thus,—*I thank you, countrymen:*
And thus still doing, thus he pass'd along.

* * * * *

As in a theatre, the eyes of men,
After a well-graced actor leaves the stage,
Are idly bent on him that enters next,
Thinking his prattle to be tedious:
Even so, or with much more contempt, men's eyes
Did scowl on Richard; no man cried, God save him;
No joyful tongue gave him his welcome home:
But dust was thrown upon his sacred head;
Which with such gentle sorrow he shook off,—
His face still combating with tears and smiles,
The badges of his grief and patience,—

* Long passed away.

That had not God, for some strong purpose, steel'd
The hearts of men, they must perforce have melted,
And barbarism itself have pitied him.

Violets.

Who are the violets now,
That strew the green lap of the new-come spring?

Richard's Soliloquy in Prison.

I have been studying how I may compare
This prison, where I live, unto the world:
And, for because the world is populous,
And here is not a creature but myself,
I cannot do it;—yet I'll hammer it out.
My brain I'll prove the female to my soul,
My soul, the father: and these two beget
A generation of still breeding thoughts,
And these same thoughts people this little world:*
In humours, like the people of this world,
For no thought is contented.

* * * * * *

Thoughts tending to content, flatter themselves,
That they are not the first of fortune's slaves,
Nor shall not be the last; like silly beggars,
Who, sitting in the stocks, refuge their shame,—
That many have, and others must sit there:
And in this thought they find a kind of ease,
Bearing their own misfortune on the back
Of such as have before endured the like.
Thus play I, in one person, many people,
And none contented: sometimes am I a king;
Then treason makes me wish myself a beggar,
And so I am: then crushing penury

* His own body.

Persuades me I was better when a king:
Then am I king'd again: and, by and by,
Think that I am unking'd by Bolingbroke,
And straight am nothing.—But, whate'er I am,
Nor I, nor any man, that but man is,
With nothing shall be pleas'd, till he be eas'd
With being nothing.

Bolingbroke's Remorse at Richard's Death.

They love not poison that do poison need,
Nor do I thee: though I did wish him dead,
I hate the murderer—love him murdered.
The guilt of conscience take thou for thy labour,
But neither my good word nor princely favour;
With Cain go wander through the shade of night,
And never show thy head by day nor light.
Lords, I protest my soul is full of woe,
That blood should sprinkle me to make me grow.
Come, mourn with me for what I do lament,
And put on sullen black incontinent:*
I'll make a voyage to the Holy Land,
To wash this blood off from my guilty hand.
March sadly after; grace my mournings here,
In weeping after this untimely bier.

—ooo—

KING HENRY IV.—Part I.

The king is about to depart for the Holy Land, when he is stayed by intelligence of the defeat of Mortimer, Earl of March,

* Forthwith.

by Owen Glendower, and by disturbances in the northern parts of his kingdom, where Hotspur, son of the Earl of Northumberland, has defeated Archibald, Earl of Douglas, and taken certain prisoners, whom he refuses to deliver up to the king. This incenses the king against Hotspur, the more so as the latter has pleaded strongly for the ransom of Mortimer, whom the king declines to redeem. Hotspur thus rendered indignant, joins with the Earl of Northumberland, the Earl of Worcester, and others, to dethrone the king. The rebel forces advance to Shrewsbury, where a great battle is fought, in which the king obtains a signal victory. Hotspur is slain by Henry, Prince of Wales (afterwards Henry the Fifth), who throughout the battle has greatly distinguished himself. The serious parts of the play are relieved by the eccentricities of the Prince of Wales and his boon companions, Sir John Falstaff, Poins, and Bardolph. Speaking of the first and second parts of Henry the Fourth, Dr. Johnson says—"No two plays are more read than these; and perhaps no author ever produced two which afforded so much delight. The great events are interesting, for the fate of kingdoms depends on them; the light occurrences are diverting; the incidents are multiplied with a wonderful felicity of invention, and the characters diversified with the utmost nicety of discernment, and the profoundest skill in the nature of man."

Act I.

Peace after Civil War.

So shaken as we are, so wan with care,
Find we a time for frighted peace to pant,
And breathe short-winded accents of new broils
To be commenc'd in stronds* afar remote.
No more the thirsty Erinnys † of this soil
Shall daub her lips with her own children's blood:
No more shall trenching war channel her fields,
Nor bruise her flowrets with the armed hoofs
Of hostile paces: those opposed eyes,

* Shores. † The fury of discord

Which,—like the meteors of a troubled heaven,
All of one nature, of one substance bred,
Did lately meet in the intestine shock
And furious close of civil butchery,
Shall now, in mutual, well-beseeming ranks,
March all one way : and be no more oppos'd
Against acquaintance, kindred, and allies :
The edge of war, like an ill-sheathed knife,
No more shall cut his master.

King Henry's Character of Percy, and of his Son Prince Henry.

Yea, there thou mak'st me sad, and mak'st me sin,
In envy that my Lord Northumberland
Should be the father of so bless'd a son ;
A son who is the theme of honour's tongue ,
Amongst a grove, the very straitest plant ;
Who is sweet fortune's minion, and her pride ;
Whilst I, by looking on the praise of him,
See riot and dishonour stain the brow
Of my young Harry.

Prince Henry's Soliloquy.

I know you all, and will awhile uphold
The unyok'd humour of your idleness ;
Yet herein will I imitate the sun ;
Who doth permit the base contagious clouds
To smother up his beauty from the world,
That, when he please again to be himself,
Being wanted, he may be more wonder'd at,
By breaking through the foul and ugly mists
Of vapours that did seem to strangle him.
If all the year were playing holidays,
To sport would be as tedious as to work :

But when they seldom come, they wish'd-for come,
And nothing pleaseth but rare accidents.
So, when this loose behaviour I throw off,
And pay the debt I never promised,
By how much better than my word I am,
By so much shall I falsify men's hopes;
And, like bright metal on a sullen* ground,
My reformation glittering o'er my fault,
Shall show more goodly, and attract more eyes,
Than that which hath no foil to set it off.
I'll so offend, to make offence a skill;
Redeeming time, when men think least I will.

Hotspur's Description of a Fop.

But, I remember, when the fight was done,
When I was dry with rage and extreme toil,
Breathless and faint, leaning upon my sword,
Came there a certain lord, neat, trimly dress'd,
Fresh as a bridegroom; and his chin, new reap'd,
Show'd like a stubble land at harvest home;
He was perfumed like a milliner;
And 'twixt his finger and his thumb he held
A pouncet-box † which ever and anon
He gave his nose, and took 't away again;—
Who, therewith angry, when it next came there,
Took it in snuff:—and still he smil'd and talk'd;
And, as the soldiers bore dead bodies by,
He call'd them untaught knaves, unmannerly
To bring a slovenly unhandsome corse
Betwixt the wind and his nobility.
With many holiday and lady terms
He questioned me; among the rest demanded
My prisoners, in your majesty's behalf.

* Barren. † A box of perfumes.

I then, all smarting with my wounds, being cold,
To be so pester'd with a popinjay,
Out of my grief and my impatience,
Answer'd, neglectingly, I know not what;
He should, or he should not; for he made me mad
To see him shine so brisk, and smell so sweet,
And talk so like a waiting gentlewoman,
Of guns, and drums, and wounds (God save the mark),
And telling me the sovereign'st thing on earth
Was parmaceti for an inward bruise;
And that it was great pity, so it was,
That villanous saltpetre should be digg'd
Out of the bowels of the harmless earth,
Which many a good tall fellow had destroy'd
So cowardly; and but for these vile guns,
He would himself have been a soldier.

Danger.

I'll read you matter deep and dangerous;
As full of peril and adventurous spirit,
As to o'erwalk a current, roaring loud,
On the unsteadfast footing of a spear.

Honour.

By heaven, methinks, it were an easy leap
To pluck bright honour from the pale-faced moon,
Or dive into the bottom of the deep,
Where fathom-line could never touch the ground,
And pluck up drowned honour by the locks;
So he, that doth redeem her thence, might wear,
Without corrival,* all her dignities:
But out upon this half-faced fellowship.†

* A rival. † Friendship

Act II.

Lady Percy's Speech to her Husband.

O, my good lord, why are you thus alone?
For what offence have I, this fortnight, been
A banish'd woman from my Harry's bed?
Tell me, sweet lord, what is't that takes from thee
Thy stomach, pleasure, and thy golden sleep?
Why dost thou bend thine eyes upon the earth;
And start so often when thou sitt'st alone?
Why hast thou lost the fresh blood in thy cheeks;
And given my treasures, and my rights of thee,
To thick-ey'd musing, and curs'd melancholy?
In thy faint slumbers, I by thee have watch'd,
And heard thee murmur tales of iron wars:
Speak terms of manage to thy bounding steed;
Cry, "Courage—to the field!" And thou hast talk'd
Of sallies and retires; of trenches, tents,
Of palisadoes, frontiers, parapets;
Of basilisks, of cannon, culverin;
Of prisoner's ransom, and of soldiers slain,
And all the currents* of a heady fight.
Thy spirit within thee hath been so at war,
And thus hath so bestirr'd thee in thy sleep,
That beads of sweat have stood upon thy brow,
Like bubbles in a late-disturbed stream;
And in thy face strange motions have appear'd,
Such as we see when men restrain their breath
On some great sudden haste. O what portents are
these?
Some heavy business hath my lord in hand,
And I must know it, else he loves me not.

* Incidents.

Hotspur's ironical speech to his Wife.

Come, wilt thou see me ride?
And, when I am o' horseback, I will swear
I love thee infinitely. But hark you, Kate:
I must not have you henceforth question me
Whither I go, nor reason whereabout:
Whither I must, I must; and, to conclude,
This evening must I leave you, gentle Kate.
I know you wise; but yet no further wise
Than Harry Percy's wife: constant you are,
But yet a woman: and for secrecy,
No lady closer; for I well believe,
Thou wilt not utter what thou dost not know,
And so far will I trust thee, gentle Kate!

Act III.

Prodigies at Glendower's birth.

Give me leave
To tell you once again, that at my birth
The front of heaven was full of fiery shapes;
The goats ran from the mountains, and the herds
Were strangely clamorous to the frighted fields.
These signs have mark'd me extraordinary;
And all the courses of my life do show
I am not in the roll of common men.
Where is he living, clipp'd in with the sea
That chides the banks of England, Scotland, Wales,
Which calls me pupil, or hath read to me?
And bring him out, that is but woman's son,
Can trace me in the tedious ways of art,
And hold me pace in deep experiments

Hotspur's contempt for Rhymers.

I had rather be a kitten, and cry—mew,
Than one of these same metre ballad-mongers:
I'd rather hear a brazen canstick * turn'd,
Or a dry wheel grate on an axle-tree;
And that would set my teeth nothing on edge,
Nothing so much as mincing poetry;
'Tis like the forced gait of a shuffling nag.

Punctuality in Bargains.

I'll give thrice so much land
To any well-deserving friend;
But in the way of bargain, mark ye me,
I'll cavil on the ninth part of a hair.

A Husband sung to Sleep by his Wife.

She bids you
Upon the wanton rushes lay you down,
And rest your gentle head upon her lap,
And she will sing the song that pleaseth you;
And on your eyelids crown the god of sleep,
Charming your blood with pleasing heaviness:
Making such difference betwixt wake and sleep,
As is the difference betwixt day and night,
The hour before the heavenly-harness'd team
Begins his golden progress in the east.

King Henry's Address to his Son on his irregularities

Had I so lavish of my presence been,
So common-hackney'd in the eyes of men,
So stale and cheap to vulgar company;
Opinion that did help me to the crown,

* Candlestick.

Had still kept loyal to possession :*
And left me in reputeless banishment,
A fellow of no mark nor likelihood.
By being seldom seen, I could not stir,
But, like a comet, I was wonder'd at:
That men would tell their children, " This is he ;"
Others would say, " Where ?—which is Bolingbroke ?"
And then I stole all courtesy from heaven,
And dress'd myself in such humility,
That I did pluck allegiance from men's hearts,
Loud shouts and salutations from their mouths,
Even in the presence of the crowned king.
Thus did I keep my person fresh and new ;
My presence, like a robe pontifical,
Ne'er seen, but wonder'd at ; and so my state,
Seldom, but sumptuous, showed like a feast ;
And won, by rareness, such solemnity.
The skipping king, he ambled up and down
With shallow jesters, and rash bavin† wits,
Soon kindled, and soon burn'd ; carded his state ;
Mingled his royalty with capering fools ;
Had his great name profaned with their scorns,
And gave his countenance, against his name,
To laugh at gibing boys, and stand the push
Of every beardless vain comparative :‡
Grew a companion to the common streets,
Enfeoff'd himself to popularity :
That being daily swallow'd by men's eyes,
They surfeited with honey, and began
To loathe the taste of sweetness, whereof a little
More than a little, is by much too much.
So, when he had occasion to be seen,

* Had kept me loyal to him who possessed the crown.
† Brushwood. ‡ Competitor.

He was but as the cuckoo is in June,
Heard, not regarded; seen, but with such eyes,
As, sick and blunted with community,
Afford no extraordinary gaze,
Such as is bent on sun-like majesty,
When it shines seldom in admiring eyes:
But rather drows'd, and hung their eyelids down,
Slept in his face and render'd such aspect
As cloudy men use to their adversaries:
Being with his presence glutted, gorged and full.

Prince Henry's Defence of Himself.

God forgive them, that have so much sway'd
Your majesty's good thoughts away from me!
I will redeem all this on Percy's head,
And, in the closing of some glorious day,
Be bold to tell you that I am your son;
When I will wear a garment all of blood,
And stain my favours* in a bloody mask,
Which, wash'd away, shall scour my shame with it.
And that shall be the day, whene'er it lights,
That this same child of honour and renown,
This gallant Hotspur, this all-praised knight,
And your unthought-of Harry chance to meet:
For every honour sitting on his helm,
Would they were multitudes; and on my head
My shames redoubled! for the time will come
That I shall make this northern youth exchange
His glorious deeds for my indignities.
Percy is but my factor, good my lord,
To engross up glorious deeds on my behalf;
And I will call him to so strict account,
That he shall render every glory up,

* Fearures.

Yea, even the slightest worship of his time,
Or I will tear the reckoning from his heart.
This, in the name of God, I promise here:
The which, if He be pleas'd I shall perform,
I do beseech your majesty may salve
The long-grown wounds of my intemperance:
If not, the end of life cancels all bands;
And I will die a hundred thousand deaths,
Ere break the smallest parcel* of this vow.

Act IV.

A gallant Warrior.

I saw young Harry,—with his beaver on,
His cuisses† on his thighs, gallantly arm'd—
Rise from the ground like feather'd Mercury,
And vaulted with such ease into his seat,
As if an angel dropp'd down from the clouds,
To turn and wind a fiery Pegasus,
And witch‡ the world with noble horsemanship.

Hotspur's Impatience for the Battle.

Let them come;
They come like sacrifices in their trim,
And to the fire-eye'd maid of smoky war,
All hot and bleeding will we offer them:
The mailed Mars shall on his altar sit,
Up to the ears in blood. I am on fire,
To hear this rich reprisal is so nigh,
And yet not ours:—come, let me take my horse,
Who is to bear me, like a thunderbolt,
Against the bosom of the Prince of Wales:
Harry to Harry shall, hot horse to horse,

* Portion. † Armour for the thighs. ‡ Bewitch.

Meet and ne'er part, till one drop down a corse.—
O that Glendower were come!

Hotspur's Speech to Sir Walter Blunt before the Battle of Shrewsbury.

The king is kind; and, well we know, the king
Knows at what time to promise, when to pay.
My father, and my uncle, and myself,
Did give him that same royalty he wears:
And,—when he was not six and twenty strong,
Sick in the world's regard, wretched and low,
A poor unminded outlaw sneaking home,—
My father gave him welcome to the shore:
And,—when he heard him swear and vow to God,
He came but to be Duke of Lancaster,
To sue his livery,* and beg his peace,
With tears of innocency and terms of zeal,—
My father, in kind heart, and pity mov'd,
Swore him assistance, and perform'd it too.
Now, when the lords and barons of the realm
Perceiv'd Northumberland did lean to him,
The more and less came in with cap and knee;
Met him in boroughs, cities, villages;
Attended him on bridges, stood in lanes,
Laid gifts before him, proffer'd him their oaths,
Gave him their heirs; as pages follow'd him,
Even at the heels, in golden multitudes.
He presently,—as greatness knows itself,—
Steps me a little higher than his vow
Made to my father, while his blood was poor,
Upon the naked shore at Ravenspurg;
And now, forsooth, takes on him to reform

* The delivery to him of his lands which had been confiscated.

Some certain edicts, and some strait decrees,
That lie too heavy on the commonwealth;
Cries out upon abuses, seems to weep
Over his country's wrongs; and, by this face,
This seeming brow of justice, did he win
The hearts of all that he did angle for.
Proceeded further; cut me off the heads
Of all the favourites, that the absent king
In deputation left behind him here,
When he was personal in the Irish war.

Act V.

Prince Henry's modest Challenge to Hotspur.

Tell your nephew,
The prince of Wales doth join with all the world
In praise of Henry Percy: by my hopes,—
This present enterprise set off his head,—
I do not think a braver gentleman,
More active-valiant, or more valiant-young,
More daring, or more bold, is now alive,
To grace this latter age with noble deeds.
For my part, I may speak it to my shame,
I have a truant been to chivalry;
And so I hear he doth account me too:
Yet this before my father's majesty,—
I am content, that he shall take the odds
Of his great name and estimation;
And will to save the blood on either side,
Try fortune with him in a single fight.

Falstaff's Catechism.

Well, 'tis no matter; honour pricks me on. Yea, but how if honour prick me off when I come on? how then? Can honour set to a leg? No. Or an arm? No. Or take away the grief of a wound? No. Honour hath no skill in surgery then? No. What is honour? A word. What is in that word honour? What is that honour? Air. A trim reckoning!—Who hath it? He that died o' Wednesday. Doth he feel it? No. Doth he hear it? No. Is it insensible then? Yea, to the dead. But will it not live with the living? No. Why? Detraction will not suffer it:—therefore I'll none of it: honour is a mere scutcheon, and so ends my catechism.

Vernon's Description of Prince Henry's Challenge.

No, by my soul; I never in my life
Did hear a challenge urg'd more modestly,
Unless a brother should a brother dare
To gentle exercise and proof of arms.
He gave you all the duties of a man:
Trimm'd up your praises with a princely tongue;
Spoke your deservings like a chronicle;
Making you ever better than his praise,
By still dispraising praise, valued with you:
And, which became him like a prince indeed,
He made a blushing cital of himself;
And chid his truant youth with such a grace,
As if he master'd there a double spirit
Of teaching and of learning instantly,
There did he pause; but let me tell the world,—
If he outlive the envy of this day,
England did never owe so sweet a hope,
So much misconstrued in his wantonness.

Life demands Action.

O gentlemen, the time of life is short;

To spend that shortness basely, were too long,
If life did ride upon a dial's point,
Still ending at the arrival of an hour.

Prince Henry's Speech on the Death of Hotspur.

Fare thee well, great heart!
Ill-weav'd ambition, how much art thou shrunk!
When that this body did contain a spirit,
A kingdom for it was too small a bound:
But now, two paces of the vilest earth
Is room enough:—this earth, that bears thee dead,
Bears not alive so stout a gentleman.
If thou wert sensible of courtesy,
I should not make so dear a show of zeal:—
But let my favours* hide thy mangled face;
And, even in thy behalf, I'll thank myself
For doing these fair rites of tenderness.
Adieu, and take thy praise with thee to heaven:
Thy ignomy sleep with thee in the grave,
But not remember'd in thy epitaph!

—ooo—

KING HENRY IV.—Part. II.

The second part of King Henry the Fourth continues his reign from the battle of Shrewsbury till his death. One of the most prominent scenes in this play is that in which the Prince of Wales finds the crown by the side of his dying father, and places it on his own head. Another striking feature is the determination or the prince, on his father's death, to forsake the scenes of

* The scarf with which he covers Hotspur.

his former revels, and to cease to associate with his old roystering companions, Falstaff and the rest. His noble conduct, too, towards the Chief Justice (who for an act of violence had committed him to prison in his profligate days), imparts great interest to the conclusion of the play.

Induction.

Rumour.

Open your ears; for which of you will stop
The vent of hearing when loud Rumour speaks?
I, from the orient to the drooping west,
Making the wind my post-horse, still unfold
The acts commenced on this ball of earth:
Upon my tongues continual slanders ride;
The which in every language I pronounce,
Stuffing the ears of men with false reports.
I speak of peace, while covert enmity,
Under the smile of safety, wounds the world:
And who but Rumour, who but only I,
Make fearful musters, and prepar'd defence

Act I.

Contention.

Contention, like a horse
Full of high feeding, madly hath broke loose,
And bears down all before him.

A Post Messenger.

After him came spurring hard,
A gentleman almost forespent* with speed,
That stopp'd by me to breathe his bloodied horse:

* Spent, exhausted.

He ask'd the way to Chester, and of him
I did demand what news from Shrewsbury.
He told me that rebellion had bad luck,
And that young Harry Percy's spur was cold:
With that, he gave his able horse the head,
And, bending forward, struck his armed heels
Against the panting sides of his poor jade
Up to the rowel-head; and starting so,
He seem'd in running to devour the way,
Staying no longer question.

A Messenger with Ill News.

This man's brow, like to a title leaf,
Foretells the nature of a tragic volume:
So looks the strond,* whereon the imperious flood
Hath left a witness'd usurpation.

* * * * *

Thou tremblest; and the whiteness in thy cheek
Is apter than thy tongue to tell thy errand.
Even such a man, so faint, so spiritless,
So dull, so dead in look, so woe begone,
Drew Priam's curtain in the dead of night,
And would have told him half his Troy was burn'd—

* * * * *

I see a strange confession in thine eye:
Thou shak'st thine head, and hold'st it fear or sin
To speak a truth. If he be slain, say so:
The tongue offends not that reports his death;
And he doth sin that doth belie the dead;
Not he, which says the dead is not alive.
Yet the first bringer of unwelcome news
Hath but a losing office; and his tongue

* The strand, the shore.

Sounds ever after as a sullen bell,
Remember'd knolling a departing friend.

Description of the Death of Hotspur and Defeat of his Army.

I am sorry I should force you to believe
That which I would to heaven I had not seen:
But these mine eyes saw him in bloody state,
Rend'ring faint quittance, wearied and outbreath'd
To Harry Monmouth: whose swift wrath beat down
The never-daunted Percy to the earth,
From whence with life he never more sprung up.
In few,* his death (whose spirit lent a fire
Even to the dullest peasant in his camp),
Being bruited † once, took fire and heat away
From the best temper'd courage in his troops:
For from his metal was his party steel'd;
Which once in him abated, all the rest
Turn'd on themselves, like dull and heavy lead.
And as the thing that 's heavy in itself,
Upon enforcement, flies with greatest speed;
So did our men, heavy in Hotspur's loss,
Lend to this weight such lightness with their fear,
That arrows fled not swifter toward their aim,
Than did our soldiers, aiming at their safety,
Fly from the field: Then was that noble Worcester
Too soon ta'en prisoner: and that furious Scot,
The bloody Douglas, whose well-labouring sword
Had three times slain the appearance of the king,‡
'Gan vail his stomach, and did grace the shame
Of those that turn'd their backs; and, in his flight,
Stumbling in fear, was took. The sum of all

* Briefly. † Being reported.

‡ Had slain three persons whom he mistook for the king.

Is,—that the king hath won; and hath sent out
A speedy power to encounter you, my lord,
Under the conduct of young Lancaster,
And Westmoreland; this is the news at full.

Greater Griefs destroy the less.

As the wretch, whose fever-weaken'd joints,
Like strengthless hinges, buckle under life,
Impatient of his fit, breaks like a fire
Out of his keeper's arms; even so my limbs,
Weaken'd with grief, being now enrag'd with grief,
Are thrice themselves: hence therefore, thou nice* crutch;
A scaly gauntlet now, with joints of steel,
Must glove this hand: and hence thou sickly quoif,†
Thou art a guard too wanton for the head,
Which princes, flesh'd with conquest, aim to hit.
Now bind my brows with iron; and approach
The ragged'st hour that time and spite dare bring,
To frown upon the enrag'd Northumberland!
Let heaven kiss earth! Now let not nature's hand
Keep the wild flood confin'd! let order die!
And let this world no longer be a stage
To feed contention in a lingering act;
But let one spirit of the first-born Cain
Reign in all bosoms, that, each heart being set
On bloody courses, the rude scene may end,
And darkness be the burier of the dead!

The Fickleness of the Mob.

An habitation giddy and unsure
Hath he that buildeth on the vulgar heart.

* Feeble. † A cap worn by an invalid.

O thou fond many ! * with what loud applause
Didst thou beat heaven with blessing Bolingbroke,
Before he was what thou wouldst have him be !
And being now trimm'd in thine own desires,
Thou, beastly feeder, art so full of him,
That thou provok'st thyself to cast him up.

Act III.

King Henry's Soliloquy on Sleep.

How many thousand of my poorest subjects
Are at this hour asleep ?—Sleep, gentle sleep,
Nature's soft nurse, how have I frighted thee,
That thou no more wilt weigh my eyelids down,
And steep my senses in forgetfulness ?
Why rather, sleep, liest thou in smoky cribs,
Upon uneasy pallets stretching thee,
And hush'd with buzzing night-flies to thy slumber ;
Than in the perfum'd chambers of the great,
Under the canopies of costly state,
And lull'd with sounds of sweetest melody ?
O thou dull god, why liest thou with the vile,
In loathsome beds ; and leav'st the kingly couch,
A watch-case, or a common 'larum bell ?
Wilt thou upon the high and giddy mast
Seal up the ship-boy's eyes, and rock his brains
In cradle of the rude imperious surge ;
And in the visitation of the winds,
Who take the ruffian billows by the top,
Curling their monstrous heads, and hanging them
With deafening clamours in the slippery clouds,
That, with the hurly,† death itself awakes ?
Canst thou, O partial sleep ! give thy repose

* The common people. † Noise, clamour.

To the wet sea-boy, in an hour so rude;
And in the calmest and most stillest night,
With all appliances, and means to boot,
Deny it to a king? Then happy low lie down! *
Uneasy lies the head that wears a crown.

Act IV.

The Character of King Henry V. by his Father.

He is gracious if he be observed;
He hath a tear for pity, and a hand
Open as day for melting charity:
Yet, notwithstanding, being incens'd, he's flint:
As humorous as winter, and as sudden
As flaws congealed in the spring of day.
His temper, therefore, must be well observ'd:
Chide him for faults, and do it reverently.
When you perceive his blood inclin'd to mirth;
But, being moody, give him line and scope;
Till that his passions, like a whale on ground,
Confound themselves with working.

Fortune.

Will fortune never come with both hands full,
But write her fair words still in foulest letters?
She either gives a stomach, and no food,—
Such are the poor, in health; or else a feast,
And takes away the stomach,—such are the rich,
That have abundance, and enjoy it not.

Prince Henry's reflections on the Crown.

Why doth the crown lie here upon his pillow,
Being so troublesome a bedfellow?

* Happy low, means the humbler classes.

O, polish'd perturbation! golden care!
That keeps the ports of slumber open wide
To many a watchful-night!—sleep with it now!
Yet not so sound, and half so deeply sweet,
As he, whose brow, with homely biggen* bound,
Snores out the watch of night. O, majesty!
When thou dost pinch thy bearer, thou dost sit
Like a rich armour worn in heat of day,
That scalds with safety. By his gates of breath
There lies a downy feather, which stirs not:
Did he suspire, that light and weightless down
Perforce must move.—My gracious lord! my father?—
This sleep is sound indeed; this is a sleep,
That from this golden rigol hath divorc'd
So many English kings. Thy due, from me,
Is tears, and heavy sorrows of the blood;
Which nature, love, and filial tenderness,
Shall, O dear father! pay thee plenteously:
My due, from thee, is this imperial crown:
Which, as immediate from thy place and blood,
Derives itself to me. Lo, here it sits,—
[*Putting it on his head.*
Which Heaven shall guard; and, put the world's whole strength
Into one giant arm, it shall not force
This lineal honour from me. This from thee
Will I to mine leave, as 'tis left to me.

Vanity of Wealth.

How quickly nature falls into revolt
When gold becomes her object!
For this the foolish over-careful fathers

* Cap.

Have broke their sleep with thoughts, their brains with care,
Their bones with industry;
For this they have engross'd and piled up
The canker'd heaps of strange-achieved gold.

Scene between Prince Henry and the King his Father.

King Henry. Come hither to me, Harry:—
Depart the chamber, leave us here alone.
Prince Henry. I never thought to hear you speak again.
King Henry. Thy wish was father, Harry, to that thought:
I stay too long by thee, I weary thee.
Dost thou so hunger for my empty chair,
That thou wilt needs invest thee with mine honours
Before thy hour be ripe? O foolish youth!
Thou seek'st the greatness that will overwhelm thee.
Stay but a little; for my cloud of dignity
Is held from falling with so weak a wind,
That it will quickly drop: my day is dim.
Thou hast stolen that,* which, after some few hours,
Were thine without offence; and, at my death,
Thou hast seal'd up my expectation:
Thy life did manifest thou lovd'st me not,
And thou wilt have me die assured of it.
Thou hid'st a thousand daggers in thy thoughts;
Which thou hast whetted on thy stony heart,
To stab at half an hour of my life.
What! canst thou not forbear me half an hour?
Then get thee gone, and dig my grave thyself;
And bid the merry bells ring to thine ear,

* Alluding to Prince Henry, having placed the crown on his head.

That thou art crowned, not that I am dead.
Let all the tears that should bedew my hearse
Be drops of balm to sanctify thy head:
Only compound me with forgotten dust;
Give that, which gave thee life, unto the worms.
Pluck down my officers, break my decrees:
For now a time is come to mock at form,
Harry the Fifth is crown'd;—up, vanity!
Down, royal state! all you sage counsellers, hence!
And to the English court assemble now,
From every region, apes of idleness!
Now, neighbour, confines, purge you of your scum:
Have you a ruffian, that will swear, drink, dance,
Revel the night: rob, murder, and commit
The oldest sins, the newest kind of ways?
Be happy, he will trouble you no more:
England shall double gild his treble guilt;
England shall give him office, honour, might:
For the fifth Harry from curb'd licence plucks
The muzzle of restraint, and the wild dog
Shall flesh his tooth in every innocent.
O my poor kingdom, sick with civil blows!
When that my care could not withhold thy riots,
What wilt thou do, when riot is thy care?
O, thou wilt be a wilderness again,
Peopled with wolves, thy old inhabitants!

PRINCE HENRY. O, pardon me, my liege! but for my tears, [*Kneeling.*
The moist impediments unto my speech,
I had forestall'd this dear and deep rebuke,
Ere you with grief had spoke, and I had heard
The course of it so far. There is your crown,
And He that wears the crown immortally
Long guard it yours! If I affect it more,

Than as your honour, and as your renown.
Let me no more from this obedience rise,
(Which my most true and inward-duteous spirit
Teacheth) this prostrate and exterior bending !
Heaven witness with me, when I here came in,
And found no course of breath within your majesty,
How cold it struck my heart ! If I do feign,
O let me in my present wildness die ;
And never live to shew the incredulous world
The noble change that I have purposed !
Coming to look on you, thinking you dead,
(And dead almost, my liege, to think you were),
I spake unto the crown, as having sense,
And thus upbraided it : " The care on thee depending
Hath fed upon the body of my father ;
Therefore, thou, best of gold, art worst of gold,
Other, less fine in carat* is more precious,
Preserving life in medicine potable :
But thou, most fine, most honour'd, most renown'd,
Hast eat thy bearer up." Thus, my most royal liege,
Accusing it, I put it on my head ;
To try with it,—as with an enemy
That had before my face murder'd my father,—
The quarrel of a true inheritor.
But if it did infect my blood with joy,
Or swell my thoughts to any strain of pride ;
If any rebel or vain spirit of mine
Did with the least affection of a welcome
Give entertainment to the might of it,
Let God for ever keep it from my head !
And make me as the poorest vassal is,
That doth with awe and terror kneel to it !

KING HENRY. O my son !

* Quality of the gold.

Heaven put it in thy mind to take it hence,
That thou might'st win the more thy father's love,
Pleading so wisely in excuse of it.
Come hither, Harry, sit thou by my bed;
And hear, I think, the very latest counsel
That ever I shall breathe. Heaven knows, my son,
By what by-paths, and indirect crook'd ways,
I met this crown; and I myself know well
How troublesome it sat upon my head:
To thee it shall descend with better quiet,
Better opinion, better confirmation;
For all the soil* of the achievement goes
With me into the earth. It seem'd in me
But as an honour snatch'd with boisterous hand:
And I had many living to upbraid
My gain of it by their assistances;
Which daily grew to quarrel and to bloodshed,
Wounding supposed peace: all these bold fears
Thou seest, with peril I have answered:
For all my reign hath been but as a scene
Acting that argument; and now my death
Changes the mode:† for what in me was purchas'd,
Falls upon thee in a more fairer sort;
So thou the garland wear'st successively.
Yet, though thou stand'st more sure than I could do,
Thou art not firm enough, since griefs are green,
And all thy friends, which thou must make thy friends,
Have but their stings and teeth newly ta'en out;
By whose fell working I was first advanc'd,
And by whose power I well might lodge a fear,
To be again displac'd; which to avoid,
I cut them off; and had a purpose now
To lead out many to the Holy Land;

* Stain. † The position of affairs

Lest rest, and lying still, might make them look
Too near into my state. Therefore, my Harry,
Be it thy course to busy giddy minds
With foreign quarrels; that action, hence borne out,
May waste the memory of the former days.
More would I, but my lungs are wasted so,
That strength of speech is utterly denied me.
How I came by the crown, O God, forgive!
And grant it may with thee in true peace live!
PRINCE HENRY. My gracious liege,
You won it, wore it, kept it, gave it me;
Then plain, and right, must my possession be;
Which I, with more than with a common pain,
'Gainst all the world will rightfully maintain.

ACT V.

Appeal of the Chief Justice to King Henry V., whom he had Imprisoned when Prince of Wales.

If the deed were ill,
Be you contented, wearing now the garland,*
To have a son set your decrees at nought;
To pluck down justice from your awful bench;
To trip the course of law, and blunt the sword
That guards the peace and safety of your person:
Nay, more; to spurn at your most royal image,
And mock your workings in a second body.†
Question your royal thoughts, make the case yours;
Be now the father, and propose a son:
Hear your own dignity so much profaned,
See your most dreadful laws so loosely slighted,

* Having succeeded to the crown.

† That is, Would you be satisfied for your representative in the state to be rudely treated.

Behold yourself so by a son disdain'd;
And then imagine me taking your part,
And in your power soft silencing your son.

An upright Judge.

You are right, justice, and you weigh this well;
Therefore, still bear the balance and the sword:
And I do wish your honours may increase,
Till you do live to see a son of mine
Offend you, and obey you, as I did.
So shall I live to speak my father's words;—
"Happy am I, that have a man so bold,
That dares do justice on my proper son:
And not less happy, having such a son,
That would deliver up his greatness so
Into the hands of justice." You did commit me;*
For which, I do commit into your hand
The unstain'd sword that you have us'd to bear;
With this remembrance,—That you use the same
With the like bold, just, and impartial spirit,
As you have done 'gainst me. There is my hand;
You shall be as a father to my youth:
My voice shall sound as you do prompt mine ear;
And I will stoop and humble my intents
To your well-practis'd wise directions.

King Henry the Fifth's rebuke to Falstaff.

I know thee not, old man; fall to thy prayers;
How ill white hairs become a fool and jester!
I have long dream'd of such a kind of man,

* "You did commit me;"—that is, you committed me to prison. History records that Henry V., when Prince of Wales, struck Judge Gascoigne in open court; for which he was consigned to prison by the judge.

So surfeit-swell'd, so old, and so profane;
But, being awake, I do despise my dream.
Make less thy body hence, and more thy grace;
Leave gormandising; know, the grave doth gape
For thee thrice wider than for other men.
Reply not to me with a fool-born jest;
Presume not that I am the thing I was:
For Heaven doth know, so shall the world perceive,
That I have turn'd away my former self;
So will I those that kept me company.
When thou dost hear I am as I have been,
Approach me; and thou shalt be as thou wast,
The tutor and the feeder of my riots:
Till then I banish thee, on pain of death,
As I have done the rest of my misleaders,
Not to come near our person by ten mile.
For competence of life I will allow you,
That lack of means enforce you not to evil;
And, as we hear you do reform yourselves,
We will, according to your strength and qualities,
Give you advancement.

—ooo—

KING HENRY V.

This historical play narrates the career of Henry the Fifth, from his ascent of the throne to his marriage with the Princess Katharine. At the commencement of the play, ambassadors from France arrive in England, with an insulting message from the Dauphin to the English monarch. The ambassadors are dismissed, with a defiance to France from Henry, who, at the head of his army, proceeds to Southampton, on his way to France

Here the Earl of Cambridge, Lord Scroop, and Sir Thomas Grey are detected in a conspiracy against the king, and are ordered for execution. The English army then proceeds to France, and besieges Harfleur, which is taken. The great battle of Agincourt follows, in which Henry, though his army is vastly inferior in numbers to the French, obtains a signal victory. The play concludes with an alliance between Katharine of France and Henry, and a consequent peace between the two nations. Amongst the most prominent incidents in the play are the scenes in which Henry, in disguise, visits his soldiers on the night preceding the battle of Agincourt, the description of Falstaff's death by Mrs. Quickly, and the amusing episode of Fluellen forcing the bully Pistol to eat the leek.

Chorus.

Invocation of the Muse.

O, for a muse of fire, that would ascend
The brightest heaven of invention !
A kingdom for a stage, princes to act,
And monarchs to behold the swelling scene !
Then should the warlike Harry, like himself,
Assume the port of Mars ; and, at his heels,
Leash'd in like hounds, should famine, sword, and fire,
Crouch for employment.

Act I.

Consideration.

Consideration like an angel came,
And whipp'd the offending Adam out of him ;
Leaving his body as a paradise,
To envelop and contain celestial spirits

Perfections of King Henry V.

Hear him but reason in divinity,
And, all admiring, with an inward wish
You would desire the king were made a prelate:
Hear him debate of commonwealth affairs,
You would say,—it hath been all-in-all his study;
List* his discourse of war, and you shall hear
A fearful battle render'd you in music:
Turn him to any cause of policy,
The Gordian knot of it he will unloose,
Familiar as his garter; that, when he speaks,
The air, a charter'd libertine, is still,
And the mute wonder lurketh in men's ears,
To steal his sweet and honey'd sentences.

The Commonwealth of Bees

So work the honey bees;
Creatures that, by a rule in nature, teach
The act of order to a peopled kingdom.
They have a king and officers of sorts:†
Where some, like magistrates, correct at home:
Others, like merchants, venture trade abroad;
Others, like soldiers, armed in their stings,
Make boot upon the summer's velvet buds;
Which pillage they with merry march bring home
To the tent royal of their emperor:
Who, busied in his majesty, surveys
The singing masons building roofs of gold;
The civil‡ citizens kneading up the honey;
The poor mechanic porters crowding in
Their heavy burdens at his narrow gate;
The sad-eyed justice, with his surly hum,

* Listen to. † Different degrees. ‡ Sober, grave.

Delivering o'er to executors* pale
The lazy yawning drone.

King Henry's defiant Message to the Dauphin of France

We are glad, the Dauphin is so pleasant with us;
His present† and your pains, we thank you for:
When we have match'd our rackets to these balls,
We will, in France, by God's grace, play a set,
Shall strike his father's crown into the hazard:
Tell him, he hath made a match with such a wrangler
That all the courts of France will be disturb'd
With chases.‡ And we understand him well,
How he comes o'er us with our wilder days,
Not measuring what use we made of them.
We never valued this poor seat of England;
And therefore, living hence,§ did give ourself
To barbarous license; as 'tis ever common,
That men are merriest when they are from home
But tell the Dauphin,—I will keep my state;
Be like a king, and show my sail of greatness,
When I do rouse me in my throne of France:—
For that I have laid by my majesty,
And plodded like a man for working-days;
But I will rise there with so full a glory,
That I will dazzle all the eyes of France,
Yea, strike the Dauphin blind to look on us.
And tell the pleasant prince,—this mock of his
Hath turn'd his balls to gun-stones; and his soul
Shall stand sore charged for the wasteful vengeance,

* Executioners.

† The Dauphin of France had, in derision of the King, sent him a box containing tennis-balls.

‡ A term used in playing at tennis.

§ Having retired from the Court.

That shall fly with them: for many a thousand widows
Shall this his mock mock out of their dear husbands,
Mock mothers from their sons, mock castles down.

* * * * *

But this lies all within the will of God,
To whom I do appeal; and in whose name,
Tell you the Dauphin, I am coming on,
To venge me as I may, and to put forth
My rightful hand in a well-hallow'd cause.
So get you hence in peace; and tell the Dauphin,
His jest will savour of but shallow wit,
When thousands weep, more than did laugh at it.

Act II.

Chorus.

Martial Spirit.

Now all the youth of England are on fire,
And silken dalliance in the wardrobe lies;
Now thrive the armourers, and honour's thought
Reigns solely in the breast of every man;
They sell the pasture now, to buy the horse;
Following the mirror of all Christian kings,
With winged heels, as English Mercuries.
For now sits Expectation in the air;
And hides a sword, from hilt unto the point,
With crowns imperial, crowns, and coronets,
Promis'd to Harry and his followers.

Apostrophe to England.

O England!—model to thy inward greatness,
Like little body with a mighty heart,—
What might'st thou do, that honour would thee do,
Were all thy children kind and natural!

But see thy fault! France hath in thee found out
A nest of hollow bosoms which he* fills
With treacherous crowns.

False Appearances; the King's Reproaches to the Traitor Scroop.

O, how hast thou with jealousy infected
The sweetness of affiance! Show men dutiful?
Why, so didst thou: Seem they grave and learned?
Why, so didst thou: Come they of noble family?
Why, so didst thou: Seem they religious?
Why, so didst thou: or are they spare in diet;
Free from gross passion, or of mirth or anger;
Constant in spirit, not swerving with the blood;
Garnish'd and deck'd in modest complement;†
Not working with the eye, without the ear,
And, but in purged judgment, trusting neither?
Such, and so finely bolted,‡ didst thou seem:
And thus thy fall hath left a kind of blot,
To mark the full-fraught man, and best indued,§
With some suspicion.

Dame Quickly's Account of Falstaff's Death.

'A made a finer end, and went away, an it had been any chrisom child; || 'a parted even just between twelve and one, e'en at turning o' the tide; for after I saw him fumble with the sheets, and play with flowers, and smile upon his fingers' ends, I knew there was but one way; for his nose was as sharp as a pen, and 'a babbled of green fields.

* *i. e.*, The King of France. † Accomplishment. ‡ Sifted. § Endow'd. || A child not more than a month old.

King Henry's Character by the Constable of France.

You are too much mistaken in this king:
Question, your grace, the late ambassadors,—
With what great state he heard their embassy,
How well supplied with noble counsellors,
How modest in exception,* and, withal,
How terrible in constant resolution,—
And you shall find, his vanities forespent †
Were but the outside of the Roman Brutus,
Covering discretion with a coat of folly;
As gardeners do with ordure hide those roots
That shall first spring, and be most delicate.

Act III.

Chorus.

Description of a Fleet setting Sail.

Suppose, that you have seen
The well-appointed king at Hampton pier
Embark his royalty; and his brave fleet
With silken streamers the young Phœbus fanning.
Play with your fancies; and in them behold,
Upon the hempen tackle, ship-boys climbing:
Hear the shrill whistle, which doth order give
To sounds confus'd: behold the threaden sails,
Borne with the invisible and creeping wind,
Draw the huge bottoms through the furrow'd sea,
Breasting the lofty surge.

King Henry's Address to his Soldiers at Harfleur.

Once more unto the breach, dear friends,—once more,
Or close the wall up with our English dead!

* In making objections. † Wasted, exhausted.

In peace there's nothing so becomes a man
As modest stillness and humility ;
But, when the blast of war blows in our ears,
Then imitate the action of the tiger ;
Stiffen the sinews, summon up the blood,
Disguise fair nature with hard-favour'd rage ;
Then lend the eye a terrible aspect ;
Let it pry through the portage* of the head,
Like the brass cannon : let the brow o'erwhelm it,
As fearfully as doth a galled rock
O'erhang and jutty † his confounded base,
Swill'd with the wild and wasteful ocean.
Now set the teeth, and stretch the nostril wide ;
Hold hard the breath, and bend up every spirit
To his full height ! On, on, you noblest English,
Whose blood is fet ‡ from fathers of war-proof !
Fathers that, like so many Alexanders,
Have, in these parts, from morn till even fought,
And sheath'd their swords for lack of argument.§

Act IV.

Chorus.

Description of Night in a Camp.

From camp to camp
The hum of either army stilly ‖ sounds,
That the fix'd sentinels almost receive
The secret whispers of each other's watch :
Fire answers fire ; and through their paly flames

* Comparing the eyes to cannons placed at port-holes.

† "Jutty his confounded base"—that is, as a rock projects over its base, which is *confounded* or destroyed by the waves.

‡ Fet,—that is fetched.

§ For lack of matter.

‖ Gently, lowly.

Each battle sees the other's umber'd* face :
Steed threatens steed, in high and boastful neighs
Piercing the night's dull ear ; and from the tents,
The armourers, accomplishing the knights,
With busy hammers closing rivets up,
Give dreadful note of preparation.
The country cocks do crow, the clocks do toll,
And the third hour of drowsy morning name.
Proud of their numbers, and secure in soul,
The confident and over-lusty † French
Do the low-rated English play at dice ;
And chide the cripple tardy-gaited night
Who, like a foul and ugly witch, doth limp
So tediously away. The poor condemned English,
Like sacrifices, by their watchful fires
Sit patiently, and inly ruminate
The morning's danger ; and their gesture sad,
Investing lank-lean cheeks, and war-worn coats,
Presenteth them unto the gazing moon
So many horrid ghosts. O, now, who will behold
The royal captain of this ruin'd band,
Walking from watch to watch, from tent to tent,
Let him cry—Praise and glory on his head!
For forth he goes, and visits all his host ;
Bids them good-morrow, with a modest smile ;
And calls them—brothers, friends, and countrymen.
Upon his royal face there is no note,
How dread an army hath enrounded him ;
Nor doth he dedicate one jot of colour
Unto the weary and all-watched night :
But freshly looks, and overbears attaint,
With cheerful semblance, and sweet majesty ;
That every wretch, pining and pale before,

* Discoloured by the gleam of the fires. † Over-saucy.

Beholding him, plucks comfort from his looks:
A largess universal, like the sun,
His liberal eye doth give to every one,
Thawing cold fear.

Scene on the Field of Agincourt between the King in Disguise, and Bates, Court, and Williams.

COURT. Brother John Bates, is not that the morning which breaks yonder?

BATES. I think it be: but we have no great cause to desire the approach of day.

WILLIAMS. We see yonder the beginning of the day, but, I think, we shall never see the end of it. Who goes there?

KING. A friend.

WILLIAMS. Under what captain serve you?

KING. Under Sir Thomas Erpingham.

WILLIAMS. A good old commander, and a most kind gentleman; I pray you, what thinks he of our estate?

KING. Even as men wrecked upon a sand, that look to be washed off the next tide.

BATES. He hath not told his thought to the king.

KING. No; nor it is not meet he should. For though I speak it to you, I think the king is but a man, as I am; the violet smells to him as it doth to me; the element shows to him as it doth to me; all his senses have but human conditions: * his ceremonies laid by, in his nakedness he appears but a man; and though his affections are higher mounted than ours, yet, when they stoop, they stoop with the like wing; therefore, when he sees reason of fears, as we do, his fears, out of doubt, be of the

* Qualities.

same relish as ours are: Yet in reason, no man should possess him with any appearance of fear, lest he, by showing it, should dishearten his army.

BATES. He may show what outward courage he will: but, I believe, as cold a night as 'tis, he could wish himself in the Thames up to the neck; and so I would he were, and I by him, at all adventures, so we were quit here.

KING. By my troth, I will speak my conscience of the king; I think, he would not wish himself anywhere but where he is.

BATES. Then I would he were here alone; so should he be sure to be ransomed, and a many poor men's lives saved.

KING. I dare say, you love him not so ill, to wish him here alone; howsoever you speak this, to feel other men's minds; methinks, I could not die any where so contented, as in the king's company; his cause being just, and his quarrel honourable.

WILLIAMS. That's more than we know.

BATES. Ay, or more than we should seek after; for we know enough, if we know we are the king's subjects; if his cause be wrong, our obedience to the king wipes the crime of it out of us.

WILLIAMS. But if the cause be not good, the king himself hath a heavy reckoning to make; when all those legs, and arms, and heads, chopped off in a battle, shall join together at the latter day,* and cry all—We died at such a place; some, swearing; some, crying for a surgeon; some, upon their wives left poor behind them; some, upon the debts they owe; some, upon their children rawly† left. I am afeard there are few die well, that die in battle; for how can they charitably

* The last day, the day of judgment. † Suddenly.

dispose of any thing, when blood is their argument? Now if these men do not die well, it will be a black matter for the king that led them to it; whom to disobey, were against all proportion of subjection.

KING. So, if a son, that is by his father sent about merchandise, do sinfully miscarry upon the sea, the imputation of his wickedness, by your rule should be imposed upon his father that sent him: or if a servant under his master's command, transporting a sum of money, be assailed by robbers, and die in many irreconciled iniquities, you may call the business of the master the author of the servant's damnation. — But this is not so: the king is not bound to answer the particular endings of his soldiers, the father of his son, nor the master of his servant; for they purpose not their death, when they purpose their services. Besides, there is no king, be his cause never so spotless, if it come to the arbitrement of swords, can try it out with all unspotted soldiers. Some, peradventure, have on them the guilt of premeditated and contrived murder: some, making the wars their bulwark, that have before gored the gentle bosom of peace with pillage and robbery. Now, if these men have defeated the law, and outrun native punishment,* though they can outstrip men, they have no wings to fly from God: war is his beadle, war is his vengeance; so that here men are punished, for before-breach of the king's laws, in now the king's quarrel; where they feared the death, they have born life away; and where they would be safe, they perish: then if they die unprovided, no more is the king guilty of their damnation, than he was before guilty of those impieties for the which they are now visited. Every subject's duty

* That is, punishment in their native country.

is the king's; but every subject's soul is his own. Therefore should every soldier in the wars do as every sick man in his bed, wash every mote out of his conscience: and dying so, death is to him advantage; or not dying, the time was blessedly lost, wherein such preparation was gained; and, in him that escapes, it were not sin to think, that making God so free an offer, He let him outlive that day to see his greatness, and to teach others how they should prepare.

WILLIAMS. 'Tis certain, every man that dies ill, the ill is upon his own head, the king is not to answer for it.

The Miseries of Royalty.

O hard condition! twin born with greatness,
Subjected to the breath of every fool,
Whose sense no more can feel but his own wringing!
What infinite heart's ease must kings neglect,
That private men enjoy!
And what have kings, that privates have not too,
Save ceremony, save general ceremony?
And what art thou, thou idol ceremony?
What kind of God art thou, that suff'rest more
Of mortal griefs, than do thy worshippers?
What are thy rents? what are thy comings in?
O ceremony, show me but thy worth;
What is thy soul of adoration?*
Art thou aught else but place, degree, and form,
Creating awe and fear in other men?
Wherein thou art less happy being fear'd
Than they in fearing.
What drink'st thou oft, instead of homage sweet,

* What is the real worth and intrinsic value of adoration?

But poison'd flattery? O, be sick, great greatness,
And bid thy ceremony give thee cure!
Think'st thou the fiery fever will go out
With titles blown from adulation?
Will it give place to flexure and low bending?
Canst thou, when thou command'st the beggar's knee,
Command the health of it? No, thou proud dream,
That play'st so subtly with a king's repose;
I am a king, that find thee; and I know,
'T is not the balm, the sceptre, and the ball,
The sword, the mace, the crown-imperial,
The inter-tissued robe of gold and pearl,
The farced* title running 'fore the king,
The throne he sits on, nor the tide of pomp
That beats upon the high shore of this world,
No, not all these, thrice gorgeous ceremony,
Not all these laid in bed majestical,
Can sleep so soundly as the wretched slave,
Who, with a body fill'd, and vacant mind,
Gets him to rest, cramm'd with distressful bread:
Never sees horrid night, the child of hell;
But, like a lackey, from the rise to set,
Sweats in the eye of Phœbus, and all night
Sleeps in Elysium; next day, after dawn,
Doth rise, and help Hyperion† to his horse,
And follows so the ever-running year
With profitable labour, to his grave:
And, but for ceremony, such a wretch,
Winding up days with toil, and nights with sleep,
Had the fore-hand and vantage of a king.

* Farced is stuffed. The tumid puffy titles with which a king's name is introduced.

† The sun.

Grandpré's description of the miserable State of the English Army.

Yon island carrions, desperate of their bones,
Ill-favour'dly become the morning field:
Their ragged curtains* poorly are let loose,
And our air shakes them passing scornfully.
Big Mars seems bankrupt in their beggar'd host,
And faintly through a rusty beaver peeps.
Their horsemen sit like fixed candlesticks,
With torch-staves in their hand: and their poor jades
Lob down their heads, dropping the hides and hips;
The gum down-roping from their pale-dead eyes;
And in their pale dull mouths the gimmal† bit
Lies foul with chew'd grass, still and motionless;
And their executors, the knavish crows,
Fly o'er them all, impatient for their hour.

King Henry's Speech before the Battle of Agincourt.

He that outlives this day, and comes safe home,
Will stand a tip-toe when this day is named,
And rouse him at the name of Crispian,‡
He that shall live this day, and see old age,
Will yearly on the vigil feast his friends,
And say—to-morrow is saint Crispian:
Then will he strip his sleeve, and show his scars,
And say, these wounds I had on Crispin's day.
Old men forget; yet all shall be forgot,
But he'll remember, with advantages,
What feats he did that day; then shall our names,
Familiar in their mouths as household words,—
Harry the king, Bedford, and Exeter,

* Colours. † Ring.

‡ St. Crispin's day, on which the battle was fought.

Warwick and Talbot, Salisbury and Gloster,—
Be in their flowing cups freshly remember'd.
This story shall the good man teach his son;
And Crispin Crispian shall ne'er go by,
From this day to the ending of the world,
But we in it shall be remember'd:
We few, we happy few, we band of brothers;
For he, to-day, that sheds his blood with me,
Shall be my brother; be he ne'er so vile,
This day shall gentle his condition:
And gentlemen in England, now a-bed,
Shall think themselves accurs'd, they were not here;
And hold their manhoods cheap, while any speaks
That fought with us upon Saint Crispin's day.

King Henry's Reply to the Herald sent by the Constable of France, summoning him to surrender.

I pray thee, bear my former answer back,
Bid them achieve me, and then sell my bones.
Good God! why should they mock poor fellows thus?
The man that once did sell the lion's skin
While the beast lived, was kill'd with hunting him.
A many of our bodies shall, no doubt,
Find native graves; upon the which I trust,
Shall witness live in brass* of this day's work:
And those that leave their valiant bones in France,
Dying like men, though buried in your dunghills,
They shall be fam'd; for there the sun shall greet them,
And draw their honours reeking up to heaven;
Leaving their earthly parts to choke your clime,
The smell whereof shall breed a plague in France.
Mark then, abounding valour in our English;
That, being dead, like to the bullet's grazing,

* On monuments in brass.

Break out into a second course of mischief,
Killing in relapse of mortality.
Let me speak proudly:—Tell the constable,
We are but warriors for the working day;*
Our gayness and our gilt, are all besmirch'd
With rainy marching in the painful field;
There's not a piece of feather in our host
(Good argument, I hope, we shall not fly),
And time hath worn us into slovenry:
But, by the mass, our hearts are in the trim:
And my poor soldiers tell me—yet ere night
They'll be in fresher robes; or they will pluck
The gay new coats o'er the French soldiers' heads,
And turn them out of service. If they do this
(As, if God please, they shall), my ransom then
Will soon be levied. Herald, save thou thy labour;
Come thou no more for ransom, gentle herald;
They shall have none, I swear, but these my joints:
Which if they have as I will leave 'em to them,
Shall yield them little, tell the constable.

Act V.

The Miseries of War.

Her vine, the merry cheerer of the heart,
Unpruned dies: her hedges even-pleach'd
Like prisoners wildly over-grown with hair,
Put forth disorder'd twigs: her fallow leas
The darnel, hemlock, and rank fumitory,
Doth root upon; while that the coulter† rusts,
That should deracinate‡ such savagery:
The even mead, that erst brought sweetly forth

* Indifferently clad. † Ploughshare.

‡ To deracinate is to force up by the roots.

The freckled cowslip, burnet, and green clover,
Wanting the scythe, all uncorrected, rank,
Conceives by idleness: and nothing teems,
But hateful docks, rough thistles, kecksies, burs,
Losing both beauty and utility;
And as our vineyards, fallows, meads, and hedges,
Defective in their natures, grow to wildness;
Even so our houses, and ourselves, and children,
Have lost, or do not learn, for want of time,
The sciences that should become our country.

—ooo—

KING HENRY VI.—Part I.

This play records the strife between the English and French, which is renewed on the death of Henry the Fifth, and the contract of marriage between Henry the Sixth and Margaret of Anjou. Joan of Arc, who is a prominent character in the play, after some successes against the English, is taken prisoner, and condemned to be burnt at the stake.

Act I.

Glory.

Glory is like a circle in the water,
Which never ceaseth to enlarge itself,
Till, by broad spreading, it disperse to nought.

Act V.

The Earl of Suffolk's Admiration for Margaret of Anjou.

I have no power to let her pass;
My hand would free her, but my heart says—no.

As plays the sun upon the glassy streams,
Twinkling another counterfeited beam,
So seems this gorgeous beauty to mine eyes.
Fain would I woo her, yet I dare not speak.

The Earl of Suffolk's Description of Margaret to the King.

This superficial tale
Is but a preface of her worthy praise.
The chief perfections of that lovely dame
(Had I sufficient skill to utter them)
Would make a volume of enticing lines,
Able to ravish any dull conceit.
And, which is more, she is not so divine,
So full replete with choice of all delights,
But, with as humble lowliness of mind,
She is content to be at your command.

Marriage.

Marriage is a matter of more worth
Than to be dealt in by attorneyship.*
* * * * * *
For what is wedlock forced, but a hell,
An age of discord and continual strife?
Whereas the contrary bringeth forth bliss,
And is a pattern of celestial peace.

—ooo—

KING HENRY VI.—Part II.

In the Second Part of Henry the Sixth, Shakspere introduces us to the feud, in its incipient state, between the rival houses of York

* By the agency of another.

and Lancaster. An important episode in the play is the insurrection, headed by Jack Cade, who is at the first successful, but in the end is killed. The play concludes with the Battle of St. Albans, in which the York faction triumphs, and the king and queen fly to London.

Act I.

A Resolved and Ambitious Woman.

Follow I must, I cannot go before,
While Gloster bears this base and humble mind.
Were I a man, a duke, and next of blood,
I would remove these tedious stumbling-blocks,
And smooth my way upon their headless necks:
And, being a woman, I will not be slack
To play my part in fortune's pageant.

Act II.

God's Goodness ever to be Remembered.

Let never day nor night unhallow'd pass,
But still remember what the Lord hath done.

The Duchess of Gloster's (when doing Penance) Remonstrance to her Husband.

For, whilst I think I am thy married wife,
And thou a prince, protector of this land,
Methinks, I should not thus be led along,
Mail'd up in shame,* with papers on my back,
And follow'd with a rabble, that rejoice
To see my tears, and hear my deep-fet † groans.
The ruthless flint doth cut my tender feet;

* Wrapped up in disgrace; alluding to the sheet of penance.

† Deep-fetched.

And, when I start, the envious people laugh,
And bid me be advised how I tread.

Act III.

Silent Resentment Deepest.

Smooth runs the water, where the brook is deep;
And in his simple show he harbours treason.

A Guilty Countenance.

Upon thy eye-balls murderous tyranny
Sits in grim majesty, to fright the world.

Description of a Murdered Person.

See how the blood is settled in his face!
Oft have I seen a timely-parted ghost,*
Of ashy semblance, meagre, pale, and bloodless,
Being all descended to the labouring heart;
Who, in the conflict that it holds with death,
Attracts the same for aidance 'gainst the enemy;
Which with the heart there cools and ne'er returneth
To blush and beautify the cheek again.
But see, his face is black and full of blood;
His eyeballs further out than when he liv'd,
Staring full ghastly like a strangled man:
His hair uprear'd, his nostrils stretch'd with struggling;
His hands abroad display'd, as one that grasp'd
And tugg'd for life, and was by strength subdued.
Look on the sheets, his hair, you see is sticking;
His well-proportion'd beard made rough and rugged,
Like to the summer's corn by tempest lodged.
It cannot be, but he was murder'd here;
The least of all these signs were probable.

* The body of a person who has died a natural death is here meant.

A good Conscience.

What stronger breast-plate than a heart untainted?
Thrice is he arm'd that hath his quarrel just;
And he but naked though lock'd up in steel,
Whose conscience with injustice is corrupted.

Suffolk's remorseless Hatred of his Enemies.

A plague upon them! wherefore should I curse them?
Would curses kill, as doth the mandrake's groan,
I would invent as bitter-searching terms,
As curst, as harsh, and horrible to hear,
Deliver'd strongly through my fixed teeth,
With full as many signs of deadly hate,
As lean faced Envy in her loathsome cave:
My tongue should stumble in mine earnest words:
Mine eyes shall sparkle like the beaten flint;
My hair be fixed on end, as one distract;
Ay, every joint should seem to curse and ban:
And even now my burden'd heart would break,
Should I not curse them. Poison be their drink!
Gall, worse than gall, the daintiest that they taste!
Their sweetest shade, a grove of cypress trees!
Their chiefest prospect, murdering basilisks!
Their softest touch, as smart as lizard's stings;
Their music frightful as the serpent's hiss;
And boding screech-owls make the concert full!
All the foul terrors in dark-seated hell.

Parting Lovers.

And banished I am, if but from thee.
Go, speak not to me; even now be gone.—
O, go not yet!—Even thus two friends condemn'd

Embrace, and kiss, and take ten thousand leaves,
Loather a hundred times to part than die.
Yet now, farewell! and farewell life with thee!

Death preferable to separation from a Lover.

If I depart from thee, I cannot live:
And in thy sight to die, what were it else,
But like a pleasant slumber in thy lap?
Here could I breathe my soul into the air,
As mild and gentle as the cradle-babe,
Dying with mother's dug between its lips.

The Death-bed Horrors of a Guilty Conscience.

Bring me unto my trial when you will.
Died he not in his bed? where should he die?
Can I make men live, whe'r they will or no?—
O! torture me no more, I will confess.—
Alive again? then show me where he is;
I'll give a thousand pound to look upon him.—
He hath no eyes, the dust hath blinded them.—
Comb down his hair; look! look! it stands upright,
Like lime-twigs set to catch my winged soul!—
Give me some drink: and bid the apothecary
Bring the strong poison that I bought of him.

Act IV.

Night.

The gaudy, blabbing, and remorseful day
Is crept into the bosom of the sea;
And now loud howling wolves arouse the jades
That drag the tragic melancholy night;
Who with their drowsy, slow, and flagging wings
Clip dead men's graves, and from their misty jaws
Breathe foul contagious darkness in the air.

Kent.

Kent, in the commentaries Cæsar writ,
Is term'd the civil'st place of all this isle:
Sweet is the country, because full of riches;
The people liberal, valiant, active, wealthy.

Lord Say's Apology for himself.

Justice with favour have I always done;
Prayers and tears have moved me, gifts could never.
When have I aught exacted at your hands,
Kent to maintain, the king, the realm, and you?
Large gifts have I bestow'd on learned clerks,
Because my book preferr'd me to the king:
And—seeing ignorance is the curse of God,
Knowledge the wing wherewith we fly to heaven,—
Unless you be possess'd with devilish spirits,
You cannot but forbear to murder me.

—ooo—

KING HENRY VI.—PART III.

The Third Part of King Henry the Sixth continues the history of that monarch and Queen Margaret from the battle of St. Albans. It records the battles of Wakefield, Towton, Barnet, and Tewksbury, and concludes with the murder of King Henry the Sixth in the Tower by the Duke of Glo'ster, afterwards Richard the Third, and the occupation of the throne by Edward the Fourth.

ACT I.

The Transports of a Crown.

Do but think,
How sweet a thing it is to wear a crown;

Within whose circuit is Elysium,
And all that poets feign of bliss and joy.

A Hungry Lion described.

So looks the pent-up lion o'er the wretch
That trembles under his devouring paws:
And so he walks, insulting o'er his prey:
And so he comes to rend his limbs asunder.

The Duke of York on the gallant Behaviour of his Sons.

My sons—God knows what hath bechanced them:
But this I know,—They have demean'd themselves
Like men born to renown, by life or death.
Three times did Richard make a lane to me;
And thrice cried,—"Courage, father! fight it out!"
And full as oft came Edward to my side,
With purple falchion, painted to the hilt
In blood of those that had encounter'd him:
And when the hardiest warriors did retire,
Richard cried—"Charge! and give no foot of ground!"
And cried—"A crown, or else a glorious tomb!
A sceptre, or an earthly sepulchre!"
With this, we charged again: but, out, alas!
We bodg'd* again; as I have seen a swan
With bootless labour swim against the tide,
And spend her strength with overmatching waves.

A Father's Passion on the Murder of a Favourite Child.

O, tiger's heart, wrapp'd in a woman's hide!
How couldst thou drain the life-blood of the child,
To bid the father wipe his eyes withal,

* That is, we boggled, made bad or bungling work of our attempt to rally.

And yet be seen to bear a woman's face?
Women are soft, mild, pitiful, and flexible;
Thou stern, obdurate, flinty, rough, remorseless.
* * * * * *
That face of his the hungry cannibals
Would not have touch'd, would not have stain'd with
  blood:
But you are more inhuman, more inexorable,
O, ten times more,—than tigers of Hyrcania.
See, ruthless queen, a hapless father's tears:
This cloth thou dipp'dst in blood of my sweet boy,
And I with tears do wash the blood away.
Keep thou the napkin, and go boast of this·
And if thou tell'st the heavy story right,
Upon my soul the hearers will shed tears;
Yea, even my foes will shed fast-falling tears,
And say,—Alas, it was a piteous deed!

Act II.

The Duke of York in Battle.

Methought he bore him* in the thickest troop,
As doth a lion in a herd of neat; †
Or as a bear, encompass'd round with dogs;
Who having pinch'd a few, and made them cry,
The rest stand all aloof, and bark at him.

Morning.

See how the morning opes her golden gates,
And takes her farewell of the glorious sun! ‡
How well resembles it the prime of youth,
Trimm'd like a younker prancing to his love!

* Demeaned himself. † Cattle, cows, oxen, etc.

‡ Aurora takes for a time her farewell of the sun, when she dismisses him to his diurnal course.

The Morning's Dawn.

This battle fares like to the morning's war,
When dying clouds contend with growing light;
What time the shepherd, blowing of his nails,
Can neither call it perfect day nor night.

The Blessings of a Shepherd's Life.

O, God! methinks it were a happy life,
To be no better than a homely swain;
To sit upon a hill, as I do now,
To carve out dials quaintly, point by point,
Thereby to see the minutes how they run:
How many make the hour full complete,
How many hours bring about the day,
How many days will finish up the year,
How many years a mortal man may live.
When this is known, then to divide the times:
So many hours must I tend my flock;
So many hours must I take my rest;
So many hours must I contemplate;
So many hours must I sport myself;

* * * * *

So many years ere I shall shear the fleece;
So minutes, hours, days, weeks, months, and years,
Pass'd over to the end they were created,
Would bring white hairs unto a quiet grave.
Ah, what a life were this! how sweet! how lovely!
Gives not the hawthorn bush a sweeter shade
To shepherds, looking on their silly sheep,
Than doth a rich embroider'd canopy
To kings that fear their subjects' treachery!
O yes, it doth; a thousand fold it doth.
And to conclude,—the shepherd's homely curds,

His cold thin drink out of his leather bottle,
His wonted sleep under a fresh tree's shade.
All which secure and sweetly he enjoys,
Is far beyond a prince's delicates,
His viands sparkling in a golden cup,
His body couched in a curious bed,
When care, mistrust, and treason, wait on him.

Act III.

Fickleness of the Populace.

Look, as I blow this feather from my face
And as the air blows it to me again,
Obeying with my wind when I do blow,
And yielding to another when it blows,
Commanded always by the greater gust;
Such is the lightness of you common men.

A Simile on ambitious Thoughts.

Why, then I do but dream on sovereignty;
Like one that stands upon a promontory,
And spies a far-off shore where he would tread,
Wishing his foot were equal with his eye;
And chides the sea that sunders him from thence,
Saying—he'll lade it dry to have his way.

Gloster on his Deformity.

Why, love foreswore me,
And, for I should not deal in her soft laws,
She did corrupt frail nature with some bribe
To shrink mine arm up like a wither'd shrub;
To make an envious mountain on my back,
Where sits deformity to mock my body;
To shape my legs of an unequal size;

To disproportion me in every part,
Like to a chaos, or an unlick'd bear-whelp,
That carries no impression like the dam.
And am I then a man to be beloved?

Gloster's Dissimulation.

Why, I can smile, and murder while I smile;
And cry, content, to that which grieves my heart;
And wet my cheeks with artificial tears,
And frame my face to all occasions;
I'll drown more sailors than the mermaid shall;
I'll slay more gazers than the basilisk;
I'll play the orator as well as Nestor;
Deceive more slily than Ulysses could,
And, like a Sinon, take another Troy:
I can add colours to the cameleon;
Change shapes with Proteus for advantages,
And set the murd'rous Machiavel to school.
Can I do this and cannot get a crown?

Act IV.

Henry VI. on his own Lenity.

I have not stopp'd mine ears to their demands,
Nor posted off their suits with slow delays;
My pity hath been balm to heal their wounds,
My mildness hath allay'd their swelling griefs,
My mercy dried their water-flowing tears:
I have not been desirous of their wealth,
Nor much oppress'd them with great subsidies,
Nor forward of revenge, though they much err'd.

Act V.

Dying Speech of the Earl of Warwick.

Ah, who is nigh? come to me, friend or foe,
And tell me who is victor, York or Warwick?
Why ask I that? my mangled body shows,
My blood, my want of strength, my sick heart shows,
That I must yield my body to the earth,
And by my fall, the conquest to my foe.
Thus yields the cedar to the axe's edge,
Whose arms gave shelter to the princely eagle,
Under whose shade the ramping lion slept,
Whose top branch over-peer'd Jove's spreading tree,
And kept low shrubs from winter's powerful wind.
These eyes, that now are dimm'd with death's black
veil,
Have been as piercing as the mid day sun,
To search the secret treasons of the world:
The wrinkles in my brows, now fill'd with blood,
Were liken'd oft to kingly sepulchres:
For who liv'd king, but I could dig his grave?
And who durst smile when Warwick bent his brow?
Lo, now my glory smear'd in dust and blood!
My parks, my walks, my manors that I had,
Even now forsake me; and of all my lands,
Is nothing left me but my body's length.
Why, what is pomp, rule, reign, but earth and dust?
And, live we how we can, yet die we must.

Queen Margaret's Speech before the Battle of Tewksbury.

Lords, knights, and gentlemen, what I should say,
My tears gainsay;* for every word I speak,

* Unsay, deny.

Ye see, I drink the water of mine eyes.
Therefore, no more but this:—Henry your sovereign
Is a prisoner to the foe; his state usurp'd,
His realm a slaughter-house, his subjects slain,
His statutes cancell'd, and his treasure spent;
And yonder is the wolf that makes this spoil.
You fight in justice: then in God's name, lords,
Be valiant, and give signal to the fight.

Omens on the Birth of Richard III.

The owl shriek'd at thy birth, an evil sign;
The night-crow cried, aboding luckless time;
Dogs howl'd, and hideous tempests shook down trees,
The raven rook'd* her on the chimney's top,
And chattering pies in dismal discord sung.

—ooo—

KING RICHARD III.

This historical tragedy describes the sanguinary career of King Richard, his murder of his brother (the Duke of Clarence), and the two young princes in the Tower, and his final overthrow and death, at the battle of Bosworth Field, by the Earl of Richmond, afterwards Henry the Seventh, who unites the rival houses of York and Lancaster, and ends the wars of the white and red roses. Dr. Johnson describes this play as one of the most celebrated of Shakspere's performances, but adds:—"I know not whether it has not happened to him, as to others, to be praised most when praise is not most deserved. That this play has scenes, noble in themselves, and very well contrived to strike in the exhibition, cannot be denied; but some parts are trifling, others shocking, and some improbable."

* To rook signified to squat down or lodge on any thing.

Act I.

The Duke of Gloster on his Deformity.

Now is the winter of our discontent
Made glorious summer by this sun of York;
And all the clouds that lower'd upon our house,
In the deep bosom of the ocean buried.
Now are our brows bound with victorious wreaths;
Our bruised arms hung up for monuments;
Our stern alarums, changed to merry meetings,
Our dreadful marches to delightful measures.*
Grim-visag'd war has smooth'd his wrinkled front;
And now, instead of mounting barbed † steeds,
To fright the souls of fearful adversaries,—
He caper's nimbly in a lady's chamber,
To the lascivious pleasing of a lute.
But I, that am not shaped for sportive tricks,
Nor made to court an amorous looking-glass;
I, that am rudely stamp'd, and want love's majesty,
To strut before a wanton ambling nymph;
I, that am curtail'd of this fair proportion,
Cheated of feature by dissembling nature,
Deform'd, unfinish'd, sent before my time
Into this breathing world, scarce half made up,
And that so lamely and unfashionable,
That dogs bark at me, as I halt by them;—
Why I, in this weak piping time of peace,
Have no delight to pass away the time;
Unless to spy my shadow in the sun,
And descant on mine own deformity;
And therefore,—since I cannot prove a lover,
To entertain these fair well spoken days,—
I am determined to prove a villain,
And hate the idle pleasures of these days.

* Dances. † Armed.

Gloster's Love for Lady Anne.

Those eyes of thine from mine have drawn salt tears,
Sham'd their aspects with store of childish drops:
These eyes which never shed remorseful* tear,—
Not, when my father York and Edward wept,
To hear the piteous moan that Rutland made
When black-faced Clifford shook his sword at him:
Nor when thy warlike father, like a child,
Told the sad story of my father's death;
And twenty times made pause, to sob and weep,
That all the standers-by had wet their cheeks,
Like trees bedash'd with rain; in that sad time
My manly eyes did scorn an humble tear;
And what these sorrows could not thence exhale
Thy beauty hath, and made them blind with weeping.
I never sued to friend nor enemy;
My tongue could never learn sweet soothing word;
But now thy beauty is proposed my fee,
My proud heart sues, and prompts my tongue to speak.

Gloster's praises of his own Person after his successful Wooing of Lady Anne.

My dukedom to a beggarly denier,†
I do mistake my person all this while;
Upon my life, she finds, although I cannot,
Myself to be a marvellous proper man.
I'll be at charges for a looking-glass:
And entertain a score or two of tailors,
To study fashions to adorn my body:
Since I am crept in favour with myself,
I will maintain it with some little cost.

* Pitiful. † A small French coin.

Queen Margaret's Execrations on Gloster.

The worm of conscience still be-gnaw thy soul!
Thy friends suspect for traitors while thou liv'st,
And take deep traitors for thy dearest friends!
No sleep close up that deadly eye of thine,
Unless it be while some tormenting dream
Affrights thee with a hell of ugly devils;
Thou elvish-mark'd abortive, rooting hog!

High Birth.

I was born so high,
Our aiery buildeth in the cedar's top,
And dallies with the wind, and scorns the sun.

Gloster's Hypocrisy.

But then I sigh, and, with a piece of Scripture,
Tell them that God bids us do good for evil:
And thus I clothe my naked villany
With old odd ends stolen forth of Holy Writ;
And seem a saint when most I play the devil.

Clarence's Dream; Scene between Clarence and Brakenbury.

BRAKENBURY. What was your dream, my lord? I pray you tell me.
CLARENCE. Methought that I had broken from the Tower,
And was embark'd to cross to Burgundy:
And, in my company, my brother Gloster;
Who from my cabin tempted me to walk
Upon the hatches; thence we look'd toward England,
And cited up a thousand heavy times,
During the wars of York and Lancaster,
That had befallen us. As we paced along

Upon the giddy footing of the hatches,
Methought that Gloster stumbled; and, in falling
Struck me, that thought to stay him, overboard,
Into the tumbling billows of the main.
O Lord! methought what pain it was to drown!
What dreadful noise of water in mine ears!
What sights of ugly death within mine eyes!
Methought I saw a thousand fearful wrecks;
A thousand men, that fishes gnaw'd upon:
Wedges of gold, great anchors, heaps of pearl,
Inestimable stones, unvalued jewels,
All scatter'd in the bottom of the sea.
Some lay in dead men's skulls; and, in those holes
Where eyes did once inhabit, there were crept
(As 'twere in scorn of eyes) reflecting gems,
That woo'd the slimy bottom of the deep,
And mock'd the dead bones that lay scatter'd by.

BRAKENBURY. Had you such leisure in the time of death
To gaze upon these secrets of the deep?

CLARENCE. Methought I had; and often did I strive
To yield the ghost: but still the envious flood
Kept in my soul, and would not let it forth
To seek the empty, vast, and wand'ring air.
But smother'd it within my panting bulk,*
Which almost burst to belch it in the sea.

BRAKENBURY. Awak'd you not with this sore agony?

CLARENCE. O, no, my dream was lengthen'd after life;
O, then began the tempest to my soul;
I pass'd, methought, the melancholy flood,
With that grim ferryman which poets write of,
Unto the kingdom of perpetual night.

* Body.

The first that there did greet my stranger soul
Was my great father-in-law, renowned Warwick,
Who cried aloud, "What scourge for perjury
Can this dark monarchy afford false Clarence?"
And so he vanish'd: Then came wand'ring by
A shadow like an angel, with bright hair
Dabbled in blood; and he shriek'd out aloud,—
"Clarence is come,—false, fleeting, perjur'd Clarence,—
That stabb'd me in the field by Tewksbury;—
Seize on him, furies, take him to your torments!"
With that, methought, a legion of foul fiends
Environ'd me, and howled in mine ears
Such hideous cries, that with the very noise,
I trembling wak'd, and, for a season after,
Could not believe but that I was in hell;
Such terrible impression made my dream.

BRAKENBURY. No marvel, lord, though it affrighted you!
I am afraid, methinks, to hear you tell it.

CLARENCE. O, Brakenbury, I have done these things,—
That now give evidence against my soul,—
For Edward's sake; and see, how he requites me!
O God! if my deep prayers cannot appease thee,
But thou wilt be aveng'd on my misdeeds,
Yet execute thy wrath on me alone;
O, spare my guiltless wife, and my poor children!

Sorrow.

Sorrow breaks seasons, and reposing hours,
Makes the night morning, and the noon-tide night.

The Cares of Greatness.

Princes have but their titles for their glories,
An outward honour for an inward toil:

And, for unfelt imaginations,
They often feel a world of restless cares:
So that between their titles and low name.
There's nothing differs but the outward fame.

Act II.

Deceit.

Ah, that deceit should steal such gentle shapes,
And with a virtuous visor hide deep vice!

Submission to Heaven our Duty.

In common worldly things, 'tis call'd ungrateful,
With dull unwillingness to repay a debt,
Which with a bounteous hand was kindly lent;
Much more to be thus opposite with heaven,
For it requires the royal debt it lent you.

The Duchess of York's Lamentation for the Misfortunes of her Family.

Accursed and unquiet wrangling days!
How many of you have mine eyes beheld!
My husband lost his life to get the crown;
And often up and down my sons were tost,
For me to joy, and weep, their gain, and loss:
And being seated, and domestic broils
Clean overblown, themselves, the conquerors,
Make war upon themselves; brother to brother,
Blood to blood, self 'gainst self:—O, preposterous
And frantic courage, end thy damned spleen;
Or let me die, to look on death no more

Act III.

The Vanity of Trust in Man.

O momentary grace of mortal man,
Which we more hunt for than the grace of God!
Who builds his hope in air of your fair looks,
Lives like a drunken sailor on a mast;
Ready, with every nod, to tumble down
Into the fatal bowels of the deep.

Contemplation.

When holy and devout religious men
Are at their beads, 'tis hard to draw them thence;
So sweet is zealous contemplation.

Act IV.

Description of the Murder of the two young Princes in the Tower.

The tyrannous and bloody act is done;
The most arch deed of piteous massacre
That ever yet this land was guilty of.
Dighton, and Forrest, whom I did suborn
To do this piece of ruthless* butchery,
Albeit they were flesh'd villains, bloody dogs,
Melting with tenderness and mild compassion,
Wept like two children, in their death's sad story.
"O thus," quoth Dighton, "lay the gentle babes—"
"Thus, thus," quoth Forrest, "girdling one another
Within their alabaster innocent arms:
Their lips were four red roses on a stalk,
Which, in their summer beauty, kiss'd each other.
A book of prayers on their pillow lay;

* Merciless

Which once," quoth Forrest, "almost changed my
mind;
But, O, the devil"—there the villain stopp'd;
When Dighton thus told on,—"We smothered
The most replenished sweet work of Nature,
That, from the prime creation, e'er she fram'd."—
Hence both are gone, with conscience and remorse;
They could not speak; and so I left them both,
To bear this tidings to the bloody king.

Expedition.

I have learn'd that fearful commenting
Is leaden servitor to dull delay;
Delay leads impotent and snail-pac'd beggary:
Then fiery expedition be my wing,
Jove's Mercury, and herald for a king!

Queen Margaret's Upbraidings of Queen Elizabeth.

I call'd thee then vain flourish of my fortune;
I call'd thee then poor shadow, painted queen:
The presentation of but what I was,
The flattering index of a direful pageant,
One heav'd a-high, to be hurl'd down below:
A mother only mock'd with two fair babes;
A dream of what thou wast; a garish* flag,
To be the aim of every dangerous shot;
A sign of dignity, a breath, a bubble;
A queen in jest, only to fill the scene.
Where is thy husband now? where be thy brothers?
Where be thy two sons? wherein dost thou joy?
Who sues, and kneels, and says God save the queen?
Where be the bending peers that flatter'd thee?
Where be the thronging troops that follow'd thee?

* Flaring, conspicuous.

Decline all this, and see what now thou art.
For happy wife, a most distressed widow;
For joyful mother, one that wails the name:
For one being sued to, one that humbly sues:
For queen, a very caitiff crown'd with care;
For one that scorn'd at me, now scorn'd of me;
For one being fear'd of all, now fearing one;
For one commanding all, obey'd of none.
Thus hath the course of justice wheel'd about,
And left thee but a very prey to time;
Having no more but thought of what thou wert,
To torture thee the more, being what thou art.

Character of King Richard by his Mother.

Tetchy * and wayward was thy infancy;
Thy school-days frightful, desperate, wild, and furious;
Thy prime of manhood daring, bold, and venturous:
Thy age confirm'd, proud, subtle, sly, and bloody.

Act V.

Richmond's Address to his Army before the Battle of Bosworth Field.

Fellows in arms, and my most loving friends,
Bruis'd underneath the yoke of tyranny,
Thus far into the bowels of the land
Have we march'd on without impediment;
And here receive we from our father Stanley
Lines of fair comfort and encouragement.
The wretched, bloody, and usurping boar,
That spoil'd your summer fields and fruitful vines,
Swills your warm blood like wash, and makes his trough
In your embowell'd bosoms,—this foul swine

* Touchy, fretful.

Lies now even in the centre of this isle,
Near to the town of Leicester, as we learn:
From Tamworth thither, is but one day's march.
In God's name, cheerly on, courageous friends,
To reap the harvest of perpetual peace
By this one bloody trial of sharp war.

Hope.

True hope is swift, and flies with swallows wings,
Kings it makes gods, and meaner creatures kings.

Daybreak.

The silent hours steal on,
And flaky darkness breaks within the east.

Richmond's Prayer before the Battle.

O Thou, whose captain I account myself,
Look on my forces with a gracious eye;
Put in their hands thy bruising irons of wrath,
That they may crush down with a heavy fall
The usurping helmets of our adversaries!
Make us thy ministers of chastisement,
That we may praise thee in thy victory!
To thee I do commend my watchful soul,
Ere I let fall the windows of mine eyes;
Sleeping, and waking, O, defend me still!

Richard Starting out of his Dream.

Give me another horse,—bind up my wounds,—
Have mercy, Jesu!—Soft; I did but dream.—
O coward conscience, how dost thou afflict me!
The lights burn blue.—It is now dead midnight.
Cold fearful drops stand on my trembling flesh.

Conscience.

Conscience is but a word that cowards use,
Devis'd at first to keep the strong in awe.

Richard's Address before the Battle.

A thousand hearts are great within my bosom:
Advance our standards, set upon our foes;
Our ancient word of courage, fair Saint George,
Inspire us with the spleen of fiery dragons!
Upon them! Victory sits on our helms.

Richard's Desperation on the Battlefield.

Slave, I have set my life upon a cast,
And I will stand the hazard of the die:
I think there be six Richmonds in the field,
Five have I slain to-day instead of him:
A horse! a horse! my kingdom for a horse.

—ooo—

KING HENRY VIII.

In this play is recorded the fall of Cardinal Wolsey, who, full of anguish at losing the favour of the king, retires to Leicester Abbey, where he expires. The dying moments of Katharine, wife of the king, are depicted, and the union of the king with Anne Bullen. The christening of the Princess Elizabeth (afterwards Queen Elizabeth) concludes the play, an eloquent prophecy as to her future greatness being delivered by Archbishop Cranmer. In speaking of Shakspere's historical plays, Dr. Johnson pronounces the two parts of Henry the Fourth and Henry the Fifth to possess the greatest excellence; and "King John, Richard the Third, and Henry the Eighth, deservedly stand in the second class."

Act I.

Anger.

To climb steep hills,
Requires slow pace at first: Anger is like
A full hot horse, who being allow'd his way,
Self-mettle tires him.

Action to be carried on with Resolution.

If I am traduced by tongues which neither know
My faculties nor person, yet will be
The chronicles of my doing,—let me say,
'Tis but the fate of place, and the rough brake*
That virtue must go through. We must not stint †
Our necessary actions in the fear
To cope ‡ malicious censurers; which ever
As ravenous fishes, do a vessel follow
That is new trimm'd; but benefit no further
Than vainly longing. What we oft do best,
By sick interpreters, once § weak ones, is
Not ours, or not allow'd: || what worst, as oft,
Hitting a grosser quality is cried up
For our best act. If we shall stand still,
In fear our motion will be mock'd or carp'd at,
We should take root here where we sit, or sit
State statues only.

New Customs.

New customs,
Though they be never so ridiculous,
Nay, let them be unmanly, yet are followed.

* A thicket of thorns. † Retard. ‡ Encounter.
§ Sometimes. || Approved.

Act II.

The Duke of Buckingham's Prayer for the King.

May he live
Longer than I have time to tell his years!
Ever belov'd, and loving, may his rule be,
And, when old time shall lead him to his end,
Goodness and he fill up one monument!

A Good Wife

A loss of her,
That, like a jewel, has hung twenty years
About his neck, yet never lost her lustre:
Of her that loves him with that excellence
That angels love good men with; even of her
That, when the greatest stroke of fortune falls,
Will bless the king.

The Blessings of a Low Station.

'T is better to be lowly born,
And range with humble livers in content,
Than to be perk'd up in glistering grief,
And wear a golden sorrow.

Queen Katharine's Speech to the King, her Husband.

Alas, sir,
In what have I offended you? what cause
Hath my behaviour given to your displeasure,
That thus you should proceed to put me off,
And take your good grace from me? Heaven witness,
I have been to you a true and humble wife,
At all times to your will conformable:
Ever in fear to kindle your dislike,
Yea, subject to your countenance: glad or sorry,

As I saw it inclined. When was the hour
I ever contradicted your desire,
Or made it not mine too? Or which of your friends
Have I not strove to love, although I knew
He were mine enemy? What friend of mine
That had to him deriv'd your anger, did I
Continue in my liking? nay, gave notice
He was from thence discharg'd? Sir, call to mind
That I have been your wife, in this obedience,
Upward of twenty years.

Queen Katharine's Speech to Cardinal Wolsey.

You are meek and humble-mouth'd;
You sign your place and calling, in full seeming,*
With meekness and humility: but your heart
Is cramm'd with arrogancy, spleen, and pride.
You have, by fortune and his highness' favours,
Gone slightly o'er low steps; and now are mounted
Where powers are your retainers: and your words,
Domestics to you, serve your will, as't please
Yourself pronounce their office. I must tell you,
You tender more your person's honour than
Your high profession spiritual.

King Henry's Character of Queen Katharine.

That man i' the world who shall report he has
A better wife, let him in nought be trusted,
For speaking false in that. Thou art, alone
(If thy rare qualities, sweet gentleness,
Thy meekness saint-like, wife-like government,—
Obeying in commanding,—and thy parts
Sovereign and pious else, could speak thee out),†
The queen of earthly queens.

* Appearance. † Speak out thy merits.

Act III.

Queen Katharine on her own Merit.

Have I liv'd thus long,—(let me speak myself,
Since virtue finds no friends),—a wife, a true one?
A woman (I dare say, without vain-glory)
Never yet branded with suspicion?
Have I with all my full affections
Still met the king? lov'd him next heaven? obey'd
him?
Been, out of fondness, superstitious to him?*
Almost forgot my prayers to content him?
And am I thus rewarded? 'Tis not well, lords,
Bring me a constant woman to her husband,
One that ne'er dream'd a joy beyond his pleasure,
And to that woman, when she has done most,
Yet will I add an honour,—a great patience.

Obedience to Princes.

The hearts of princes kiss obedience,
So much they love it; but, to stubborn spirits,
They swell, and grow as terrible as storms.

Outward Effects of a Disturbed Mind

Some strange commotion
Is in his brain; he bites his lip, and starts;
Stops on a sudden, looks upon the ground,
Then lays his finger on his temple; straight
Springs out into fast gait;† then stops again,
Strikes his breast hard, and anon he casts
His eye against the moon: in most strange postures
We have seen him set himself.

* Served him with superstitious attention. † Steps.

Firm Allegiance.

Though perils did
Abound as thick as thought could make them, and
Appear in forms more horrid, yet my duty,
As doth a rock against the chiding flood,
Should the approach of this wild river break,
And stand unshaken yours.

External Effects of Anger.

What sudden anger's this? how have I reap'd it?
He parted frowning from me, as if ruin
Leap'd from his eyes: so looks the chafed lion
Upon the daring huntsman that has gall'd him;
Then makes him nothing.

Falling Greatness.

Nay, then, farewell!
I have touch'd the highest point of all my greatness!
And, from that full meridian of my glory,
I haste now to my setting: I shall fall
Like a bright exhalation in the evening,
And no man see me more.

The Vicissitudes of Life.

So farewell to the little good you bear me.
Farewell, a long farewell, to all my greatness,
This is the state of man; to-day he puts forth
The tender leaves of hope, to-morrow blossoms,
And bears his blushing honours thick upon him;
The third day comes a frost, a killing frost;
And, when he thinks, good easy man, full surely
His greatness is a ripening,—nips his root,
And then he falls, as I do. I have ventured,

Like little wanton boys that swim on bladders,
This many summers in a sea of glory;
But far beyond my depth; my high-blown pride
At length broke under me; and now has left me,
Weary, and old with service, to the mercy
Of a rude stream, that must for ever hide me.
Vain pomp and glory of this world, I hate ye;
I feel my heart new open'd: O, how wretched
Is that poor man that hangs on princes' favours!
There is, betwixt that smile we would aspire to,
That sweet aspect of princes, and their ruin,
More pangs and fears, than wars or women have;
And when he falls, he falls like Lucifer,
Never to hope again.

Cardinal Wolsey's Speech to Cromwell.

Cromwell, I did not think to shed a tear
In all my miseries; but thou hast forc'd me
Out of thy honest truth to play the woman.
Let's dry our eyes; and thus far hear me, Cromwell;
And,—when I am forgotten, as I shall be,
And sleep in dull cold marble, where no mention
Of me more must be heard of,—say I taught thee;
Say, Wolsey,—that once trod the ways of glory,
And sounded all the depths and shoals of honour,—
Found thee a way, out of his wreck, to rise in;
A sure and safe one, though thy master miss'd it.
Mark but my fall, and that that ruin'd me.
Cromwell, I charge thee, fling away ambition;
By that sin fell the angels; how can man then,
The image of his Maker, hope to win by't?
Love thyself last: cherish those hearts that hate thee.
Corruption wins not more than honesty.
Still in thy right hand carry gentle peace,

To silence envious tongues. Be just, and fear not:
Let all the ends thou aim'st at be thy country's,
Thy God's, and truth's; then, if thou fall'st, O
Cromwell,
Thou fall'st a blessed martyr. Serve the king;
And,—pr'ythee, lead me in;
There take an inventory of all I have,
To the last penny; 'tis the king's: my robe,
And my integrity to Heaven, is all
I dare now call mine own. O Cromwell, Cromwell,
Had I but serv'd my God with half the zeal
I serv'd my king, he would not in mine age
Have left me naked to mine enemies.

Act IV.

Applause.

Such a noise arose
As the shrouds make at sea in a stiff tempest,
As loud, and to as many tunes: hats, cloaks,
(Doublets, I think,) flew up, and had their faces
Been loose, this day they had been lost. Such joy
I never saw before.

Cardinal Wolsey's Death.

At last, with easy roads,* he came to Leicester,
Lodg'd in the abbey; where the reverend abbot,
With all his convent, honourably receiv'd him;
To whom he gave these words,—"O father abbot,
An old man, broken with the storms of state,
Is come to lay his weary bones among ye;
Give him a little earth for charity!"
So went to bed; where eagerly his sickness

* By short stages.

Pursued him still; and, three nights after this,
About the hour of eight (which he himself
Foretold should be his last), full of repentance,
Continual meditations, tears, and sorrows,
He gave his honours to the world again,
His blessed part to heaven, and slept in peace.

Wolsey's Vices and Virtues.

So may he rest; his faults lie gently on him!
Yet thus far, Griffith, give me leave to speak him,
And yet with charity,—He was a man
Of an unbounded stomach,* ever ranking
Himself with princes; one that by suggestion
Tied all the kingdom; simony was fair play;
His own opinion was his law: i' the presence†
He would say untruths; and be ever double,
Both in his words and meaning; he was never,
But where he meant to ruin, pitiful:
His promises were, as he then was, mighty;
But his performance, as he is now, nothing.
Of his own body he was ill, and gave
The clergy ill example.
* * * * *

This cardinal,
Though from an humble stock, undoubtedly
Was fashion'd to ‡ much honour. From his cradle
He was a scholar, and a ripe and good one;
Exceeding wise, fair spoken, and persuading;
Lofty and sour to them that lov'd him not;
But, to those men that sought him, sweet as summer:
And though he were unsatisfied in getting,
(Which was a sin), yet in bestowing, madam,
He was most princely. Ever witness for him

* Pride. † Of the king. ‡ Formed for

Those twins of learning that he raised in you,
Ipswich and Oxford! one* of which fell with him,
Unwilling to outlive the good that did it;
The other, though unfinish'd, yet so famous,
So excellent in art, and still so rising,
That Christendom shall ever speak his virtue.
His overthrow heap'd happiness upon him;
For then, and not till then, he felt himself,
And found the blessedness of being little:
And, to add greater honours to his age
Than man could give him, he died fearing God.

Act V.

Archbishop Cranmer's Prophecy of the Future Greatness of the Infant Princess, afterwards Queen Elizabeth.

Let me speak, sir,
For heaven now bids me; and the words I utter
Let none think flattery, for they'll find them truth.
This royal infant (Heaven still move about her!)
Though in her cradle, yet now promises
Upon this land a thousand thousand blessings,
Which time shall bring to ripeness; she shall be
(But few now living can behold that goodness),
A pattern to all princes living with her,
And all that shall succeed: Sheba was never
More covetous of wisdom and fair virtue
Than this pure soul shall be: all princely graces,
That mould up such a mighty piece as this is,
With all the virtues that attend the good,
Shall still be doubled on her: truth shall nurse he
Holy and heavenly thoughts still counsel her;
She shall be lov'd and fear'd: her own shall bless her;

* Ipswich.

Her foes shake like a field of beaten corn,
And hang their heads with sorrow : good grows with
 her ;
In her days, every man shall eat in safety,
Under his own vine, what he plants ; and sing
The merry songs of peace to all his neighbours :
God shall be truly known ; and those about her,
From her shall read the perfect ways of honour,
And by those claim their greatness, not by blood.
Nor shall this peace sleep with her ; but as when
The bird of wonder dies, the maiden phœnix,
Her ashes new create another heir,
As great in admiration as herself,
So shall she leave her blessedness to one,
(When Heaven shall call her from this cloud of dark-
 ness)
Who, from the sacred ashes of her honour,
Shall star-like rise, as great in fame as she was,
And so stand fix'd : peace, plenty, love, truth, terror,
That were the servants to this chosen infant,
Shall then be his, and like a vine grow to him ;
Wherever the bright sun of heaven shall shine,
His honour and the greatness of his name
Shall be, and make new nations : he shall flourish,
And, like a mountain cedar, reach his branches
To all the plains about him ;——Our children's chil-
 dren
Shall see this, and bless Heaven.

—*ooo*—

PERICLES, PRINCE OF TYRE.

This play describes the wanderings of Pericles, Prince of Tyre, to avoid the anger of Antiochus, King of Antioch, who was seeking to kill him. It has been generally conjectured, that portions only of the drama were written by Shakspere's hand. The play, however, appears in every edition of the great dramatist's works. Malone says of Pericles—"The numerous expressions bearing a similitude to passages in the undisputed plays, some of the incidents, and in various places the colour of the style, all combine to set the seal of Shakspere on the play, and furnish us with proofs that a considerable portion of it was written by him."

Act I.

Sanctity of a Good Man's Word.

I'll take thy word for faith, not ask thine oath;
Who shuns not to break one, will sure crack both.

Description of a Prosperous City.

This Tharsus, o'er which I have government,
(A city, on whom plenty held full hand),
For riches, strew'd herself even in the streets;
Whose towers bore heads so high, they kiss'd the clouds,
And strangers ne'er beheld, but wonder'd at;
Whose men and dames so jetted* and adorn'd,
Like one another's glass to trim† them by;
Their tables were stor'd full, to glad the sight,
And not so much to feed on, as delight;
All poverty was scorn'd, and pride so great,
The name of help grew odious to repeat.

Sorrows never come singly.

One sorrow never comes but brings an heir,
That may succeed as his inheritor.

* Jet, to strut. † Trim, to dress.

Act III.

Pericles' Prayer during the Storm at Sea.

Thou God of this great vast,* rebuke these surges,
Which wash both heaven and hell; and thou that hast
Upon the winds command, bind them in brass,
Having call'd them from the deep! O still thy deaf'ning,
Thy dreadful thunders, gently quench thy nimble sulphurous flashes.

Virtue and Knowledge superior to Nobility and Wealth.

I held it ever,
Virtue and cunning† were endowments greater
Than nobleness and riches; careless heirs
May the two latter darken and expend;
But immortality attends the former,
Making a man a god.

—ooo—

THE MERRY WIVES OF WINDSOR.

It is generally supposed that this comedy was written at the command of Queen Elizabeth, who was so much amused at the humours of Sir John Falstaff in the historical plays, that she desired to have a representation of the fat knight in love. Shakspere is said to have written this play in fourteen days. The escapades of Falstaff occupy the most conspicuous place in it, whilst the episode of the loves of Fenton and Anne Page form a pleasing variety. Dr. Johnson says—"This comedy is remarkable for the variety and number of the personages, who exhibit more characters, appropriated and discriminated, than perhaps can be found in any other play."

---

* This vast extent of ocean. † Knowledge.

Act III.

Inequality of means and position between lovers an obstacle to marriage.

He doth object, I am too great of birth;
And that, my state being gall'd with my expense,
I seek to heal it only by his wealth:
Besides these, other bars he lays before me,—
My riots past, my wild societies;
And tells me, 'tis a thing impossible
I should love thee, but as a property.

The sincerity of Fenton's love for Anne Page.

I will confess, thy father's wealth
Was the first motive that I woo'd thee, Anne:
Yet, wooing thee, I found thee of more value
Than stamps in gold, or sums in sealed bags;
And 'tis the very riches of thyself
That now I aim at.

Act IV.

Legend of Herne the Hunter.

There is an old tale goes, that Herne the hunter,
Sometime a keeper here in Windsor forest,
Doth all the winter time, at still midnight,
Walk round about an oak, with great ragged horns;
And there he blasts the tree, and takes* the cattle;
And makes milch-kine yield blood, and shakes a chain
In a most hideous and dreadful manner:
You have heard of such a spirit; and well you know,
The superstitious idle-headed eld
Received, and did deliver to our age,
This tale of Herne the hunter for a truth.

* Strikes with disease.

Act V.

Evils of a forced Marriage.

You would have married her most shamefully,
Where there was no proportion held in love.
The truth is, she and I, long since contracted,
Are now so sure, that nothing can dissolve us,
The offence is holy, that she hath committed:
And this deceit loses the name of craft,
Of disobedience, or unduteous title;
Since therein she doth evitate* and shun
A thousand irreligious cursed hours,
Which forced marriage would have brought upon her.

* Escape, avoid.

INDEX.

—o—

www.ingramcontent.com/pod-product-compliance
Lightning Source LLC
LaVergne TN
LVHW010210110826
845151LV00002B/655

* 9 7 8 1 4 2 5 5 3 4 9 3 6 *